THE VOLUNTEERS

By the same author

Stannary Tales (Twelveheads Press, Twelveheads, Nr Truro) 1980

Talvisodan Kanarialinnut (The Winter War Canaries) 1984 (Werner Söderström Osakeyhtiö)

THE VOLUNTEERS

THE FULL STORY OF THE BRITISH VOLUNTEERS IN FINLAND 1939 – 41

"History is not what you thought.
It is what you can remember."
(W.C. Sellar and R.J. Yeatman:
"1066 And All That", Methuen,
London, 1929)

Justin Brooke

Published in 1990 by
The Self Publishing Association Ltd
Lloyds Bank Chambers,
Upton-upon-Severn, Worcs.
A MEMBER OF

in conjunction with
JUSTIN BROOKE
Chymorvah Vean,
Marazion Cornwall.

British Library Cataloguing in Publication Data
Brooke, Justin *1920-*
The Volunteers: the full story of the British volunteers in Finland 1939-41.
1. Russo-Finnish War. Role of Allied forces
I. Title
948.97032

ISBN 1 85421 084 X

Produced and Designed by The Self Publishing Association Ltd.
Printed and Bound in Great Britain by Billing & Sons Ltd, Worcester.

To the brave people of Finland,
who, despite all their difficulties,
endured us as well.

CONTENTS

Harold Gibson, M.C., Director, Finnish Aid Bureau, 1940-41

FOREWORD

Much of the information in this book is taken from the Official Report on the Finnish Aid Bureau and the British Contingent of the International Volunteer Force for Finland, which the late Harold Gibson, M.C., Director of the Finnish Aid Bureau, drew up in two parts. The first part is dated 30th September 1940 and the second, which is the longer of the two and which contains a number of appendices, is dated 22nd August 1941.

Historically equal in importance to this report and in detail more so are the files of the War Archives in Finland, to which access was specially granted by the Finnish Ministry of Defence. Further useful detail came from the microfilms of Finnish newspapers at the Library of the University of Helsinki, from the Swedish State Archives in Stockholm, and from the Public Record Office at Kew, to all of whose staffs I express my sincere gratitude. A list of all the people and organisations who have assisted me in the preparation of this book is given at the end.

As readers will appreciate, fifty years of inflation have made it difficult to relate the cash sums mentions in this book to modern conditions. The exchange rates in 1940-41 were £1 = 220 Finnish marks = 19.69 Swedish kronor.

Marazion, 1990 Justin Brooke

INTRODUCTION

Finland formed part of the Kingdom of Sweden for about six centuries before the Russo-Swedish war of 1808-09, and after the war it became an autonomous Grand Duchy of Russia. Following the outbreak of the Russian revolution in 1917 Finland declared herself a Republic, and in 1920 joined the League of Nations. Under the Treaty of Tartu (Dorpat), in neutral Estonia, concluded the same year with the Soviet Union, the latter country recognised Finland's independence, and on her own initiative made a non-intervention treaty with her in 1932. The treaty included provisions for settling disagreements between the two countries, and provided for those which could not be settled through the normal diplomatic channels to be submitted to a mixed conciliation commission of two members from each country. In 1933 a protocol was added to the treaty, which defined the concept of attack. In so doing Finland, who had joined the Scandinavian bloc of neutral countries, hoped she would be giving the Soviet Union adequate guarantees that Finnish territory would not be permitted to be used for the warlike purposes of another State. In 1934 the Soviet Union joined the League of Nations, reaffirmed the 1932 Treaty with Finland, and agreed that it should remain in force until 1945.

Meanwhile, between 1921 and 1929 Germany made a number of treaties with the Soviet Union, eight of them of major importance, and none of which were denounced when Hitler came to power in 1933. In that year Germany ratified the extension of the non-aggression pact with the Soviet Union, which had been signed in Berlin in 1926. In mid-August 1939, while an Anglo-French military delegation was discussing a tripartite non-aggression pact in Moscow, Joachim von Ribbentrop, the German Foreign Minister, arrived there. On 19th August he signed a trade agreement, by which Germany undertook to supply the Soviet Union with machinery and manufactured goods, in return for oil, timber and minerals, all of which were vital to the German economy. Four days later the two countries signed a ten-year non-aggression pact, which effectively made them allies. A secret protocol to the pact was drawn up and signed on 28th August, which recorded that the two countries agreed to have specific areas of interest in the Baltic, Germany taking Lithuania and Soviet Russia taking Estonia, Finland and Latvia. Poland was divided between the two, roughly along the Curzon line. As a result of the negotiations, the Anglo-French Mission returned home empty-handed.

Germany invaded Poland early in September 1939, and France and the United Kingdom declared war on her in accordance with the terms of their treaties with Poland. By 17th September Germany had occupied the western half of Poland, and the Soviet Union had begun to occupy the eastern part, ostensibly to "protect" the Ukrainian and White Russian minorities there. At the same time the Soviet Union gave guarantees of neutrality to a number of states, including Finland and the Baltic states, while a meeting of the Scandinavian prime ministers held on 18th and 19th September, at which Finland was represented, made a fresh declaration of their countries' desire to remain neutral.

While the division of Poland proceeded, the Soviet Union began to strengthen its position in the Baltic, and demanded of each State in turn the granting of military bases and the signing of non-aggression treaties, which would effectively bring them into the Soviet sphere of influence. Estonia came first, on 28th September, Latvia on 5th October, and Lithuania, despite being within the agreed German area of influence, on 11th October. Meanwhile, on 5th October, Finland was invited to send representatives to Moscow with a view to negotiating "concrete political questions", which the Soviet Union stated on 8th October were of the same nature as the demands being made on the other Baltic states. To lead the three-man delegation Finland appointed her Minister in Stockholm, Dr J.K. Paasikivi, well-known for his support of the policy favouring friendly relations with the Soviet Union, and later President of Finland. His government instructed him that he must stress Finland's adherence to the Russo-Finnish non-aggression pact of 1932 and to other international agreements to which she was a party, as well as Finland's wish to maintain her neutrality as part of the neutral Scandinavian bloc. He was also instructed to state that Finland had resolved to defend her neutrality by all the means at her disposal, and to reject any proposals which conflicted with his country's political position of neutrality, including mutual aid pacts, and the ceding of bases, harbours or territory. He was, however, authorised to negotiate over certain islands in the Gulf of Finland, in exchange for which he was to seek compensating land transfers elsewhere.

It turned out that the Soviet Union wanted much larger concessions than the Finnish government had anticipated. Besides land-transfers totalling some 1,725 square miles it wanted the defences on the Carelian isthmus and elsewhere to be dismantled. It wanted Hanko for use as a naval base, as well as the nearby Lappvik harbour for a naval anchorage. In fact, the Soviet Union wanted so much that to agree to its demands would have left Finland defenceless, and would in effect have put an end to her independence and neutrality, in exchange for which the Soviet Union offered some 3,455 square miles of desolate land adjacent to Finland's eastern frontier. The delegation did not approve of this, and therefore offered some islands in the Gulf of Finland, a small part of the Carelian isthmus which would have the effect of straightening out the frontier, and the Fishermen's or Rybachi Peninsula in Petsamo, on Finland's arctic coast. In exchange for these Finland sought land elsewhere.

Negotiations lasted until 13th October, when they were broken off without a decision having been reached, and the Finnish delegation returned to Helsinki for further discussions with the government. It reappeared in Moscow a few days later with fresh proposals, but these, too, were rejected, and the delegation left for home on 24th October. For about a month the Finnish representatives made repeated visits to Moscow in an attempt to reach a fair and honourable solution to the problem that confronted the two countries, leaving Moscow for the last time on 14th November. Two days later a particularly unpleasant propaganda war was started against Finland in the Soviet press and wireless. Despite this the Finnish government was still hopeful of being able to maintain the peace, but as time went on it became clear that the propaganda war was a prelude to military operations.

On 26th November the Soviet Union claimed that Finnish artillery had fired on a Carelian village called Mainila, on the Russian side of the frontier, killing one soldier and wounding twelve others. The Finnish government showed that its observers had noted and immediately reported that seven shots had been fired on the Russian side of the frontier, and that since early November, anticipating just such an incident, there had been no Finnish artillery within range of Mainila. Despite this explanation the Soviet Union abrogated the non-aggression pact with Finland, in direct defiance of its terms, on 28th November. The next day it broke off diplomatic relations, claiming that a Finnish army patrol in Petsamo had penetrated into Soviet territory. The truth was that a Russian detachment had crossed the border into Finland and had kidnapped three Finnish frontier guards.

Finland then proposed to the Soviet Union that they should follow the procedures for settling their differences in accordance with their non-aggression pact, or should alternatively ask an independent party to mediate. She also offered to withdraw her forces on the Carelian isthmus far enough from Leningrad, which lay only 20 miles from the frontier, so as to make sure that that city did not feel threatened. These representations were of no avail, as the Soviet Union had already decided to go to war with Finland. On 30th November its forces crossed the frontier on all the available roads and penetrated into the country. At the same time its air force bombed Helsinki and other undefended places in the south of the country. Thus began the Winter War, "an act of aggression hardly ever equalled in the history of the world".

The outcry in the rest of the world was immediate, and virtually unanimous, and one country after another joined in condemning the actions of the Soviet Union. Sympathy for Finland in the United Kingdom was so great that even the technical press gave an opinion. For instance, the *Mining World*, a London weekly, wrote: "The unjustifiable attack upon a peace-loving people has shocked the world, for it is laughable to suppose that even though Leningrad is only 20 miles from the Finnish border, that Finland, with 300,000 troops, could menace the might of Russia with 15,000,000 troops." The paper added a week later that the Russians had attacked Finland deliberately for the sole purpose of prolonging the war started by Hitler in September, and that Russia's attitude, in the view of many thoughtful persons, was more dangerous to the peace and security of the world than were even the aggressive designs of Germany.

On the outbreak of the Winter War the British Red Cross immediately allocated £10,000 for assistance to relieve suffering caused by the war, and made a grant of £1,000 towards the cost of a consignment of chloroform, which was urgently needed. This was followed by vast medical stores, comprising x-ray apparatus, operating tables, dressings, surgical instruments and drugs, all needed in a hurry, which were promptly found and sent off.

On 2nd December the Finnish government appealed to the League of Nations, and a week later the League called on its members to help Finland with material and humanitarian aid, and to refrain from any action which might weaken her ability to resist the aggressor. On 14th December a meeting of the Council of the League appealed to the Soviet Union to cease hostilities and to accept mediation by the League. Molotoff, on behalf of his country, refused to discuss the Finnish question, and the same day the Soviet Union was expelled from the League.

OSASTO SISU

"The Tough Detachment"

In order to place the British volunteers in their proper light, as members of a larger formation, it is appropriate at this stage to record the arrangements made in Finland for the reception and training of foreign volunteers who arrived there during and after the Winter War. Field-Marshal Baron C.G. Mannerheim, the Supreme Commander of Finland's Defence Forces, realised that without a knowledge of either of Finland's two languages, Finnish and Swedish, the best that a foreign volunteer could hope to do would be to release a Finn for the front. So on 1st December 1939 he made an Order that the Headquarters of the Home Forces should arrange for their reception and training. Two days later orders went out that records of volunteers should be kept at ports of arrival, and that linguists should be posted to all ports and to Tornio, on the Finnish side of the frontier with Sweden, at the head of the Gulf of Bothnia. Here the Finnish and Swedish rail systems meet, and here numbers of Scandinavian and other volunteers were expected. Esko Riekki, a senior civil servant and former Head of the State Police, was appointed Home Forces Liaison Officer at Tornio, while in Helsinki a Volunteer Office was set up at General Staff Headquarters. The office was under Professor Lönnrot, with General Oskar Enckell, a former Chief of Staff, in overall command of all the foreign volunteers. On 21st December the Finnish Diet agreed that volunteers should be entitled to rations, accommodation, pay or salary, and pilots' bonuses on the same basis as Finnish conscripts. Ordinary privates received 10 marks a day and monthly-paid officers 500 marks.

The Headquarters of the Home Forces were in

Hämeenlinna, 67 miles north of Helsinki on the main railway. Here it was arranged that foreign volunteers should be quartered and trained in Lapua, 275 miles north of Helsinki on the same line. Home of the State Ammunition Factory, "the celebrated parish of Lapua" already had a barracks, as it had been a garrison for Russian troops until 1917. It had also been the scene of important events in Finland's history, for during the 1808-09 Russo-Swedish war, Adlercreutz defeated Rayevski near the town, and troops raised there in 1917 played a significant part in the Finnish War of Independence.

Captain (later Major) Bertil Walter Nordlund, then 36 years of age, who spoke five languages fluently, was assistant to the military attaché at the Finnish Legation in Stockholm at the outbreak of the Winter War. Returning to active service in Finland on 6th January 1940 he reported to General Malmberg of the Finnish General Staff. The General told him that he was entrusting to him a difficult but interesting command, but without assistants, without funds, and without precise instructions. He was to collect the foreign volunteers together and to knock them into shape, first a platoon, then a company, battalion or brigade, whatever was possible. Captain Nordlund arrived in Lapua on 9th January. He later wrote that his first job there was to invent a suitable cover-name for his detachment. He finally chose *Osasto Sisu* (The Tough Detachment), because *sisu* was a word then internationally known as a symbol of Finnish toughness and strength, and because foreigners could pronounce it. He then took command of the first eight foreign volunteers who had arrived before him.

The Headquarters of the Helsinki Military District arranged to recruit volunteers from among the foreigners resident in Finland. A man offering his services at the Reception Centre for Foreign Volunteers was given a movement order and a rail pass to Lapua, where he reported to Osasto Sisu, signed on, received his army number, and handed in his civilian identity card. The cards were then forwarded to various authorities for inspection, sometimes to the State Police in Helsinki or Vaasa, sometimes to the

Ministry of Defence, or to the Headquarters of the Home Forces. Pilots volunteering for the Air Force, however, were sent to Air Training Regiment 2 at Parola, near Pori.

The first foreign volunteer to arrive in Lapua and sign on was a Canadian Finn named Grönberg, who had seen service as a captain in the War of Independence in 1917-18, and who was made a Captain in the Reserve. Captain Nordlund, who had the powers to hire and fire, discharged him a few days later for unmilitary conduct. During the next few days seventeen others arrived, including the first Finnish-born British subjects, Hancock W. and Beck. Beck was really the very first British volunteer of all, for on the outbreak of the Winter War he offered to assist the British Consul in Helsinki, and worked as a clerk at the Consulate up to Christmas 1939, dealing with enquiries about volunteering. Other British subjects to arrive in Lapua included two brothers born in Russia before the revolution and described as stateless British, and Bamford, who was also born in Russia.

The Finnish constitution stipulates that the language of the country's defence forces is Finnish. This was quietly disregarded in Osasto Sisu, which had a No. 1 or International company, using Finnish words of command but with instruction in French and German, a Hungarian company using Magyar, and a British company using English. By 20th February there were about a hundred volunteers in Lapua, quartered in the former Russian barracks near the church. During the next ten days a further twenty or so arrived. There was now a total of 23 different nationalities, the largest group being Estonians. A Hungarian company comprising 18 officers, 10 NCOs and 341 men arrived on 3rd March via London, Bergen and Tornio, and brought the total up to about five hundred. One of the Hungarians, Illo von Walzel, arrived on his own, and later recorded that it looked as though all the world's adventurers and confidence tricksters had by some mutual agreement decided to hold a meeting in Lapua. All sorts of people turned up, he noted, from lion-tamers to doctors of law. Two Yakuts arrived from Helsinki, and, although liable for service in the Finnish army they were sent to Lapua because it was thought that their Mongoloid features might cause them to be mistaken for Russian spies if they joined a Finnish unit. A Dutchman came from as far away as Batavia, the modern Jakarta; and many of those who had only joined up for the duration of the war left as hastily as they had come when the armistice was signed.

Much of the history of Osasto Sisu was recorded in the unit's War Diary, which was kept (in Swedish, anonymously) between 3rd March and 10th May. Meanwhile, a second-in-command to Captain Nordlund arrived in Lapua on 17th February. This was Bror-Leo Lerche, a landowner with property on the island of Nauvo, near Turku. He subsequently employed several volunteers on his estate, including Rattigan (as a gun-dog trainer), Budd, and, in the spring of 1941, three volunteers released from protective custody.

One of the officers in No. 1 company was Captain John Joseph Jack O'Brien Hitching. On 22nd February he arrived in Lapua, five days after the London *Daily Sketch* had reported him to be an Englishman and a company commander in the Finnish Foreign Legion, and had credited him with the Military Cross. A Roman Catholic, born in Portsmouth of Irish parents, he served in the first World War in France, Belgium, Salonika and Archangel, and acted as liaison officer between the British and Finnish General Staffs in 1920. He married and settled down in Helsinki about 1932, where he worked as a free-lance journalist, using a green ribbon in his typewriter to stress his Irishness. In March, in Captain Chandor's absence, he interviewed and wrote a report on each of the nine men in Winter's draft, who were quartered in the High School, and signed it Officer Commanding the British Contingent. He returned to No. 1 company when Captain Chandor returned to Lapua a few days later, and on demobilisation later in the month went home to Helsinki. To the British volunteers who subsequently met him in that city he used to say that he did not dare to return to England, but never said why. Having lived in Finland through the Russo-Finnish wars of 1939-40 and 1941-44 it was not unnatural that he should have been accused of working for countries other than his own. In 1944, for instance, the Finnish State Police knew that he was reporting both to their Ari Kauhanen and to the German Büro Cellarius, the German intelligence office in Helsinki. He left Finland for Sweden after the United Kingdom concluded peace with Finland in the summer of 1944.

A man who had a profound influence on the British volunteers through his long association with them was posted to Lapua as assistant to Captain Norlund and Lieut. Lerche on 12th March. This was Lieut. Count Peter Nicholas von der Pahlen, born in 1896 in the then Russian Baltic province of Courland. The son of a big landowner and senior public servant, he was educated in St Petersburg, now Leningrad, and fought in the White Army which defended Courland after the Russian revolution in 1917. Courland then became part of Latvia and the family estates were nationalised, so the Count moved to Finland and managed an aunt's property, the manor and park of Monrepos, near Viipuri. As he had had no military training in Finland he was not called up on the outbreak of the Winter War, so he asked Field-Marshal Mannerheim, who was a personal friend of the family, to give him something to do. He was made a lieutenant on the reserve, and before being posted to Lapua he acted as interpreter at the interrogations of Russian prisoners of war. He spoke fluent German, French, Russian and English, in addition to Finnish and Swedish, and was an ideal choice for Osasto Sisu, as subsequent events showed.

In the second week of March, when Captain Nordlund was discussing with his superiors the sending of a volunteer company to the front, rumours of an armistice began to circulate, and on the morning of 13th March the volunteers collected in the barracks to hear the noon wireless bulletin. The signing of the armistice was announced, and the war diarist recorded that the rumour was confirmed, "and all sorts of unthinkable and unexpected scenes occurred in the barracks – old warriors could not conceal their tears, and for the first time it seemed that Osasto Sisu had lost the reason for existing and the right to be." Taylor H., who had only just arrived in Lapua with Winter's draft, whose members also heard the broadcast, wrote: "I shall never forget the bitter tears which were shed by the Finns, men as well as women, when they heard that all their fine efforts against the Russians had been in vain." But notwithstanding the armistice, volunteers of all nationalities continued to turn up. On 16th March a Spaniard, an Italian, a Luxemburger, a Jugoslav and two Estonians arrived, and later came the two British drafts, some Belgians, and several Frenchmen. The last volunteers arrived on 26th March via Tornio, and included Albert John Hart, an Englishman, Messrs. Hawkins and Johnston from the U.S.A. (the last-named without proper identity documents), and a Canadian pilot named Newhouse.

With only a day's notice General Enckell arrived in Lapua on 22nd March, with a view to settling the future of the volunteers. After reviewing the three companies he attended a dinner given in his honour at the Hotel Simsiö, now the Hotel Lapua. Those present included Captains Nordlund and Chandor, Lieuts. Kemesi and Celmins, and officer-cadet Miklosz. After the meal there was a long discussion on the fate of Osasto Sisu, and late in the evening it was announced that those who had compelling reasons to return to their homelands or to resume their civilian occupations in Finland could obtain their discharge. Estimates showed that about 60 men from the British company and about 70 from No. 1 company wanted to go home.

On 27th March a return was made of the strength of Osasto Sisu. Of twenty-two nations then represented, including three stateless men, there was a total of 717 volunteers, of which the No.1 company had 155, the Hungarian company 341, the British company 158, cadre personnel 24, and sick, on leave, etc. 39. Of the 717 men, 639 took part in the parade for Field-Marshal Mannerheim on that day. When the British and Hungarian units left Lapua on 17th April only a skeleton staff remained, consisting of Captain Nordlund, his adjutant Lieut. K. Rings, Lieut. Count von der Pahlen, and a mechanic, the others having been demobilised. On 10th May Captain Nordlund was posted to

Helsinki to take charge of the Headquarters Volunteer Office, and Osasto Sisu came to an end. The other three members of its staff were posted to the Swedish School on Kulosaari, an island suburb of Helsinki, presumably for demobilisation.

FINNISH AID BUREAU

While Osasto Sisu was getting organized in Finland, things began to move in London. On 2nd January 1940 the British government promised the League of Nations that the United Kingdom would do all it could to help Finland resist Soviet Russian aggression. The same day Harold Gibson, M.C., then working in the secretariat of the War Cabinet, suggested to Lord Halifax, the Foreign Secretary, that permission should be granted to raise a volunteer force of a thousand men. The matter was submitted to the War Cabinet, which decided that the British government could not raise a volunteer force, but that it could allow an Aid for Finland Bureau to be opened. Its functions would be twofold, first to be a central Bureau for aiding Finland in her prosecution of the war against Russia, and second to be a recruiting office for raising a British contingent for the international volunteer force in Finland. News of this decision was passed to the Finnish government, which informed Lord Chatfield, First Lord of the Admiralty and Chairman of the War Cabinet, on 21st January, that it would welcome a token force of British volunteers, as it would have a wonderful effect in raising civilian morale after the recent heavy bombing. It would also set an example to neutral countries, particularly to the United States, who might reasonably be expected to follow the British example.

The Finnish Minister in London, Georg Achates Gripenberg, whose wife Peggy was Welsh, was unable to carry out Gibson's proposals unaided. He therefore sought the advice of Lords Halifax and Chatfield, who recommended that Gibson should undertake the organization of the Bureau as its Director. The War Cabinet gave its approval for the formation of a Committee to Aid Finland on Friday 26th January, and the Committee's first meeting was held the same day. On this and on all subsequent occasions Gripenberg chaired the meetings of the Committee, which was composed of the Rt. Hon. L.S. Amery, M.P. (Secretary of State for India), Lord Balfour of Burleigh, the Earl of Lytton, Lieut-General Sir George McDonough (a former Director of Military Intelligence and Chairman of the Anglo-Finnish Society in London), Colonel Gösta Serlachius (a Finnish industrialist, who left for Finland in February and who did not return), and Richard Temple, K.C., with Gibson as Director. Subsequently Lord Davies, Lord Dawson of Penn (the Royal Physician), Lord Nuffield, Lord Phillimore, Harold Macmillan, M.P. (later Lord Stockton), and Raymond Needham, K.C. (an eminent tax counsel and honorary counsel to the Finnish Legation in London) joined the Committee.

The Committee was unofficially formed some days before 26th January, for its promoters had time to invite several leading representatives of the Labour party to join it, with a view to giving it as wide a political base as possible. For no stated reasons the invitations were declined, only Philip (later Lord) Noel-Baker, M.P., admitting that he felt he could be of more help if he were not on the committee. He had recently visited Finland, and had had the distinction of taking a sauna close to the front line. As regards the others, who included Clement R. (later Lord) Attlee, M.P., and Sir Walter (later Lord) Citrine, of the T.U.C., who visited Finland together in February 1940, one can only conclude that the Labour party's then fondness of all things Russian, and particularly for what they called "socialism", and possibly the remote fear that the sending of volunteers to Finland might involve the United Kingdom in a war with the Soviet Union, overcame any desire that may have had to assist actively in opposing one of their country's enemies. Of all the Labour peers invited to join the Committee, only Lord Snell accepted. He was a member from about 20th February to 4th March, for which gesture his name is still remembered in Finland. It is worth noting, however, that despite the hostility of individual "socialists" to the Finnish Aid Bureau, both Mrs Barbara Ayrton-Gould, Chairman of the Labour Party, and T. Holmes, Chairman of the T.U.C., were members of the Executive Committee of the Finland Fund, whose chairman was Lord Phillimore and whose Honorary President was Gripenberg.

The day the British Committee for Finland was formed it accepted Lord Davies' offer of Thorney House, Smith Square, London, S.W.1, for its offices, and the Bureau opened there the same day. Lord Davies generously agreed to charge no rent, to pay the rates himself, and to lend the necessary office furniture. Thanks to the assistance of Colonel Serlachius and the generosity of three firms in the timber trade who had close business ties with Finland (Price & Pierce Limited, Plywood and Timber Products Limited and Corke, Sons and Company Limited), a nucleus of staff was already at Thorney House on 26th January and started work immediately after the first committee meeting had been held. The Bureau paid the salaries of this nucleus, except for five which the three firms paid.

The first Committee meeting agreed that Gripenberg should staff and finance the recruiting office, which would be under his chairmanship. An age limit of forty years was set for volunteers, except for those with special qualifications, though this rule was not very closely observed. Finally, it was agreed to use a supply of badges and buttons already in existence, and that uniforms should be sent out to Finland in advance.

Within a few days Thorney House was fully staffed. In addition to the Director there was a Deputy Director, George Faber (the managing director of the management company of Investment Trust Units, a well-known Unit Trust), who had three chief personal assistants and a second personal assistant, respectively John Watson, Major Walter Creighton, W. Dwight Whitney (an American), and Marshal Buchan. Secretary to Gibson was Miss Trevor, and to Faber, Miss Smart. Major R.E. Crane acted as Equipment Officer and Mr McLeod as Transport Officer, while G. Edmunds was Paymaster. Liaison Officer between the Bureau and the Finnish Legation, and resident at Thorney House, was Peter Cederholm, a multi-lingual Finnish officer who had served with Gibson in Spain. Mrs Tatton-Brown was Registrar, and Miss Foreshall was Special Equipment Officer. She was instrumental in the formation of knitting groups, whose activities were so successful that every volunteer who went to Finland had a thick soft white knitted woollen scarf to keep out the cold. The three receptionists were Colonel Butler-Stoney, Colonel Powell and Major Deverell, who were backed up by fifteen clerical staff, two telephonists, two commissionaires, two caretakers and two cleaners, as well as several members of the Military Transport Corps and the Women's Voluntary Services. The majority of the officers gave their services free.

On 2nd February the Bureau received a message from the Finnish government that mechanics and technicians were urgently needed to help with the supply and repair of war materials, and for service in mills and factories to release Finns for the army. A scheme was finally approved by the Ministry of Labour on 27th February, and a large number of technicians were enrolled. Dozens of them were granted transit visas through Sweden, though it seems unlikely that more than a few reached their destination.

As part of the Bureau's function of obtaining material aid, Gibson and Lord Ismay had discussions in February with General Oskar Enckell, who had arrived in London as a special envoy to seek help from the British government. Apart from the discussions he appears to have achieved little.

On 10th February Lord Davies and Macmillan went to Finland with Colonel Serlachius to make enquiries on the spot, and Lord Davies telegraphed nine days later asking for a hundred field-guns, fifty howitzers, and ammunition, which Gripenberg and Gibson discussed with Sir Walter Citrine, who had also just returned from Finland. The latter urged that the Labour party should do all it could to secure the guns and aeroplanes which Finland needed. After much discussion the Air Ministry somewhat grudgingly released eight Blenheim bombers and asked the Bureau to provide the necessary aircrews. On 11th March the Committee made a further appeal to Neville Chamberlain, the Prime Minister, to assure Britain's immediate, effective and full support in the event of Soviet Russia offering unacceptable terms to the Finns. But it was too late, as the armistice was signed on the evening of the following day, and the bombers were not delivered until well after peace had been concluded.

Lord Nuffield, meanwhile, gave generously to the Bureau and joined the Committee just before its meeting held on 9th February. The meeting agreed that volunteers should receive 2s. a day, and while in Finland should have Finnish army pay of 10 marks a day, the balance being kept to the volunteer's credit in London, under the control of the Committee. The meeting also agreed that 500 men should be sent out at first (a figure increased ten days later to 1,000), that publicity was essential, and that an account should be opened at the District Bank (now part of the National Westminster Bank) at its Cornhill branch in the City. Arrangements were made with the Passport Office to issue passports free of charge to volunteers. This appears to have been done against the production of a civilian identity card and a statement from the volunteer in lieu of a proper birth certificate. Evidently adopted to save time, this bending of the rules permitted several volunteers, including two eighteen-year-olds from the same house at the same minor public school as the writer, to add six years to their true ages and to ensure their acceptance for service overseas. Only one, Owbridge, made the journey; and his correct year of birth is given in Appendix "A". At the same time the Norwegian and Swedish authorities agreed to issue transit visas to volunteers without charge, and, following the example of the French government, the War Cabinet agreed that British volunteers should be transported free by rail in Britain, while the Finnish government undertook to provide free rail transport in Scandinavia.

Gibson estimated that it would cost £200 to equip and arm each volunteer, and to maintain him in the field for six months. Transport to and from Finland would cost a further £200, so that the money needed for the first 500 volunteers would be £100,000. Realising that the success of the movement depended on the speed with which it was carried out, Lord Nuffield guaranteed this money so that the Committee could enlist and despatch them without having to wait while the necessary funds were collected. As the British government was anxious to avoid publicity a public appeal was impossible, so Needham undertook to seek large donations from his wealthy friends to cover Lord Nuffield's guarantee. To assist Needham, Lord Nuffield very generously promised that when £400,000 had been raised he would make a gift of his original guarantee and so bring the total up to £500,000.

Meanwhile, on 21st February, after visiting Mänttä, the home of Colonel Serlachius and his industrial complex, Harold Macmillan was taken on an official tour of the Suomussalmi and Kuhmo fronts where, in addition to a captured Russian helmet, he obtained the Finnish officer's white fur hat later beloved of cartoonists. Lord Davies went to Lapua to see what arrangements were being made for the volunteers. He made a brief speech to the volunteers in the assembly hall of the International Barracks, and then took coffee with the officers. In the evening he dined in the canteen. Word soon went round that he was arranging billets for his fellow-countrymen.

A Committee meeting held on 26th February was told that the ban on publicity had been lifted, and decided to launch a public appeal for one million pounds, under the title of "The Fighting Fund for Finland", to bring it into line with General John O'Ryan's appeal in the United States, launched some weeks earlier. Temple worked out a scheme for launching the appeal, but the armistice came before it could be carried into effect. In the meantime, considerable sums were being sent direct to Gripenberg at the Finnish Legation in London; in Leeds, for instance, a local collection made in mid-February produced £4,200. Support for the appeal came from some unusual quarters: at the request of Professor Tancred Borenius, the eminent Finnish art historian who had lived many years in Britain, the septuagenarian artist John Hassall designed a poster to advertise the Finland

Fund, while Charles Thomas, another artist, designed and produced stamps with the inscription *Finlandia Invicta* (Finland unvanquished), which were sold in aid of the Fund. And a Mr Goodwin offered to write a book about Finland and to give the profits from it to the Fund.

In addition to the infantry volunteers, there was also a group of sixteen anti-aircraft fire control specialists, temporarily discharged from the Royal Artillery and Royal Army Ordnance Corps. They were enrolled at Vickers Limited, head office in London as civilian employees of De Jersey & Company, Vickers' Helsinki associate. The first six, who were R.A.O.C. Sergeants – Dorey, Frisby, Hartgrove, Hurst, Ongley and Sturgess – left London about 20th February and arrived in Finland three days later, where they were placed under the Ministry of Defence. Of the remainder Best was a member of Captain Blew-Jones' draft as far as Bergen, and he and the others – George, Lazarus, Mason, Parcell, Silverwood-Cope, Smith A.M., Sutton, Taylor and Webb – reached Helsinki by various means. Like the infantry volunteers they received the Finnish Winter War Service Medal with the bar *Kotijoukot* (Home Forces). Towards the end of March Silverwood-Cope was given a commission as Acting Captain in the Royal Artillery and took up the post of Acting Assistant Military Attaché at the British Legation in Helsinki, where he became known as Captain Cope, and took over responsibility for the technicians. Most of them returned home later in 1940, but Frisby and Hurst stayed in Helsinki for about a year, working for De Jersey & Company.

A group whose activities were not mentioned in print until 1975 were sixteen ground staff volunteers from the Royal Air Force, drawn from the 56 and 151 Squadrons at North Weald in Kent. The party comprised sergeants Bennett and Galpin, corporals Bristow, Martin, Russell, Sayce and Short, and leading aircraftmen Biltcliffe, de la Plain, Duckworth, Inward, Marshall, Merrells, Mitchell, Reid and White. All were temporarily discharged from the R.A.F. and travelled as civilians working for the Gloster Aircraft Co. Ltd. There was some delay in obtaining Swedish visas, and it was not until 22nd February that the first twelve men left. The other four – Bennett, de la Plain, Marshall and Mitchell – left Perth by air for Stavanger in Norway on 3rd March, and continued by train to join the main party in Stockholm. On arrival by air at Turku the party was posted to Säkylä, on the shores of Pyhäjärvi (Holy Lake), some forty miles north of Turku. The lake was frozen over and used as a landing-strip. After spending three weeks servicing Hurricanes they were transferred on similar duties to Hollola, near Lahti, on the shores of Vesijärvi (Water Lake). Here they remained until early April, when they were released for repatriation. They arrived in Stockholm on 10th April, the day the Germans occupied Norway, and other plans for their repatriation had to be made. Bennett and Mitchell flew home from Stockholm in the diplomatic plane, and Biltcliffe, de la Plain and Marshall reached home early in 1941 via Russia, the Middle East and the Cape of Good Hope. The remaining eleven, of whom eight had been sentenced to extradition and interned for allegedly planning to sabotage installations loading iron ore for Germany at Oxelösund, south of Stockholm, were sent to Petsamo, in northern Finland, at the end of August, as noted later. There a Swedish vessel took them to Iceland, then under British occupation.

The Bureau also assisted three civilian parties who had volunteered to help Finland. Largest of these groups was the Friends' Ambulance Unit, 56 strong, which arrived in Finland in two parties early in February and which worked on the front north of Lake Ladoga, notably at Tohmajärvi and Leppäsyrjä. After the end of hostilities it left for Sweden, with a view to joining up with the British forces in northern Norway, but only a few managed to get through, and the others returned to Stockholm and were repatriated through Russia in October.

The second-largest civilian group was a unit of the First Aid Nursing Yeomanry, or F.A.N.Y, affectionately known as Fannies, whose eighteen civilian nurses and their ten ambulances were in charge of Miss Mary Runciman, an adopted niece of the late Lord Runciman. The party travelled via Newcastle and Oslo to Stockholm, where it arrived on 27th February, and Umeå, half-way up the coast of the Gulf of Bothnia. The vehicles arrived there in the first week of March, and the convoy drove round the top of the Gulf and down to Helsinki, where the party split up, one part going to Lahti and the main part to a hospital at Punkaharju. After the invasion of Norway the party was reunited in Helsinki, and after some delay was shipped out through Petsamo on an American freighter which had come to collect Finnish-American volunteers.

Charles Anthony Gilkison, a film director, organized and planned the third and smallest civilian group, a party of eight London Fire Brigade volunteers. With a Brigade officer named Locke in charge, its members were chosen from about four hundred candidates. It left London by air for Sweden on 12th March, after a farewell party at the offices of the Finland Fund in 9 Upper Belgrave Street, S.W.1. The equipment was sent by sea to Umeå in Sweden, and the vehicles followed the same route as the F.A.N.Y. convoy to Helsinki, where the party arrived three days after the armistice but still in time to be of considerable use, and to be photographed against a background of burnt-out ruins. The members worked with the Helsinki Fire Brigade on special jobs until the early spring of 1941, when they were "demobilised" and took up jobs teaching English, either individually or for the British Council in Helsinki and various provincial towns. Gilkison worked for a while as a cartoonist for a Swedish-language newspaper in Turku. Seven of the party eventually left Finland at the end of June 1941 with the main body of ex-military volunteers, the eighth, who had been injured, being flown home. A grateful Finnish government awarded each man the Winter War Service Medal with the bar "Home Forces", and Gilkison received in addition the Freedom Cross, 4th Class (Civil). For many years after the Winter War the Helsinki Fire Brigade used a bright red van with the inscription "London Fire Volunteers" on its sides. When the Germans protested about it in 1942 the Finns replied cheerfully that they were satisfied that vehicle still had some years of useful life left, and that in any case it did not need repainting. It was finally scrapped in the 1950s.

Last of the volunteer groups, but one which failed to leave the country, was a Skiers' Corps under the command of J.L. Coats, formerly an officer in the Grenadier Guards. It managed to get a little training, but was disbanded after the armistice and its members, many of whom were serving officers, returned to their units.

RECRUITING

Sympathy for Finland ran high in the British press, which at the time had few good stories to cover. The Finnish Legation in Smith Square, London, soon found that so many people were coming forward to offer their services that it opened a register of men and women volunteers, as did Finnish vice-consuls in the northern towns. Details of volunteers were passed to the Finnish Aid Bureau when it opened its doors at the end of January. People arriving and leaving there had to negotiate a crowd of journalists and photographers who, as might be expected, managed to interview a large number of volunteers who were not accepted. Notable among these were Percy Jerred, 19, son of the fencing-master at Eton, and Leslie Wallace, 15, of Kingsbury, the youngest applicant recorded. Predictably, Britain's only communist daily, the *Daily Worker,* was strongly pro-Soviet and anti-Finnish. Under the heading "Mannerheim Recruiting in London?" it reported on 7th February "on the best possible authority" that the London representative of the White Guard Finnish Government had received official permission to recruit soldiers for General Mannerheim in London. Ten days later it asked "Are British lives to be sacrificed in an intervention which will lead to war against the Soviet Union?" Among the opponents of the Finnish cause was George Bernard Shaw, the self-made millionaire playwright.

Under the Foreign Enlistment Act of 1870 it is against British law to recruit volunteers for service in foreign countries. However, the Act contains a power to grant dispensations, and so to legalise its recruiting activities the Finnish Aid Bureau applied for a special Royal licence, which H.M. King George VI granted on 8th February. Under the licence Gibson enlisted every volunteer, each of whom took an oath of allegiance to Finland in Gripenberg's presence, as embodied in the Agreement of Service.

"Probably the first man in Great Britain to hold a Royal licence for enlisting British subjects for service in a foreign country", Harold Gibson, M.C., was described as tall, grey-haired, and "that rather rare combination, a sportsman who is also a linguist." After a distinguished career in the army during the first World War he became a Commissioner for the League of Nations in southern Russia, and during the Spanish Civil War he served as Deputy Director of Supplies to the International Board for Non-Intervention in Spain. When not concerned with international affairs he bred horses, for which he had a particular flair, and with Lord Manners, founded the New Forest Cavaliers, a well-known riding and driving association, of which he was secretary.

By 14th February, when it was announced in Parliament that Britons would be allowed to volunteer for Finland and that the Foreign Office would grant exit permits for men over the age of 27, the Finnish Legation in London had received between two and three thousand applications. Meanwhile, the second meeting of the Committee took place on 30th January, when it changed the name of the organization to the Finnish Aid Bureau. It noted that about 300 names had been selected from the best of the applicants to volunteer. The third meeting, held on 2nd February, arranged for the first detachment to be interviewed on 7th February, at which time applications were coming in at the rate of 400 a day. Among the first volunteers to apply were a great many Scots and Irish, and the Committee decided that it could save time and expense if branch offices were opened in Glasgow, Edinburgh and Dublin. With the assistance of Lord Balfour an office was opened in Glasgow early in March, but the armistice intervened before offices could be opened in the other two cities. A good many applicants had some experience of flying, and were anxious to offer their services to the Finnish Air Force. They agreed, however, to enlist as infantry privates on the understanding that they would be given the opportunity to transfer to that branch of the Finnish Defence Forces on arrival in Finland.

Every applicant was given a form to fill in, giving the fullest possible information about himself, with space for two reliable references. From the details thus supplied the Bureau staff were able to determine which of the applicants were worth interviewing. Some were rejected on account of age and some because they were in reserved occupations or had relatives financially dependent upon them. In the case of the latter the Committee felt that it would be impossible to pay an allowance to relatives in the event of the volunteer being killed, although according to the Agreement of Service this was intended to be a liability of the Finnish government. All rejected applicants received a letter telling them why they had been turned down; among their number were several born in Russia before the revolution, one of whom wished to go to prisoner-of-war camps to try to persuade Russian prisoners to defect, and another who wanted to spread anti-Russian propaganda over the wireless. Only two Russian-born volunteers were accepted, under assumed names, and only one of them actually reached Finland.

Successful applicants were given an appointment at Thorney House for interview and medical examination. On arrival there the applicant was taken in charge by a messenger who had a file bearing the applicant's name and number and containing his application form, a form for the interviewing officers, a form for the medical officers, and an equipment measurement form. Two members of the interviewing panel interviewed the applicant. The panel combined a wealth of experience and talent: The Rt. Hon. L.S. Amery, M.P., The Rt. Hon. Lord Balfour of Burleigh, Admiral T.P.H. Beamish, Brigadier-General Lord Croft, Sir Iain Colquhoun, The Rt. Hon. Lord Esher, Lieut-General Sir W.T. Furse, Sir Hubert Gough, General Sir Alfred Knox, Colonel C.C. Leveson-Gower, Lieut-General Sir George Macdonough, Colonel C. Ponsonby, M.P., and Brigadier-General A.C.M.G. Symons. After the interview the two panel members decided whether the applicant was suitable for military service in Finland. "Well, Mr Pearce", was one question put to an applicant, "and why do you want to go to Finland?" – "Fight the bloody Finns, of course", came the unexpected reply. Pearce was accepted.

From the interview the applicant went for a medical inspection. Lord Dawson of Penn, who was President of the Royal College of Physicians as well as a member of the Committee of the Finnish Aid Bureau, built up and assisted a panel of some forty doctors for the purpose. Being well acquainted with the young consultants who had recently been elected to the Fellowship of the College he had no difficulty in obtaining candidates. They generally worked in pairs for a morning or an afternoon at a time; and later many of them became internationally famous. As might be expected, in the hurry to build up the panel one or two names were inserted in error, including that of a gynæcologist.

One of the inspecting specialists wrote many years later that there was no dearth of recruits, some of whom rejected any suggestion that they were physically unfit to serve. Sometimes they practised guile and deception to avoid rejection, by adjusting their ages and concealing their scars. "In one instance the loss of one eye was countered with the argument that one eye had to be closed anyway when taking aim with a rifle, especially, as he emphasised, 'it is only my left eye'." They were, indeed, the specialist continued, "a grand bunch of variegated beings, some misfits in society, some dwellers below stairs, but all imbued with sympathy for the maltreated, and ready to forfeit life in a just cause where wrong needed to be righted."

Among those passed at the medical inspection as fit for military service, or for what was euphemistically described as "indoor duties" were three men with seriously defective hearing, one man with a stiff leg, one with an artificial leg, two blind in the left eye (one of whom turned out later to be a crack shot), several with poor eyesight, and single cases of double hernia scars, hernia and hydrocœle, lack of a finger, lack of a thumb, crippled hands and curvature of the spine (who had a pilot's licence), and mitral stenosis. There were also cases of weak hearts and lungs, pleurisy adhesions and neurasthenia, and two were found on arrival in Lapua to have contracted a venereal disease. The writer had the flattest feet (then considered an affliction) the inspecting specialist had ever seen, and he called his colleague's attention to them.

The poor physical condition of many of the volunteers who reached Finland and served there aroused the attention of the Finnish authorities, who were highly critical of the apparently haphazard selection methods employed in London and other capitals. As a result of their own medical examination of some thirty British volunteers attached to the Finnish Air Force, they not unnaturally concluded that the rest of the unit was of a similarly low physical standard. The matter should, however, be seen against the background of the general mobilisation of all able-bodied men between twenty and twenty-eight years of age at the outbreak of war in September 1939. A month before that event *The Times* quoted an Army Council report, made after a quarter of a century of medical benefit under the National Health Insurance Act, which showed that out of the last million men who had volunteered to serve in the British armed forces between the wars, one in three was rejected on sight, the second was rejected on physical, medical or educational grounds, and the third was accepted only after standards had been lowered as regards height, vision and teeth. It therefore seems likely that a large proportion of the volunteers of military age were chosen from among those whom the British army had rejected.

If the medical panel and the interviewing officers recommended that a volunteer be accepted, he was photographed. He then went for an interview with Gibson, who told him the result. Then he was sent to Lillywhite's, in Lower Regent Street, to be measured for his uniform, and one of an appropriate size was packed with other items in a canvas bag bearing his number, and was sent off separately.

After the volunteer had been accepted at Thorney House, his personal details were sent to the Home Office, the Military Intelligence Department, and the Ministry of Labour, as well as to Scotland Yard, whose "satisfactory assurances" were necessary before the volunteer could be finally permitted to go overseas. The purpose of these checks, which in some instances seem to have been somewhat cursory, was to prevent criminals and communists, who might engage in sabotage, from going to Finland, and in this they were fairly successful, since a number of known members of the British Communist Party were refused permits to leave, and only one, Weaver, got through. The checks were also intended to identify volunteers who had dependents, but here again a number of married men, some with small children, managed to slip through.

The volunteers were equipped with the standard issue British army uniform, webbing-belt, pouches, large and small packs, and respirators. Although special Arctic equipment such as Balaclava helmets, special boots, special gloves, windcheaters, snow-glasses, field-dressings and snow camouflage cloaks (but not camouflage trousers) were on the equipment list, only the gloves, which turned out to be ski gloves, and the snow-cloaks, were issued. It was not until the end of March that the deficiencies were made good, and there was an issue of Finnish jackboots, fur caps, dubbin, field-dressings, and a blue and white cockade to go in the fur caps. In lieu of windcheaters a non-uniform leather waistcoat or a British army leather jerkin was issued in London before departure. The list of equipment which found its way into Gibson's Report made no reference to a hussif (an important item), or to knife, fork and spoon, the British soldier's "fighting irons". Not all the specially-made camouflage cloaks were issued, and when on 18th April the War Office asked for the pattern the Bureau was able to supply 400 cloaks from stock for the British forces in northern Norway. Being made of a good-quality heavy duty cotton cloth, many of the cloaks issued to volunteers in Finland were later made into shirts.

The cap-badge was a chromium-plated rose, two inches in diameter, bearing the letters "NI". The greatcoat and battledress shoulder-badges were of a similar but smaller design, and the buttons, in two sizes for greatcoat and cap, bore the same rose and initials. The badges and buttons had originally been made in 1936 for the International Board for

Non-Intervention in Spain, and the letters "NI" stood for "Non-Intervention". Turned up the other way they became "IN" for "International", and the Tudor Rose of England became the White Rose of Finland. Their acquisition was due to Gibson, who sent his wife to collect them from a warehouse on Poole Harbour, Dorset, where they had been stored since the end of the Spanish Civil War.

The Committee had considerable difficulty in finding the right men to act as officers to command their unit, and the accounts of its deliberations in Gibson's Report suggests that there were very few to choose from and that the Committee made the choice first and then found criteria to fit it, an old Civil Service trick. So to command the volunteers it claimed that it had been essential to secure the services of an up-to-date soldier, "full of the spirit of adventure and with an international reputation, possessed of the highest gifts of leadership." It picked 2nd Lieut. Kermit Roosevelt, the fifty-year-old son of the late Theodore Roosevelt and a relative of President Roosevelt. He had won the Military Cross in Mesopotamia (now Iraq) during the first World War, and had recently become a British subject. At the time he was serving in the Middlesex Regiment, but on 17th February, with the approval of the War Cabinet, he relinquished his commission in the British army. On 29th February the War Office gazetted him a Temporary Major with effect from 31st January, and on 3rd March he was appointed Commanding Officer of the British Volunteers, with the rank of Colonel. As he was temporarily indisposed at the time it was agreed that he should help with the staff work in London and should go to Finland with a large draft due to leave on 16th March. The cessation of hostilities upset his plans, and four days after the armistice he resigned his appointment and was reinstated as a field officer in his old regiment. He attended all the attestation ceremonies and made brief speeches of welcome to the volunteers, a sad, quiet-voiced, portly little figure in an ill-fitting uniform. His enthusiasm for Finland's cause was such that he recruited several volunteers himself, one, Gee, in a West End bar. In an interview with the *Daily Telegraph* on the day of his appointment, he said: "What threatens the world today is the force of evil. That is what the defence of Finland means to me."

Brigadier-General Sir Ormonde Winter, 65 years of age, was chosen as officer to command the base depot. He was an old friend of Gibson, having served with him on the Non-Intervention Board in Spain. His selectors wrote that the man for the job should be a soldier of wide experience, a stern disciplinarian capable of dealing with raw recruits and old soldiers alike with equal ease, and of inspiring them with enthusiasm. Unfortunately, on the journey out, three pilots in his draft refused to stand watch on deck at night, so the General took the watch instead. The result was that he caught a bad cold, and when he arrived in Finland with his draft he was taken to Tornio hospital with a high temperature. There he was found to have developed a double mastoid, and was sent to Stockholm, where an eminent surgeon operated on him – at a cost of £253. The doctors refused to let him join the unit while he was convalescing, and on 9th July he was flown home on the diplomatic plane. After his departure from Sweden Victor (later Sir Victor) Mallet, the British Minister in Stockholm, wrote: "This elderly, retired officer seems to me to be the sort of dud who ought never to have been employed at all, still less on an expedition which required a youthful, tough, and physically strong leader."

The Committee also decided that it was essential that the Commanding Officer should have experienced and up-to-date officers under him, and as early as 30th January asked the War Office to provide a good second-in-command, four good company commanders, and a good adjutant. The War Office waited until 7th March before submitting a list, and it was only possible to interview the candidates before the Winter War ended. In the meantime, however, the Committee had realised that it would have to rely on volunteers already enlisted for its officers and NCOs. As it was impossible to make a selection of suitable candidates in London, due to the ban on instruction there, it was decided for convenience to enlist all the volunteers as privates, to let Gibson appoint acting officers and acting NCOs for the journey to Finland, and for the final appointments to be confirmed after Colonel Roosevelt's arrival there. In the intervening period it was hoped that General Winter would be able to advise which of the temporary appointments should be confirmed.

After a volunteer had passed through all the Bureau's departments and had been accepted and measured for his uniform, he attended an attestation. Gripenberg presided at these ceremonies, with some members of the Committee and staff also present, and which were held in the Assembly Room at Thorney House. The room was decorated with the Finnish flag and the Union Jack, and those to be sworn in were paraded there. Gibson read out the terms of the Agreement of Service and thanked the volunteers for coming to Finland's aid. Each volunteer then took the oath, kissed the Bible, and undertook honestly and faithfully to defend the cause of Finland against all enemies and to obey the orders of his military superiors. The Agreement was then signed in triplicate, Gripenberg signing for the Finnish government, Gibson for the Finnish Aid Bureau, and the volunteer for himself, one copy being given to each. Each volunteer then held himself in readiness to leave within twenty-four hours.

The Agreement stated the terms on which each volunteer undertook to serve as a member of the British Contingent of the International Volunteer Force in Finland, and was identical in detail to the one provided in Finland for overseas volunteers who enlisted there. It contained two extra clauses covering the obligations of the Finnish Aid Bureau, and in drawing it up the Committee had the expert advice of Needham. Although the interviewing of volunteers began on 7th February it was not until twelve days later that the Committee finally approved the wording of the Agreement* and enabled attestation to begin.

In one of its more enlightened moments the Bureau appointed Canon F.R. Barry as Honorary Chaplain to the

---

* see Appendix "B"

volunteers. He supplied New Testaments to all who wanted them. Special prayers for the volunteer force were regularly offered in St John's Church, Smith Square. Two Roman Catholic chaplains were also appointed, with a view to serving in the Catholic company which was being raised with the blessing and help of the Cardinal Archbishop of Westminster, and of the Bishop of Southwark. The Catholic company, however, failed to materialise. None of the chaplains accompanied the volunteers to Finland, and it was not until a month or so had passed after they had been demobilised there that the volunteers had a visit from anyone able to offer spiritual guidance. Suffice it to say that of those who elected to serve in the army in Finland after being offered the chance to go home, there was a high proportion of Roman Catholics.

Early in March 1940 volunteers were still coming in, at a rate of about 150 a day. On the news of the armistice a large draft which had gone on board a ship at Hull disembarked again, after drinking six barrels of beer which Colonel Whitbread, the eminent brewer, had sent them. Recruiting was stopped on 15th March. Among the volunteers accepted but stranded in London or Hull were some regular army officers who had obtained leave to volunteer, several seamen, some engineers, four pilots, two gunners and two navigators, most of whom had been rejected by the army or the Royal Air Force.

In his Report Gibson thought that it would have been difficult to improve on the system of recruiting, or to have recruited a better body of men. In Osasto Sisu the view was that the volunteers were an exceptionally motley crowd, and that in general their military capabilities were below average. All classes of society were represented, from baronets to bricklayers and from plumbers to pickpockets. Of the 228 volunteers recruited in London who reached Finland, 13 or 6% were under 20 years of age at 1st January 1940, 43 or 19% were in the 20-25 age group, 71 or 31% were between 26 and 30, 45 or 20% between 31 and 35, 22 or 10% between 36 and 40, and 31 or 13% were over 40, leaving only three (1%) whose date of birth has not been ascertained. The oldest was

Grant, an Old Etonian who had been a major in the Indian army and who was two months short of his sixtieth birthday when he volunteered. The youngest was Babbs, who celebrated his eighteenth birthday a month after he arrived in Finland. Out of the 228, 162 or 71% elected to serve in the Finnish armed forces, and of these it was later ascertained that 15, or just over 9%, were physically unfit for active service. Here it should be noted that Davidsen, a Scandinavian, did not require repatriation from Finland, and was therefore omitted in Gibson's report from the number it was intended to bring home, as were the sixteen anti-aircraft volunteers and the sixteen R.A.F. ground staff.

Of all the volunteers who did not reach Finland, or, having arrived there, did not serve in the army or air force, the oldest was General Winter, late of the Royal Field Artillery, born in 1875, and the youngest was John Smith, a clerk in the bus company at Norwich, born in May 1922. After excluding any typing errors which may have been made in foreign consulates, it appears that three volunteers added six or seven years to their ages when applying for passports, that two others held both British and Canadian passports, and that all but one of the Irish volunteers travelled on British passports.

An examination of the army numbers issued to the 228 volunteers who reached Finland shows that the lowest number, 2, was issued to Archer-Shee and the highest, 1390, to Arter. Adding to the 228 the 751 volunteers accepted and awaiting transport as at 15th March 1940, only 76 of whom had transit visas for Sweden, this suggest an acceptance rate of about 70% of the 1,390 interviewed. In addition to these a further 1,207 had been interviewed and medically examined but not accepted, and 6,300 awaited interview, making a grand total of some 8,900 who had offered their services. This may include the "several thousand" women volunteers mentioned in Gibson's Report but nowhere else, and is well below the figure of "about 10,000" given in the British and Scandinavian press. Gibson, however, in a letter to the volunteers, gave a figure of "over 7,000".

DRAFTS

Captain Hugo Henry Chandor, an Old Etonian in his 45th year, was the 249th volunteer to be interviewed. During the first World War he served as a Captain in the Lovat Scouts, attached to the King's Own Scottish Borderers, and later served on the Staff in France. An accomplished linguist, he spent some of the years between the wars farming in Brazil. When he called at Thorney House on 22nd February he was told he was to command the first draft of fifty volunteers on its arrival in Finland, and that he was to go out a day or two ahead of it, with 2nd Lieut. Guthrie as his second-in-command. This was to enable him to obtain first-hand knowledge of the arrangements made for the volunteers, and to contact the British Military Attaché in Helsinki. At Thorney House he interviewed a number of men who were to come under his command, and also met Colonel Paul Rodzianko, an old friend of Field-Marshal Mannerheim from their days together in the Imperial Russian White Cavalry. Now a British subject, the Colonel was interviewed in the press, and gave his opinion briefly: "Volunteers make excellent troops," he said, "they fight like blazes for an ideal."

Captain Chandor and Lieut. Guthrie left London the same evening, and arrived in Edinburgh the following day. Here they were held up for four days, and eventually embarked on the s/s *Cara*, in convoy for Bergen, on 27th February. The next day the *Daily Telegraph* reported that an advance party of volunteers was on its way to Finland, having left some time ago by a route that was being kept a closely-guarded secret. But while Captain Chandor and Lieut. Guthrie were waiting in Edinburgh the list of the first fifty volunteers was vetted at the Home Office and at Scotland Yard, who refused forty permission to leave the country, apparently just as the ship was about to leave. In the confusion which followed the remaining ten volunteers were divided between two drafts, the first of which left London on 29th February under Brigadier-General Sir Ormonde Winter. Described in Gibson's Report as the first proper draft, it travelled via Middlesborough to Narvik, and from thence by train to Tornio. The Report was understandably silent on the story of the forty stranded volunteers, which appeared in the Finnish and Swedish press in the middle of March. It then became apparent that of those volunteers on the list of men coming under his command and given to Captain Chandor, Harrison and some others had come out in Winter's draft and Lieut. Nurk had been placed in command of the next draft, which included, among others, Aitken-Quack, Archer-Shee, Carwithen, Connolly, Graham E.M., Patterson, the Prince de Liguori, and Shaw-Kennedy.

The immediate effect of the refusal of exit permits for the forty men was the tightening-up of Thorney House's selection procedures, and as a result Lieut. Nurk's and Captain Blew-Jones' drafts only included a very small number of people who had left their country for their country's good. They included two communists, two fascists, two or three professional thieves, a couple of kleptomaniacs, and one or two with drink problems. To cover up the setback Gibson's Report stated that the difficulty of obtaining transport had caused three weeks' delay in getting the first volunteers to Finland, and that Captain Chandor had been appointed Base Supply and Transport Officer, an appointment the latter described in a letter home as transport and supply officer, which was something different. Those transport difficulties, however they had arisen, were exacerbated when the Hungarian volunteer company arrived in the United Kingdom, since it travelled from Leith to Bergen on the s/s *Meteor,* the vessel which carried Captain Blew-Jones' draft on her next voyage.

Captain Chandor and Lieut. Guthrie arrived in Tornio on 6th March, and donned their uniforms. They acquired Finnish army roses for their collar insignia, and, finding that the British forage-caps issued to them were quite unsuitable for the 27°F (– 15°C.) frost which met them on their arrival, they obtained Finnish army fur caps with proper protection for the ears and the back of the neck. After a fruitless four-day wait for his draft Captain Chandor became impatient, and left by train for Lapua (to the British volunteers "lap ewer"), leaving Lieut. Guthrie behind. On arrival in Lapua on 11th March he reported to Captain Nordlund, who introduced him to Captain Rodolphe Eric Miville, a Swiss, and Lieut. Fontenoy, a Frenchman, whom he had appointed as liaison officers to be attached to the British unit. Captain Miville, a horse-breeder who lived in Ireland, had the reputation of being one of the finest horsemen in the world, a born soldier, and a grand talker, but despite these gifts he had been in Lapua since 1st February, idle most of the time. Captain Chandor told Captain Nordlund that about 350 British volunteers were in transit (it is a mystery how he arrived at this figure), and that even more had offered their services. The two agreed that the quartering of so many might cause insurmountable problems, and the two left on the night train for Hämeenlinna to obtain orders from the Headquarters of the Home Forces.

During the two captains' absence from Lapua Winter's draft, which had left Middlesborough on 1st March, arrived in Tornio on 12th March and in Lapua the following day, under the command of Taylor H. and with Sergeant Rehunen as interpreter. It was quartered in the High School. Meanwhile, the two officers continued their journey from Hämeenlinna to Helsinki and saw Major (later Lieut.-Col.) J.H. Magill, the newly-appointed Military Attaché, and Gordon (later Sir Gordon) Vereker, the Minister. He travelled north again in no doubt that the Legation (and, he presumed, the Foreign Office as well) was very much opposed to the volunteers, and that he could expect little assistance from the Minister.

Captains Nordlund and Chandor returned to Lapua on 15th March with instructions to turn the Workers' House into a barracks for the British unit. This wooden building, which contained among other things a stage and auditorium and a number of smaller rooms, stood near the railway station and had formerly been in the hands of the local communists. During that time it was the scene of a riotous assembly in the winter of 1929, which led to the formation of the extreme right-wing Lapua Movement and the subsequent outlawing of the Finnish communist party.

A second draft of 69 volunteers left Middlesborough for Trondeim early in March under the command of Lieut. Karl Nurk. An Estonian by birth, and a gifted linguist, he had seen active service against the Bolsheviks in his native country at the age of only fourteen, and had subsequently become a big-game warden in Kenya, from whence he came to London to volunteer. His draft reached Lapua on 16th March. About twenty of them were without kits, which had been sent out with medical supplies for the doctor with Winter's draft, and "lost" at Narvik, since there had been a delay in unloading them from the s/s *Briarwood*. In fairness to the General, however, who was eager to get to Finland, it should be noted that, even fifty years later, the Norwegian State Railways office at Narvik still refuses to allow "goods" to travel by passenger train; and army kits and medicines were, in their eyes, "goods". On arrival in Lapua the members of the draft were "all dead tired, and ravenous, and very bad-tempered", and there was "a quartet of real bad hats" who, in Captain Chandor's view, should never have come out. To add to his troubles the Osasto Sisu feeding arrangements (if ever they had been made) broke down, but Captain Chandor used the situation to advantage and obtained Captain Nordlund's permission for the British unit to do its own catering. On a brighter note Captain Chandor found that Taylor H. (whom Gibson intended should be commissioned) was an hotel proprietor who knew all about catering, so he appointed him quartermaster and reduced him to the rank of sergeant. Captain Miville and Lieut. Fontenoy were appointed to do the bulk buying of food. There were one or two others with special qualifications to form the nucleus of the headquarters organization, including Ryder, an accountant, who was made sergeant and who kept the unit finances in exceedingly good order. At about this time, Field Post No. KPK 16-4934 was alloted to the unit.

When he returned to Lapua Captain Chandor found that

the "Marta man", about whom he had already complained to Captain Nordlund, was still there, though in different clothes, so he went to see Captain Nordlund, who promised to have the man removed. Who this figure may have been remains a mystery, but it is possible that he may have been either an English-speaking volunteer from Helsinki or a representative of the Finnish State Police. The name Captain Chandor gave to him could have been taken from "Mata Hari", the Malay for the eye of day (the sun) and the name given to a notorious female spy in the first World War, or from Mata-mata (many eyes), the Malay for a policeman. Certainly in the conditions then prevailing there could have been a sprinkling of people in Lapua, working for countries beyond Finland's frontiers, and Captain Chandor must have been well aware of this.

Thanks to a handful of malcontents and trouble-makers at Lapua (and, one suspects, to a lack of proper leadership and discipline), discontent began to spread in Captain Chandor's absence in Helsinki. All hands had been turned to converting the Workers' House into a barracks, an urgent task which included equipping a cook-house and breaking frozen ground to bring in water-pipes, which had to be buried a metre deep and insulated against the frost with a foot and a half of sawdust. Ignoring the orders from Osasto Sisu that Sunday 17th March was to be a rest-day Captain Chandor ordered the work of conversion and equipping to continue on that day. Most of the unit worked with a will except for two, who refused to work and who were put into the guard-room for three days. The first two drafts, totalling 77 volunteers, moved in on Monday 18th March, when Lieut. Guthrie, who had also grown impatient of waiting, turned up from Tornio, two days before the third and largest draft arrived. Standing orders for the unit, posted soon afterwards, stated that all the hotels in Lapua (there was only one, the Simsiö, where the officers were billetted) were out of bounds to other ranks.

The most unusual member of Lieut. Nurk's draft, and, in fact, of the whole unit, was E.P. Loureiro, a Portuguese who spoke no English. How he managed to pass the interview at

Thorney House will never be known, but he was recruited at a time when the Committee felt that it would be a good thing to give the unit as international a nature as possible, and at the same time recruited two Italians, Boselli and the Prince de Liguori. Loureiro found on arrival at Lapua that Captain Chandor spoke Portuguese, so he became his batman. After two and a half weeks in the unit, during which time he picked up some very useful and unusual English phrases, Loureiro left for home, with Sergeant Francis and interpreter von Essen to accompany him as far as Helsinki.

The third and largest draft was placed under the command of Captain Douglas Holden Blew-Jones. He had seen eight years' service as a regular Captain in the Life Guards and six years in the Nottinghamshire Yeomanry, and was reported to be a good officer. Before his draft left London on 9th March eight officers and eight NCOs were temporarily appointed for the journey. The draft embarked at Leith early in the morning of 10th March, and after breakfast was divided up into platoons, as follows:

> Headquarters: Captain Blew-Jones, Lieut. Boddam-Whetham, Lieut. Herford (medical officer). NCOs: Howard, Grant (quartermaster), von der Leith, Roberts R.A., total 7.
>
> Platoon 1: Lieut. Joyce, M.C., Lieut. Fraser. NCOs: Nicholls, Davidsen (interpreter), total 4, plus 36 men.
>
> Platoon 2: Lieut. Ninnis, Lieut. Watson. NCO: Pooke, total 3, plus 32 men.
>
> Platoon 3: Lieut. Hopkinson, Lieut. Lenox-Conyngham. NCOs: Vessey, Golby, total 4, plus 33 men.

Platoon 4: Lieut. Ruck-Keene. NCOs: Kilgour, Kingcote, Smith M.L., total 5, plus 24 men.

This made a grand total of 148, from which two duplicated names and Best (an anti-aircraft specialist) should be deducted, leaving 145. There were also 21 Belgian and French volunteers, two of whom, on the journey out, having (to the cockney ear) unpronounceable names, acquired nicknames, and answered to the names of Meeses Smeeth and Meeses Chones.

The armistice between Finland and the Soviet Union was signed in Moscow in the evening of 12th March, and news of it reached the draft when it was half a day's sail from Bergen. On arrival there several volunteers sought their commanding officer's permission to leave the draft and to make their own way home, but they were ordered to accompany the others to Finland. In London Gripenberg cabled the Finnish Foreign Ministry to ask what their wishes were with regard to the volunteers in Finland and those in transit. On 16th March a reply was received to the effect that as there was a possibility of further fighting (the Finnish cabinet not having ratified the armistice at the time the cable was sent), those in Finland should remain there for the time being and those in transit should proceed thither. Lord Chatfield was consulted in his official capacity, and with his approval telegrams were sent to the volunteers in Tornio and Bergen. But there were none in either place, for after a day's delay Captain Blew-Jones' draft had left Bergen by the night train, on the instruction of a senior official at the Finnish Foreign Ministry to whom he had telephoned, while the second draft had already arrived in Lapua. When Captain Blew-Jones' draft arrived in Lapua the War diarist recorded the arrival of 144 men, of whom two were officers, though there were, in fact, 145 men.

The leader of each draft was given an adequate sum of money to meet any unforeseen circumstances which might arise on the journey, and Captain Blew-Jones' draft was provided with £500 in sterling and Norwegian and Swedish currency. The money was entrusted to Dr Herford at Thorney House within minutes of the departure of the draft, with instructions to pay the unexpended balance to the paymaster on arrival, together with an account of the money spent. Captain Blew-Jones knew nothing of the money until Dr Herford told him of it as the ship approached Bergen, and ordered him to hand it over to Lieut. Fraser, which he did under protest. On the journey through Sweden each volunteer was given five kronor (about 5s.)

Captain Blew-Jones heard of Brigadier-General Winter's illness when his draft arrived in Tornio on 18th March. Here he decided that, with Lieut. Fraser, to whom he had already given complete authority, he was going to run the whole unit. He had already refused to take the other officers into his confidence, an act which Gibson described in his Report as cancelling all the temporary appointments of officers and NCOs, except that of Lieut. Fraser. The draft left for Lapua by train on 19th March, and at Kemi Lieut. Fraser asked Lieut. Joyce what was the French for winter. Lieut. Joyce, who had served with distinction in France during the first World War as a Major commanding a machine-gun company, replied *hiver*. In the evening of the same day, when Brigadier-General Winter was in hospital and Captain Blew-Jones' draft was in the train between Kemi and Lapua, Lieut. Fraser sent the following telegram:

COLONEL BLEW JONES
BRITISH SECTION INTERNATIONAL
VOLUNTEER FORCE
LAPUA TEL. 306

INSTRUCT YOU TAKE OVER FULL COMMAND ALL BRITISH VOLUNTEERS LAPUA AND REORGANIZE.

D'HIVER, G.H.Q.

About half-past seven in the evening of 19th March Captain Chandor was informed of the arrival of the telegram, and with Captain Nordlund's authority collected it from the telegraph office on the railway station. He noted that the name and address on it were similar to those of the officer commanding the draft expected later that evening. After reading it Captain Chandor decided to take his three henchmen (his own words), Captain Miville, Lieut. Fontenoy and Lieut. Guthrie, into his confidence. First, it was obvious that D'Hiver was either Winter with a higher temperature than he ought to have, or was Captain Blew-Jones himself. "The point I had to decide was this", he wrote, "was this man a fool, fraud, a gent. with odd ideas, or – ?" Early the following morning Dr Herford and Lieut. Joyce called on Captain Chandor and asked to speak frankly about Captain Blew-Jones and Lieut. Fraser. Meanwhile, the last-named took the opportunity to put the money into a safe-deposit at the bank in Lapua before matters came to a head.

Although much against his will, Captain Chandor decided, at the insistence of Dr Herford, to go to discuss the matter with Captain Nordlund, even though he did not wish to trouble him with the internal affairs of the unit. Captain Nordlund agreed that Captain Blew-Jones and Lieut. Fraser had better leave at once, and arranged for them to go to Helsinki by the night train. Captain Chandor, however, was apparently willing to overlook the attempted embezzlement of the unit funds until Dr Herford pointed out that he, Dr Herford, was responsible for the money, and insisted on seeing Captain Nordlund and demanding an account. He had already agreed with Sergeant Howard for guards to be placed on the bank – Volunteer Medlicott and Sergeant Vessey – so that neither Captain Blew-Jones nor Lieut. Fraser could take the money out. Lieut. Fraser was then ordered to hand over the key to the safe deposit, and Lieut. Fontenoy and Dr Herford escorted him to the bank, where the money was all recovered, despite Lieut. Fraser's attempts to conceal some of it. After he and Captain Blew-Jones had been discharged from the unit, which took place at Captain Chandor's request without an enquiry, they were sent to Kemi to join the homebound party which left Lapua on 23rd March. Captain Chandor, meanwhile, realising that apart from the quiet-voiced Lieut. Joyce there was no-one else capable of taking command of the unit, of which he, Captain Chandor, had been acting commander since his arrival in Lapua, obtained Captain Nordlund's permission to continue in that position. On 26th March General Enckell telegraphed Gibson to ask for the appointment to be confirmed, and the following day Lieut. Fontenoy, en route for his native France, delivered explanatory dispatches to Gibson at Thorney House.

Captain Chandor, who had spoken to Captain Blew-Jones on the telephone when the latter was in Tornio, noted in his letters home that he thought that Captain Blew-Jones was going to try to take charge of everything. But he seemed to be quite hopeless, and hardly knew the number of officers in his draft who would require billets, two, four, five or seven. This lends some colour to the suggestion in Gibson's Report that Captain Blew-Jones had cancelled their appointments. "Blew-Jones turned out to be utterly incompetent, and Fraser seems to have been his evil genius", Gibson wrote, "Their extraordinary conduct on the outward journey produced discontent and indiscipline, and on arrival at Lapua they were dismissed from the unit and ordered to return home."

The last the volunteers heard of the sorry affair was at the pay parade on 5th April, when each member of Captain Blew-Jones' draft received an extra 30 marks, as the rate of exchange on the Swedish kronor issued on the journey out had been wrongly calculated.

HOMEBOUND PARTY

The party of sixty-two volunteers who had decided to return home left Lapua on 23rd March in charge of Boddam-Whetham and Lieut. Ruck-Keene. During its fortnight's stay in Kemi, pending the granting of transit visas for Sweden and Norway, the two venereal disease cases joined it, making sixty-four. When at last it left for Oslo, on Sunday, 7th April, Lieut. Ruck-Keene returned to Lapua. The next day the Finnish Foreign Ministry telegraphed to Gibson to say that the party was on its way to embark on the s/s *Bessheim* at Oslo. Meanwhile, Volunteer Owbridge, whose transit visa for Sweden had been granted on 30th March, arrived in Oslo ahead of the main party on 4th April, and reported to Ch. Nyberg, Secretary at the Finnish Legation, saying that he had accompanied General Winter to Stockholm. Nyberg arranged accommodation for him and the party at the City Hotel, 19 Skippergate, near the railway station. On 8th April Nyberg recorded that everything was quiet in Oslo, but that in the evening, when a general mobilisation was announced, the sirens were sounded and communications between the capital and the rest of the country were cut. It was thus impossible for him to get in touch with the station at Kongsvinger on the Norwegian side of the frontier with Sweden, so as to intercept the volunteers and return them to Sweden.

Everything went well for the party until 9th April, when the train reached Charlottenberg, on the Swedish side of the frontier. Here its members heard rumours of an impending German invasion of Norway. The train left at six in the morning, and when it was about ten miles from Oslo it came to a sudden stop. Word was passed down that the Germans were bombing the airport and the docks. A German bomber flew the length of the train, but all the passengers, including some Norwegian soldiers, remained inside under orders, and the train was not bombed. After about half an hour the train continued its journey to Oslo, and on arrival at half past eleven the party went to the City Hotel. After a meal some of them went out for a walk, and on returning found the Germans had occupied the General Post Office, which was opposite the hotel. In the light of these developments Owbridge, Boddam-Whetham, von der Leith (a U.S. citizen) and Watson went to the Finnish Legation to see Nyberg, who told them that the American Vice-Consul, Easton T. Kelsey, was in charge at the British Consulate, whose staff had fled the country the previous day. Kelsey suggested that the party should return to Sweden, and Nyberg bought third-class railway tickets to Stockholm for the whole party. He then instructed the leaders of the party to order its members to destroy all documents and badges which might render their journey difficult or compromise them. It was agreed that the volunteers should leave their luggage at the City Hotel, where the Finnish Legation would collect and store it until the situation cleared, as suitcases might attract the Germans' attention. Nyberg also suggested that the party should be divided into small groups which could try to reach the station. He handed 65 tickets to Owbridge for distribution, and told him he had ascertained from the Swedish Minister in Oslo, Mr Beck-Friis, that the Swedish frontier guards would not prevent the party from crossing into Sweden without return visas. He then telephoned Counsellor Soravuo at the Finnish Legation in Stockholm and asked him to clear the matter with the Swedish Foreign Ministry.

The instructions were duly repeated to the members of the party, who were advised to try to cross into Sweden in small groups as best they could, after destroying their passports and paybooks and taking only enough clothing to keep warm on the journey. Some of the party set off straight away on foot for the frontier, intending to cross it by road and then to board the train. Jones W.C. and another decided to wait until it was dark. About six in the evening Kelsey turned up, made sure that each man had a railway ticket, and gave each one ten Norwegian kroner (about 10s.). About twenty decided to take the 8.20 pm train. Luckily the Germans did not visit the hotel; and about half past seven the party began to leave the hotel, in twos and threes, at intervals, having agreed with each other that they would not recognise each other or speak. "We managed to get past the sentries into the station," wrote Jones, "and then our ordeal began again, as the train was an hour late and we had to stand in a queue. All the time we were being subjected to a scrutiny from two officers with binoculars who were up on a platform by the station clock with a machine-gun section. At last the train arrived, and we boarded her and got seats or stood in the corridor as it was fairly full. After an endless wait we steamed out of Oslo at 9.20, and after about three hours we saw the passport people get aboard. This was another sticky moment, but a man who had an American passport managed to get the officials on their own and told them our story. They were very nice about it, and let us over the border without further trouble."

About one o'clock in the morning of 10th April the Passport Control at Charlottenberg telephoned the Foreign Ministry in Stockholm to say that about forty British volunteers had arrived on the late night express from Oslo, with an American (who was not named) carrying a letter from the Finnish Minister in Oslo. The following day the Swedish Minister in London sought residential visas for the forty-five volunteers who had reached Stockholm under "Captain" Watson. On arrival there part of the party was quartered in the Hotel Patricia, Vasagatan 37, and the rest at the Hotel Excelsior, Birger Jarlsgatan 79.

In Oslo Nyberg called at the City Hotel in the morning of 10th April, and found to his surprise a rearguard of ten volunteers optimistically awaiting the arrival of the British forces. Two of them called at the Finnish Legation in the evening, when arrangements were made for the group to leave for Stockholm on 11th April by the night train. However, the railway connection with Kongsvinger had already been cut in several places, and the volunteers were accordingly advised to leave the same evening by the Oslo-Kornsjö route, which was the only rail link with Sweden still open.

When it became possible to make a head-count in Stockholm it was found that nineteen volunteers had been left behind in Norway. The ten left in Oslo were taken prisoner, their German captors accusing them at first of being English soldiers intending to commit sabotage in Norway under the pretext of being volunteers for Finland: Averill, Ford J.H., Gee, Henderson, Johnston, Lavey, Lowe, Munday, Seccombe and Stephenson. The remaining nine managed to get away. Munro, Smith J. and Tosh hitch-hiked to Andalsnes, where they picked up a British warship. From there they were transferred to a Polish vessel which landed them in Scotland on 23rd April. Olivo, who according to a British newspaper had fought his way through a German patrol with a "Colt automatic", was taken off on a British transport vessel at Ålesund, transferred to an Italian ship, and returned home at the end of April. The five others were in a group which included Arter, Boddam-Whetham, Carwithen, Farragut, Johnson, Porte, Seilerne and Young, managed to slip over the frontier into Sweden.

The British press treated the affair with considerable imagination, and on 16th April reported that the Germans in Oslo had captured nineteen volunteers, who had been shot for espionage and sabotage. Ten days later the Finnish press stated more accurately that three volunteers had reached a Scottish port, seven had arrived in London, and nine were missing. Unluckiest of the escapers from Norway was an Australian named Bowman, who on arrival in Stockholm saw the British Minister, who engaged him as a doorkeeper for the British Legation in Kovno, Latvia. When the news reached London that the Germans had taken him off the ship carrying him across the Baltic to Riga, the Finnish Aid Bureau promptly disowned him.

The Finnish Aid Bureau made payments for the maintenance of the fortunate forty-five on a generous scale, the money being remitted through the Foreign Office and the British Consul in Stockholm. The latter also paid each volunteer five kronor "minimum relief" a day. As soon as

Gibson heard that the volunteers were safe he saw the Swedish Minister in London and arranged with him that they should not be interned as they were really civilians, and had travelled as such. Gibson later admitted that at first they were treated too well and had been given too much pocket-money, but on instructions he telegraphed to Mallet they were subsequently treated on the same basis as British naval ratings and merchant seamen stranded in Sweden, and were transferred to a Y.M.C.A. hostel. On 2nd July the Swedish Minister in London agreed to recommend to his government that they should be moved away from Stockholm to "some agricultural district" where they could be given suitable employment.

Gibson agreed with the War Office in July that the volunteers should return through Russia via Odessa, Istanbul and Haifa to Palestine, on condition that they joined the British forces there. The Committee accepted the quotation of Thomas Cook & Son of £32 and £27.10s. per head for transporting volunteers from Stockholm and Helsinki respectively to Haifa. Transit visas for Russia, Turkey and Syria were also required, and in Stockholm there was already a queue for Russian visas for twenty-five members of the Friends' Ambulance Unit, which had arrived from Finland early in April. Four volunteers, including Owbridge, managed to get Russian visas on their own, applying direct to the Soviet Legation in Stockholm. Anticipating rightly that authority for his action would be forthcoming from London, Mallet applied on 20th July to Madame Kollontay, the Soviet Minister, for visas for thirty men. No reply was received, so on 27th July W.H. Montague-Pollock, Mallet's First Secretary, wrote to Madame Kollontay and "blew" the cover of the thirty men for whom Mallet had sought visas, most of whom had recently-issued "clean" passports not showing where they had been, stating that they had all been volunteers in Finland. As no notice had been taken of his Minister's letter of 20th July to Madame Kollontay, he sent copies of the correspondence to the Swedish Foreign Ministry, with a request to ask Her Excellency to make up her mind. Ultimately, after a ballot,

Blew-Jones, Budden, Cook, Coughlan, Fleming, Fraser, Johns, Kingcote, Lansdown and Williams succeeded in getting visas with the help of the British Legation, and the last of this group, Coughlan and Fraser, left Sweden in November and December respectively. Although Gibson had told the Foreign Office that he did not think that Blew-Jones, Fraser and Fleming should travel via Russia to Palestine, the Foreign Office claimed afterwards that Gibson had not asked for "this opinion" to be telegraphed to Stockholm, and had therefore done nothing about it. Most of the rest of the party were apparently sent home by the diplomatic plane before the arrival of the contingent from Finland the following summer.

In mid-August the Swedish Foreign Ministry informed its Berlin envoy that it was sending 112 British military personnel home via Petsamo, on the Swedish s/s *Göteborg*. These were all men who, following the fighting in Norway, had escaped over the border into Sweden. At the same time the Ministry stated that it would send eight former British volunteers with the party, who had been sentenced to deportation in a Swedish court, and in anticipation of which they were being held in close arrest. These were drawn from the R.A.F. ground crews and the anti-aircraft volunteers already referred to. In November only twenty-four of the original forty-five remained in Sweden, Haddleton, Henley, Walker W.E. and Zipfel (who had acquired some Swedish) having returned to Finland to rejoin the contingent during the summer. Of the others who had left the country by various means, including De Burgh-Thomas, who stowed away at Petsamo on the Finnish s/s *Kastelholm* on 24th August, and who was found, as was Boswell, when German naval search-parties came aboard at Vardö and Kirkenes respectively, and Bowman, already mentioned, only eleven had left Sweden via Russia. Meanwhile, during the summer, one or two of the party in Stockholm incurred debts, but Lt-Col. Sutton-Pratt, the British Military Attaché, kindly helped them out, and was reimbursed from Thorney House funds. Of the others, Geddes married and settled down in Stockholm, one volunteer got into trouble with the

Swedish authorities but was declared to be unbalanced and was detained in a mental home, and another was convicted of larceny and sentenced to three months' hard labour. The following March Burch, who had been working part-time as a gardener and Dixon R. were recruited as "consular agents", and may have been sent to Finland.

By the middle of August 1940, nineteen volunteers had managed to travel through Russia, Turkey, Syria and Palestine to Egypt. On being granted their Russian visas, each volunteer had to sign a written undertaking to join the British forces in the Middle or Near East before he was given his tickets and travelling allowances. This arrangement was agreed with the War Office just before 28th July, when a telegram was sent to Sir Stafford Cripps, the British Ambassador in Moscow, asking him to try to obtain the necessary transit visas. In spite of the fact that the War Office also telegraphed the British General Headquarters in Cairo about this arrangement, the first six volunteers sent to the Middle East from Stockholm repudiated their agreements. Wrongly using their original Agreements of Service they succeeded in obtaining sums of money for subsistence from various British Consuls and in persuading the British Consul in Cairo to send them home via the Cape of Good Hope. Of the six, Owbridge left the ship at Durban and was married there in 1943, while the other five reached London after giving interviews to the South African press. The next ten to travel through Russia joined the British forces as they had undertaken to do. Gibson, meanwhile, sent a list of volunteers still in Finland to the British Legation in Helsinki, arranged in order of priority for Russian transit visas, based on their estimated usefulness in the Middle East. In October, after taking legal advice, the Finnish Aid Bureau regarded as lapsed the clause in the Agreement of Service which provided for the repatriation of volunteers on the cessation of hostilities.

By mid-August "at least four" of the homebound volunteers, some of whom may have been cashiered from the British army before volunteering, had rejoined or joined the British army and had attained the rank of lieutenant-colonel. Kingcote, born in Monmouth but claiming to be Australian, obtained a position as an army canteen manager, and one of the men who had been in trouble with the police both in Sweden and Egypt attempted to claim compensation for having contracted "a serious skin disease" while on service in Finland. A skin specialist who examined him in London said the volunteer was "perfectly fit to work and there was no ground whatever for compensation."

Meanwhile, other volunteers in and around Stockholm obtained work, and some of them were still there in 1941-42, such as Reed C.J.M., who was at the Brazilian Legation. Evans E.V. was working as a gardener for Major Johnstone, noted later, and Snodin was teaching at St Sigfrids Internatskola, a boarding-school.

LAPUA

On the conclusion of the trouble over Blew-Jones and Fraser, Captain Chandor selected his officers, and confirmed first of all the temporary appointments of Lieuts. Guthrie, Nurk and Ruck-Keene, the last-named on Lieut. Joyce's recommendation. Dr Herford's appointment as Lieutenant was a firm one and needed no confirmation; of the others, temporary Captains Boddam-Whetham and Watson had decided to accompany the homebound party, and the temporary commissions of Hopkinson, Lenox-Conyngham and Ninnis were not confirmed. Captain Chandor wanted to make Howard an officer, as it had been intended that he should be Colonel Roosevelt's aide-de-camp, but Gibson refused permission on the grounds that the now much-reduced unit had enough officers. So Howard was made Orderly Room Sergeant instead.

The Blew-Jones draft had hardly settled in at the Workers' House before Captain Chandor was overwhelmed with requests from volunteers who wanted a private word with him. Some twenty applied for immediate repatriation; and while he was trying to select NCOs he found that under his command he had baronets who would not accept responsibility or a stripe, pilots who wanted to know why they were not flying, ski-ing champions who wanted to teach ski-ing, men who had been in the Spanish Civil War who wanted to choose their own officers publicly, architects who wanted to rebuild bombed houses, and so on. The book which was sent out at the end of March, containing personal details of the men under his command, never reached him; but ultimately the NCOs were chosen, the best that could be obtained in the short time available. Among those who had come out as NCOs in the Blew-Jones draft only Golby, Grant, Nicholls, Pooke, Roberts and Vessey, together with Howard, kept their temporary appointments, while Kilgour and

Smith M.L. were reduced to the ranks and Davidsen, Kingcote and von der Leith opted to return home. All but two of the NCOs chosen had previous military experience, and several had fought in the first World War, including Commins and Humphries. Also on Lieut. Joyce's recommendation Captain Chandor selected Asling, a former Guards sergeant, as company sergeant-major. This was a very happy choice, as Asling turned out to be an exceedingly capable drill instructor, and under his guidance the unit rapidly became smart and proficient on the parade-ground. Sergeant Seyler, also an ex-Guardsman, who had a fine flow of invective for backsliders, assisted him most ably.

Captain Chandor wrote later that he regretted some of the appointments, which were made without dossiers and without personal knowledge of the men he was promoting. Each of the appointments was subject to the approval of Captain Nordlund and Gibson. He admitted that among the volunteers there were "some really unsuitable elements; agitators, men with criminal records, men who were physically quite unfit for the life and climate they might be expected to undergo . . . The large majority was *excellent;* I cannot speak too highly of them . . . My main preoccupation always was to endeavour to produce a trained and efficient company as quickly as possible, and so to interest and inspire all ranks with the wish to uphold our country's name, that we should never give cause for trouble, and that any disciplinary action I might be compelled to take would not be public." Only one of the men he promoted gave trouble later, when, as a civilian, the Finnish authorities found it necessary to place him in protective custody. Following the promotions the company was divided into three rifle platoons and a machine-gun platoon, and training began.

On 21st March Captain Chandor addressed the volunteers and stated that a commission would arrive the following day to enquire into the state of affairs and to decide whether or not to let the volunteers go home. Passports were collected the following day for safe-keeping, and the first rumours of thefts of clothing and rifles from the unguarded quartermaster's stores led to a kit inspection, at which nothing was found. Only fifteen volunteers had their own kits at this time, but during the day a further 115 kits arrived, supplementing some surplus kits which had come out earlier, so the company was fitted out after a fashion, mostly in uniforms that were too large, and was drilled to form a guard of honour. In the evening there was a reception for all the volunteers in the canteen at the International Barracks, with coffee, cakes, songs, and speeches.

General Enckell arrived on 22nd March, and Captain Chandor was in the party which met him at the station. In the morning the general had private conversations with Lieut. Ruck-Keene, Sergeants Howard and Vessey, and Volunteer Lenox-Conyngham, the last three being candidates for commissions. In the afternoon there was a parade, and the British company, in its ill-fitting uniforms, marched over to the International Barracks in twos and re-formed in threes. A white car with two staff officers in it drove up, and General Enckell got out and made speeches to each of the three companies of Osasto Sisu, thanking each one in turn for coming to Finland to fight. Meanwhile, a Hungarian cook took over the British cook-house for the day, and prepared a splendid goulash for the lunch which preceded the parade. Unsure of how it would be received he put his head cautiously round the door of the canteen when the meal was half-finished, and was met with loud and prolonged cheers.

As already noted, on 23rd March the volunteers who had opted to go home left. Most of them went north to Kemi, but four of their number, Davidsen, the Prince de Liguori, Forbes and Way, went south to Helsinki, whence they managed to return home by air some days later, Davidsen having stayed long enough in Helsinki to sign the visitors' book at the Grinzing restaurant, as "flight luftenant". Meanwhile, back at Lapua, rumours began to fly around as to the possible movements of the unit. One thought that within three days it was to go "down to the frontier near Helsinki", a geographical impossibility, another that the unit was to be only two hours' journey from the country's capital and would have Lewis-gun and machine-gun training. On

25th March a pile of Finnish army skis was delivered to the Workers' House, and many of the volunteers tried them out. It took a little time to get used to the bindings, which were rawhide thongs which passed over the instep, but after a little instruction in German from a Polish volunteer sergeant named Justschenko several volunteers became proficient in their use, to the extent that they subsequently skied the three miles to the top of the nearby Simsönvuori, Mount Simsiö, all of 356 feet above sea-level.

Diaries kept by the volunteers at this time show that one of the main preoccupations was food, and that there was much dissatisfaction at the apparent lack of urgency in setting up a training programme during the first week or ten days. During the first few days the training consisted largely of foot-drill. Rifle-drill began on Tuesday, 26th March. A selection was made, and those who had done drill before or who showed aptitude for it were separated from those who hadn't and didn't. The latter were put into the Awkward Squad under L/Cpl. Humphries, who knocked his recruits into shape with great good humour and patience.

The same day Captain Nordlund issued an Order of the Day to the men under his command. To those with no immediate prospects of returning home he stated: "You can be assured that the Republic of Finland will take as good care of you as of her own sons, since you have all earned it", a promise which was later most generously fulfilled. The day was spent drilling the four platoons into which the British company had been divided, for Field-Marshal Mannerheim's visit the following day. At a quarter to nine in the morning of 27th March a trial parade took place on the square in front of the International Barracks. There was a frost of between 18° and 27° Fahrenheit, and the British unit, in British army boots with metal studs, metal heel and toe caps, and in forage caps giving no protection to the ears, very soon began to feel the cold. So after the trial parade the unit was dismissed and ordered into the warmth of the canteen, which overlooked the barrack square. Every twenty minutes or so they were called out, lined up, called to attention, and then dismissed and sent indoors again. This happened four or five times, until finally word was brought that the Field-Marshal was on his way. The unit then went outside and formed up.

While all this was going on Field-Marshal Mannerheim arrived in his special train punctually at ten o'clock, and was greeted by Captain Nordlund. After inspecting a guard of honour he declined the offer of a car and proceeded on foot through the town to the barracks, being greeted by the townsfolk along the route. The parade began at 10.20, twenty minutes late. Captain Nordlund called Osasto Sisu to attention, and the Field-Marshal inspected the No.1 and Hungarian companies, and made a speech to each. Then he inspected the British unit and addressed it in English. He thanked the British volunteers for coming out to fight alongside the Finnish army in their heroic struggle for the principles for which England, too, was fighting. His Order of the Day No. 38 of 24th March was read out in various languages, and those of Osasto Sisu who knew it, mainly in No.1 company, sang the Finnish National Anthem. After giving three rousing cheers for the Field-Marshal the three companies marched past him at the salute, which the war diarist noted "must be regarded as completely successful". The fourth and last British platoon consisted of the Air Force volunteers led by their commander Lace, who at the appropriate moment gave the order "Royal Air Force: eyes right!" After the march-past Osasto Sisu was formed up as a guard of honour around the military graves in the nearby churchyard, and the Field-Marshal and Captain Nordlund laid wreaths while a bugler sounded a salute and Osasto Sisu presented arms. A total of 639 men took part, as noted earlier, of which 158 were in the British unit, out of a possible 162. The British unit was warmly congratulated on its appearance.

The British unit marched back to the Workers' House in good order, and Captain Chandor had a long talk with Field-Marshal Mannerheim and his Chief of Staff. Of the discussion Captain Chandor wrote: "He asked me what we wanted to do, and I said that if we were wanted we had come out to try and be of some assistance to Finland and would like to do this; but that if he did not want us we would go home. There was a feeling amongst some of the men that we were no longer wanted in Finland, and I myself knew that the whole volunteer movement was disapproved of by the Legation, and so presumably by our government whom the Legation represented, so that it did seem as if perhaps the wisest plan would be to endeavour to get home as soon as possible. This, however, was not my business; I was sure that decisions of this nature would be taken by the Finnish authorities, in conjunction with the Committee, and my job, it seemed to me, was to continue our training as swiftly and efficiently as possible, and keep the men as happy as I could." Nevertheless, Captain Chandor did not inform his officers of the gist of his conversation with the Field-Marshal, and, as we shall see, this sowed the seeds of an unfortunate division among them.

While the Field-Marshal and Captain Chandor were conferring, a small party of journalists and interested civilians interviewed Captain Nordlund and inspected the barracks. Early in April the newspaper *Vaasa,* published in the town of that name on the coast some twenty miles from Lapua, printed a full-page account of Osasto Sisu. "The English drill in close order on the square in front of their barracks", the paper noted. "At the entrance on the main road stands a sentry, motionless, with a rifle on his shoulder. He turns mechanically as we approach, and salutes the commander smartly. From the square come English words of command, shouted by a khaki-clad sergeant in typically British fashion. The rifles are firm in the men's grip, and they move as a single man". The visitor entered the Workers' House, which was crowded, but there was ample evidence of discipline, cleanliness and tidiness. "The freedoms offered by war have been used by some to write their thoughts on the ends of their bunks", a visitor noted. "What was the son of Albion thinking of, I wonder, when he christened his bunk 'The House of Love'?"

In another part of the building was the sick-bay, where there was a couple of influenza patients. The only "wounded" man the visitors met was an Englishman.

Without thinking of the snow and ice they had arranged a football match against the Hungarians, in which the Englishman dislocated his wrist. The visitors were told that the discipline was good and that there had been only eight or nine cases requiring punishment. "A foreign legion, in a democratic country, without foreign legion discipline, was a miracle, and that miracle has been seen of late in Lapua" was the comment of one. Dean Kares, former Secretary of the Lapua Movement, who was one of the party, must have had mixed feelings on revisiting the scene of his activities of less than ten years earlier, when he noticed that on the roof of the building was a Finnish flag, in whose upper corner was stitched a small Union Jack.

The canteen in the Workers' House was used for meetings and instructional sessions. One day the volunteers were ordered there for a lecture by Lieut. Joyce. A number of them stood round the walls. The meeting was called to attention, and Lieut. Joyce had just started speaking when Volunteer Pearce, who was standing in front of the automatic gramophone, slipped a mark into the slot, unobserved. The machine obeyed, and a couple of seconds later there was a loud click and the sounds of the Beer Barrel Polka filled the room. Confusion reigned until one of the sergeants had the presence of mind to pull out the plug and cut off the current to the infernal machine.

After ten days' or a fortnight's training in Lapua a Suomi machine-pistol, an improved form of the Thompson sub-machine-gun, was issued to the volunteers for practice. Then a captured Russian Degtaryev DP.1928 rapid rifle was issued, and several old soldiers handled it to get the "feel" before the machine-gun platoon tried it out on the rifle-range. Early in April a captured Russian machine-gun was issued, a PM.1910 Maxim-type, which was known to the Finns as a Model 09. The belt fed in on the right-hand side, and it had a tripod, wheels, and a removable protective shield. Most of the unit had an opportunity to try it out in the succeeding weeks, and found it to be fairly accurate, but clumsy to handle. Two more of a slightly different design were later issued to the unit, which hitherto had only been armed with rifles sent out from home.

The main body of 34 Air Force volunteers left Lapua on 1st April. The eight qualified pilots and eight aspiring pilots were stationed at Air Regiment 2 at Parola, in south-west Finland not far from the port of Pori, under the command of Major E.E. Nuotio, while the eighteen aspiring air-gunners went to Air Training Regiment 1 at Karvia, under the command of Lt-Col. L. Schalin. At Parola there were four Canadian volunteers, Hall, Taylor H.S. (who had volunteered in London), Waller (who had joined up direct in Finland), and Walker J.S. Out of Winter's draft of eleven who had arrived in Lapua on 13th March Dalton, Harrison and Wellmon continued their journey southwards to Parola, also to join Air Regiment 2. Graham E.M., and possibly others, followed the same route when Nurk's draft arrived in Lapua. As he travelled south Dalton decided to make his own way home, and arrived back in London on 24th March, the first volunteer to do so. Wellmon followed him a few days later. Here it is relevant to mention a British volunteer named Windton, in Air Regiment 3, who ferried aircraft over from Sweden to Finland, and to another named Barrington, who was in Air Regiment 2 in February, neither of whom were recruited in London.

Unfortunately, all but the qualified pilots were found to be unsuitable on account of their poor physique, and were sent back to Lapua on 15th April. The eight who remained at Parola, including Lieut. Aitken-Quack, were either employed there or transferred to other units such as Air Regiment 4 at Luonetjärvi, near Jyväskylä in the middle of the country, where Captain Lace, Lieuts. Armstrong and Maund, 2nd Lieuts. Elliott and Taylor H.S., and CSM Walker J.S. were stationed. Captain Waller was transferred to Joroinen, some distance east of Jyväskylä, though Captain Kenworthy, a former Schneider Trophy test-pilot and the first volunteer pilot, left no record of his movements.

Some of the Air Force volunteers who were posted back to Lapua returned to Parola when the British unit left for Savonlinna, including Lieuts. Armstrong, Sir G.D.P.

Sinclair-Lockhart, Stead, Sergeant Mackie and Volunteers Perowne and Summers. On 4th May Lt-Col. Schalin's adjutant, Fagerholm, wrote to Captain Nordlund in Lapua to say that after the eighteen Englishmen training as air-gunners had been posted back to Lapua, several of them had arrived in the barracks without reporting or presenting any kind of leave or movement order. In addition, "G. Sinclair-Lockhart appeared in the uniform of a lieutenant in the Finnish Air Force Reserve, without it having been mentioned in the daily orders of the Commander-in-Chief that he had been taken into the Air Force." He was given a rail warrant, and rejoined the unit at Savonlinna as a private. Lace, the writer added in a postscript, was a nice chap.

Among the ex-Air Force volunteers who returned to Lapua Corporal Brown and Sergeant Butt asked to retain their Finnish ranks and pay. This was refused, and they were reduced to the ranks, the story of the attempt of Brown and Bowhay-Saunders to steal a Blenheim bomber and fly home not having preceded them. However, Scott A.H.W., who had served as a captain in the first World War, kept his Finnish rank of lieutenant, McKay, who had fought in the same war, was made a platoon sergeant, and Archer-Shee was made a lance-corporal. The odd man out was Le Mee-Power, who returned to Parola and obtained his discharge on 24th April. Having some knowledge of Norwegian he invited several of the Air Force volunteers to join him in an attempt to reach the British forces at Narvik. None of them were good enough skiers, however, an essential qualification for the journey, so Le Mee-Power went on his own to the north of Finland. He went into Norway via Karesuvanto, and presumably Skibotn, but, finding that there was no chance of reaching Narvik, he returned to Finland the way he had come, and crossed the frontier into Sweden near Pajala, about fifty miles north of the Arctic Circle. Here the Swedish police picked him up, and sent him to a camp at Hälsingmo. The following year he rejoined the contingent when it was transferred to Sweden.

Back in Lapua, on Sunday evening, 7th April, the British

volunteers gave a stage show in the Workers' House, to which the Osasto Sisu officers were invited. The bunks of the barrack-room were pushed back to the walls to make room for seats for the audience, and the stage was cleared of bunks for the performers. The performance was distinctly mixed and almost a disaster, though the war diarist politely described it as a concert, since a choir from the Hungarian company sang some folk-songs. It did, however, have one flash of humour. Read, who claimed kinship with the actor Ernest Thesiger, now famous for his portrayal of doddering old gentlemen, was found to have so much talent for female impersonation (then rare) that he was promptly nicknamed Phyllis.

Meanwhile, the Finnish Aid Bureau, apart from corresponding with Captain Chandor, appears to have done little to plan for the volunteers' future, and so on 8th April, twenty-six days after the armistice, the Finnish Foreign Office took the initiative and telegraphed Gibson to ask if the Committee would extend the operation of the Agreement of Service, for those remaining in Finland, until 31st May, with which the Committee agreed. This meant that until that date the volunteers would receive accommodation and rations from the Finnish government and 2s. per day from the Committee, as hitherto, of which 10 marks would be paid in Finland and the balance would be credited in London.

The 9th April was a busy day. Three German measles cases returned from hospital to hear the news of the German invasion of Denmark and Norway, the Norwegian declaration of war on Germany, and the planning of a British expeditionary force to Norway. In Lapua the machine-gun platoon carried the Maxim gun to the firing range, some two miles away, and practised target firing. The three infantry platoons took part in field exercises elsewhere. Their objective was a slightly raised piece of ground which, backed by extensive woods, had to be captured. The purpose of the exercise was to maintain communications and to find cover on exposed and snow-covered ground. The following day three platoons paraded for saluting drill, and a class in rifle-drill was held for the NCOs. At the second parade there was rifle-drill under section leaders, and the machine-gun platoon practised target firing with the Degtaryev and the Maxim. Fatigues took up most of the afternoon, and the volunteers aired their sleeping-bags as the weather was fine and a thaw had set in. There was no information as to the unit's future movements, but the sergeant-major announced that everything had to be got ready for a possible move at a day's notice. Gas-masks and other equipment were issued the following day, and instruction was given in their use, as well as in target recognition on a landscape target made by Sergeant Seyler.

April 12th was fine and calm, but the news of the German invasion of Norway was already having an upsetting effect of all ranks. Speaking on behalf of a majority of the officers Lieut. Joyce asked Captain Chandor if he would try to arrange for the volunteers to go to Norway immediately, if the Finns did not want them. Captain Chandor replied that as far as he could see nobody had thought of the details, such as how to get there, would the Finns welcome such a move after putting in so much staff work, how useful would the unit be with 70% completely untrained, would it not be murder to lead such a body against specialised troops, how was the Agreement of Service to be settled, and so on. Captain Chandor wrote home: "I feel that Joyce is rather a nuisance, the sort of nuisance I do not intend to tolerate much longer!" Nevertheless, he had appointed him as his second-in-command, a post which Joyce retained for another five weeks. But then volunteers Bristow and Nightingale requested a move to Norway, and Sergeant Howard also discussed the matter with him.

Realising that there were now strong feelings in the unit, Captain Chandor discussed the Norwegian question with Captain Nordlund, in the light of the unit's impending move. Captain Nordlund then discussed it with Professor Lönnrot and General Enckell, and with Field-Marshal Mannerheim. The last-named promised an answer the following day. In the evening Captain Chandor received a telegram from Major Magill, summoning him to Helsinki, and left on the night train. Before he left, orders came from

Captain Nordlund that the unit was to hold itself in readiness to move the following day. The sergeant-major announced that new classes of Finns were being called up, that all army leave had been stopped, and that a state of grave emergency existed, as it was thought that hostilities between Russia and Finland might start again. Company orders were changed, causing much disappointment, as everyone wanted to be on the rifle-range for the first firing, as originally intended, since it was now four weeks since the arrival of the first draft, and no-one had yet fired a rifle. Instead, there was company and platoon drill and some bayonet instruction with dummies. Kits were packed and ready for a possible departure by 4 pm., and the volunteers were confined to barracks after the last parade. At tea the sergeant-manor announced that permission was granted for all ranks to go to the town until 10 pm., and kits were unpacked again. No explanation was given, and rumours began to circulate. An issue of cigarettes was made; and Sergeant Howard noted in his diary that the craving for cigarettes did not seem to get less with the lack of them, and that many were definitely unhappy unless they had a regular issue. High prices were paid for single ones; and it was a common sight to see five or six volunteers sitting in a circle, with a lighted cigarette-end mounted on a pin (there were no such luxuries as filter-tipped cigarettes available then), taking turns at having a "drag" until the cigarette had been smoked down to the last quarter inch.

On 14th April company orders cancelled the previous day were put up on the notice-board again. Reveille was at six, and an advance party left for the rifle-range to fix the targets. No. 1 platoon followed at half past eight and the others later. The volunteers were in good humour. The range was about two hundred yards, and each had two sighting and five scoring rounds. The ammunition had been made locally to the English rimless pattern, and the rifles were Lee-Enfield models of the type used in the British army. This international combination may have accounted for the occasional misfires. After the first section had had its turn on the range it went forward into the butts to relieve the section that had been marking the targets there. While one of the volunteers in the second section was sitting down waiting for the action to begin, a French letter fell out of his pocket. He let it lie where it fell. One of the others, however, took it up and unrolled it, and, unnoticed by the owner of the weapon fixed it to the muzzle of a rifle left leaning against the wall of the butts. The next section fired its turn, and the time came for the change-over. The outgoing section climbed out of the butts, lined up, and was called to attention. It sloped arms, and was marched back to the firing point, one of its members with his rifle adorned with the French letter flapping gaily in the breeze. The sergeant-major was one of the last to notice it, and ordered the offender to "remove that disgusting thing" from his rifle.

While all this was going on, the War Office in London asked the Committee of the Finnish Aid Bureau if the volunteers could be sent to Norway, having apparently heard of the feeling among them. The Committee, which in turn had heard that some of the volunteers had become troublesome, consented to this, and it was decided that Gibson should go to Finland to see Field-Marshal Mannerheim and discuss the future of the volunteers with him, as well as to explain the position to the volunteers and to take any necessary action to maintain the good reputation of the unit. It so happened that Lord Balfour of Burleigh had to go to Finland on other business, whose nature was not stated, and he undertook the task intended for Gibson, who never left London. One suspects that another reason for sending his Lordship was that he had a "handle" to his name which might carry more weight with the Field-Marshal (a Baron) and others than that of a mere Mister.

Meanwhile, Captain Chandor arrived in Helsinki around noon on 11th April. He went to the Legation and saw someone, probably Vereker or Major Magill, and then saw General Enckell. The upshot of his discussions was that he found that it was quite impossible for the unit to go to Norway. He then dined with Lord Carlow, the Air Attaché, who said that he had just come back from inspecting the Air Force volunteers, who were far from satisfactory. Captain

Chandor replied that he was not in the least surprised, and that he feared he might be saddled with them again. He returned to Lapua about midday on 14th April, in time to take a turn on the rifle-range. He came with the news that the homebound party had arrived in Oslo the day the Germans invaded Norway, but that about thirty of them had succeeded in getting back to Stockholm, and that the remainder had taken to the woods in twos and threes. Of his discussions in Helsinki he told his officers nothing, except to say that he had been treated like royalty and that no other member of the unit was to visit the city. The following day 28 Air Force volunteers returned to Lapua.

On arrival in Helsinki early in April Lord Balfour had discussions with the diplomatic staff of the British Legation, and also with the Field-Marshal. In mid-April he visited Lapua, where he was photographed with the Air Force volunteers and Captains Nordlund and Chandor. Chandor later told Lord Balfour that the unit was not fit to fight under its present officers, only three of whom (Joyce, Scott and Nurk) had any previous military experience, and would first need intensive training under other officers. On hearing this the War Office decided not to send the volunteers to Norway.

On 16th April reveille was early again, and the volunteers were put on fatigues preparatory to departure. They were called out a platoon at a time and asked to sign an amendment to Clause 10 of the Agreement of Service, prolonging it to 31st May 1940 or to such earlier time as the Finnish authorities might decide. Only about ninety signed the amendment, though the rest recognised that they were under the same discipline as those who had signed, and this was duly reported to General Enckell. Two who did not sign had already sought Captain Chandor's permission to leave the unit and find their own way home when the unit left Lapua. Knowing that one of them had visited Finland before the war and knew his way around the country, Captain Chandor took no chances, and when the unit left Lapua on 17th April he placed the two under close arrest, from which they were released on arrival in Savonlinna after undertaking to stay with the unit until 31st May.

After the departure of the British and Hungarian companies from Lapua, Captain Nordlund reported on them to the Headquarters of the Home Forces. He noted that outwardly the British unit had made a comparatively favourable impression, perhaps partly due to the uniform equipment which they had brought with them. But its inner spirit, its *esprit de corps,* and the unit's general military bearing was not, as far as he could see, anywhere near the high level of the Hungarian unit, for instance. He may not have known that whereas the Hungarians had come out as a trained unit, the British had not, or that Britain does not have conscription in peace-time, or that few of the volunteers knew how to handle a rifle properly when they arrived; and that none of them were used to the extreme cold found in Finland in the late winter and early spring.

SAVONLINNA

On 15th April the first preparations for the unit's departure from Lapua were made when a sergeant and party were sent to collect the horses and carts. The best chestnut horse was allotted to Captain Chandor. This upset the Hungarians, who sent an officer to intervene. He ordered a new deal, took all the best horses, and gave the sergeant the duds. As this took place about ten o'clock at night the Hungarians thought that it would be too late to fetch Captain Chandor from his billet. As soon as he heard what had happened Captain Chandor asked Captain Nordlund to order a parade of all the horses, so that there could be a new share-out the following morning. This Captain Nordlund arranged, but he gave the Hungarians the first choice. With 350 of them even Captain Chandor felt they were entitled to it, and they at once chose the chestnut horse. Although Captain Chandor didn't mind personally, he felt that the honour of his unit was affected, and walked away from the parade. Seeing he was upset Captain Nordlund told Captain Miville to choose a horse for Captain Chandor, who had to make do with the best of a bad bargain.

The next day Taylor H., the quartermaster-sergeant, was put in charge of arrangements for packing the unit's kit and equipment and transferring the baggage to the station. Loading it on to the special train went without a hitch, despite the sleet, though the train did not arrive until an hour after its intended departure time of three in the afternoon. The British unit managed to get the only first and second class carriage, while the Hungarians had one with only second and third classes, "in return for their horse behaviour", Captain Chandor noted. The sick Britons travelled with the sergeants in the second class part. The others were in goods wagons, fitted up as dormitories with plank shelves and each with a central stove for heating, and not very comfortable. The horse platoon was crowded in with its horses, and the machine-gunners were in a van with the Maxim gun and a quantity of ammunition. The train finally left Lapua at about half-past eight, and spent the next fourteen hours on its journey, standing for long periods in station sidings to let the regular trains pass. Breakfast was at Jyväskylä, and lunch was at Pieksämäki, where there was a wait of nearly four hours while the Hungarian part of the train was taken off to continue its journey to Lappeenranta, on the southern shores of lake Saimaa. The British unit arrived at Savonlinna around midnight on 17th/18th April.

Savonlinna – savver leaner to the volunteers – had a population of just over 8,000 on the outbreak of the Winter War, but this was considerably increased on the arrival of evacuees from territory ceded to the Soviet Union after the armistice. It lies on islands and a cape joined by bridges, between lakes Pihlajavesi and Haapavesi, and one is seldom far from water when one wanders in the town. It grew up around the castle of Olavinlinna, which was built in 1475. Then as now an important industrial and cultural centre and a popular holiday resort, it was the home of the volunteers for the last six weeks of their army service.

The train pulled in at the station and the kits and equipment were unloaded, the horses were moved to stables, and the carts were taken off. The volunteers were then marched to an army canteen, where soup awaited them. A couple of Lottas (the Finnish equivalent of the Auxiliary Territorial Service), were working in the canteen when the party arrived, and were singing a little Finnish ditty to the tune of the Lambeth Walk. The volunteers took this as a compliment; but it made the interpreters smile. Subsequently enquiries showed that it was a tribute to Major-General Hjalmari Siilasvuo, victor of the battle of Suomussalmi and Commander of the highly-successful Finnish III Army Corps, to which the British unit was now attached. The song can be roughly translated as follows:

General Siilasvuo's my name,

I'm a teetotaller of fame.
Whisky and gin? Oh, no!
I'm General Siilasvuo. Hoi!

The volunteers were then marched to their billets which were in the theatre-cum-ballroom of the Hotel Seurahuone. The officers and interpreters were quartered in the hotel, which was a wooden building in the main street. As if to celebrate their safe arrival in the town a record number of volunteers reported sick later in the day. Six were admitted to Military Hospital 19, suffering from such things as a fractured knee, feverish pains, stomach pains, lung catarrh, vaccination swelling, and a sore throat. Breakfast on the first day was in the canteen again, and included porridge without milk or sugar, brown bread, and sausage. Later the same day Field Post No. KPK 27-T.9300 was issued to the unit.

As there was no ground attached to the theatre, apart from a small sloping yard at the back, the unit paraded near the harbour, where there was a wide open level space large enough for the whole company at once. A great crowd assembled to watch the British unit drilling on its first day; and Captain Chandor noted in his letters home at the time that the arms and foot drill were getting noticeably better day by day.

The unit still did its own catering, but now based on Finnish army rations, which were found to be less in quantity than those which had been enjoyed in Lapua, though the unit had a small fund available for outside purchases, so it was possible to vary the monotony. Much of the hot food consisted of soups and stews cooked on a field-kitchen in the yard behind the barracks, which vehicle accompanied the unit to the rifle-range and on manœuvres. The efforts of the cooks, Volunteers Moore, Alexander, Haywood and Thompson, were sometimes supplemented by such things as fried eggs, which Punshon cooked on a smoky stove in the theatre's diminutive kitchen. For bread the volunteers had unlimited supplies of Finnish army rye biscuit, named vaneri (plywood) in the land of its birth.

These biscuits were about a foot square and had a hole in the middle, and within a few days of the unit's arrival every man had his own rye biscuit hanging on a nail on his bunk. On several days the catering officer managed to get fish, and on another the III Corps Headquarters staff sent a huge block of milk chocolate, a delicacy which had not been seen since leaving home. It took considerable skill to divide it into equal-sized lumps for each volunteer.

The day after the unit arrived in Savonlinna Captain Chandor thought it would be a good idea to take the volunteers out on a route march. The Finnish guide who was procured to lead them thought they wanted to see the local sights, so he led the party from the barracks, northwards under the railway, over a wooden bridge, past the Casino, and into a park on the edge of lake Haapavesi. Here the narrow rocky paths brought confusion to the columns of three, and after coming to a halt and having some altercation with the guide, Captain Chandor left him to his own devices and led the unit back the way it had come. It turned right and marched westwards along the main street to the outskirts of the town, where there was a sign pointing to Hautausmaa. Thinking this was the name of the next village Captain Chandor boldly led the column of men up the hill, where the road ended – at the cemetery, this being Hautausmaa in Finnish. Here he halted the unit, turned it round, and marched it back to the barracks.

It rained hard on 20th April, and as it was Saturday the morning was spent cleaning up the barrack-room. Bath, in civilian life a carpenter, knocked up a counter for the canteen, which adjoined the kitchen. The unit was given a second typhoid injection, and the Finns told them the town's drinking-water had been polluted by dead Russians. While this was going on Captain Chandor went to III Army Headquarters with the unit's newly-appointed liaison officer, Lieut. Stig Brunow, to meet Major-General Siilasvuo and his chief-of-staff Lieut-Col. Gustav Ehrnrooth, and to thank them for all the arrangements made for the unit's reception. There he learned that Colonel Ehrnrooth wanted a parade and inspection the following day, which was Sunday, to be followed by a march-past, a sight-seeing tour of the castle, and a meal of beer and sausages. To make sure that everything went off properly there was a practice parade in the morning. Captain Chandor wrote: "I inspected so as to get the men and uniforms right, as per Finnish arrangement. We also had to practise a shout; for when a Finnish inspecting officer arrives he greets his troops with *Hyvää päivää, komppania!* (good day, company!), and the answer *Hyvää päivää, herra eversti!* (good day, Mr Colonel!). Not an easy thing to teach them."

"We had lunch", Captain Chandor continued, "and then went out to the parade. A band was waiting for us, and punctual to time Colonel Ehrnrooth arrived and held his inspection. He made a very good speech, read by Brunow in English, then we cheered him and he went off in his car to the saluting base, and we marched past. The parade was really quite a success, I think; anyhow, one simply would not recognise the troops now as the same men who were wandering round like half-baked tramps a week ago. I won't say they are quite the equals of the Brigade of Guards yet, but when *God Save the King* was played while they were presenting arms one could see their chests going out, and not a man moved; and every cook and servant clamoured to come on parade."

The unit marched past the saluting base and up the street towards Kyrönsalmi bridge. There it halted, piled arms, and walked down to the ferry which took the volunteers over the straits to the castle. The band came too, and played while the volunteers were entertained to sausages and beer and were shown round the fortifications.

The III Army Corps Order of the Day No.14 of 21st April 1940 welcomed the British contingent under its own commanding officer, with effect from 17th April, as an independent company of the Corps. Circumstances beyond the control of the Finnish government, the Order stated, might prevent the volunteers from returning to their own country. The Finnish High Command would, however, "do everything in their power to solve these problems in a mutually satisfactory manner, and will keep in continual touch with the British Minister in Helsinki," to whom the volunteers themselves could always apply.

The people of Savonlinna accepted the volunteers with great good humour, and it was not long before the local children had named the dark-skinned Purves The Indian Prince, a compliment they did not pay to Butler, who was also born in India. Sergeant Seyler, who was lean and about six feet six inches tall, was nicknamed The Outline. The volunteers as a body, on account of the fact that they were often heard singing selected (and polite) songs such as John Peel, Cock Robin and The Quartermaster's Stores (the latter with additional verses referring to their officers and NCOs), both while marching through the town and while washing in the town's sauna, became known as The Canaries. This was an apposite description of men who, like birds in a cage, were unable to get out of Finland but were still able to sing. In turn, an elderly bearded man who lived on the eastern outskirts of the town and who watched the manœuvres of the volunteers with great interest was nicknamed The Lama, a reference to a character in the film *Lost Horizon*.

As if to remind the unit that winter was not yet over, a flurry of snow came on 22nd April. Among the volunteers on orders that day for breaches of discipline were three NCOs who had got lost exploring one of the islands and "a man who is quite obviously cracky" who had attacked another man with a knife. Captain Chandor was going to punish him severely, but changed his mind while he was talking to him because he felt it might finish him off altogether. The next day Captain Miville gave a dinner-party for the members of the F.A.N.Y. ambulance unit, who were due to leave Savonlinna the following week. Captain Chandor and Lieut. Brunow were invited, and the former noted that the dinner was a complete nightmare owing to the fact that they had to wait so long for everything.

The unit spent 24th April on the rifle-range just west of the town. Here the volunteers made the acquaintance of the Finnish rapid rifle, the Lahti-Saloranta M. 1926, which, unknown to them at the time, had been offered to the Royal Air Force in 1934 but turned down. Of a 7.62 mm. calibre, and using Russian-type rim cartridges, the weapon was about 4 lbs. lighter than the British Bren gun. It worked on recoil, and had a choice of a 20-round magazine or a 75-round drum, both fixed underneath the weapon. With the same cyclical rate of fire as the Bren, 500 rounds a minute, it was made obsolete in Finland at the end of 1940; and when in 1942 the writer was trained to use the Bren gun he found it to be the inferior of the two weapons.

The next day the unit went on a seventeen-mile route march, westwards from the town and towards Mikkeli, in full marching order. After the first hour a halt was called, and the volunteers sat down in the ditches on either side of the road to rest, some distance west of Laitaatsilta. While they were resting a gipsy family came over the brow of the hill, with a horse and cart containing their belongings. For some reason or other the horse took fright and tried to bolt into the forest. The cart overturned in the ditch, and the horse fell over. Not knowing that in Finland at that time gipsies were considered to be "untouchables" a dozen volunteers jumped to their feet, got the horse and cart back on the road, and loaded up the cart. The gipsies went on their way shouting *Kiitos!* (thank you) to them. And ever afterwards, when any gipsy came into Savonlinna and saw a volunteer he would wave to him and say hullo, how are you, and so on, in Finnish. It remained a puzzle for the good people of the town how it was that these foreigners could have acquired such a strange power over the people they called *mustalaiset* (the black people).

The field kitchen met the unit at the rendezvous and provided a most welcome meal. Then the unit marched back to barracks, still able to sing (outside the town) such rude songs as are usually sung in the British army on route marches and never in mixed company. Taxed almost to the limit the unit marched into the yard behind the barracks at attention, and, to quote Captain Chandor again, "looking really good; I was simply delighted."

On 26th April the platoons were divided into squads for the purpose of arms drill. On the square at the end of Satamakatu (Harbour Street), just east of the bank, a lance-corporal in charge of a squad forgot to inspect each man's ammunition before the drill began, to ensure that he only had blank practice ammunition. An onlooker wrote: "I was one of the two guards at Field Post Office 27 in the Orthodox Church (which lay almost opposite the barracks) in the summer of 1940. An incident which I recall from those times was when the British volunteers were drilling down on Satamakatu. They were practising loading and firing their rifles. I don't know whether they had blank ammunition. A shot rang out. The onlookers were scared out of their wits; they were watching from both sides of the road. The bullet struck the upright of a twin door in a building on the other side of the street. It had been well aimed between two people's heads! The soldier who fired the shot was disarmed and marched away in the grip of two strong men. The drill was over for the day. It was just lucky that no-one was hurt." The lance-corporal concerned was reduced to the ranks and spent the rest of the day in detention. The hole became known as Roper's Hole, after the volunteer who fired the shot. Roper was unmoved by the incident, and returned to Finland after the war and married a Finnish girl.

Lord Balfour of Burleigh made a second visit to the volunteers, in Savonlinna. On 26th April, after Major Magill had telephoned his Lordship's expected time and place of arrival to Captain Chandor, the latter drove with Lieut. Brunow and Miss Runciman to the airfield at Joroinen, some fifty-five miles from Savonlinna, with an empty car for Lord Balfour and for Mrs Vereker, who came as her husband's representative. They were expected to arrive at noon, but at one o'clock a telephone call came from Helsinki to say that the party would arrive at three. The plane came in, and out stepped four Finnish officers, but no Lord Balfour or Mrs Vereker. After making enquiries Captain Chandor discovered that his visitors had landed at Juva airfield, some distance to the south, and had driven direct to Savonlinna.

Mrs Vereker and Lord Balfour took a march-past of the unit on the quayside. Back in the barracks Lord Balfour spoke to the volunteers. He said he wanted to consider with them the best course to be adopted in the present difficult circumstances, and stressed that he would not discuss the legal aspects of the Agreement of Service, but rather its spirit. The Committee, he added, having arranged transport to Finland so that the volunteers could fight there, undertook to bring them back to England. But it was "quite possible" that the Russians might attack again, and if the volunteers were to fight the Russians they would have to wait in Savonlinna. Field-Marshal Mannerheim had made it perfectly clear to Lord Balfour that he could not in any circumstances agree to the transfer of the unit to Norway, because it would be an infringement of Finland's neutrality. However, it might be possible to arrange for transport home via Petsamo, but if this was impossible the alternative was to continue training, as the waiting period could be a long one.

Lord Balfour then had a discussion with the officers, who, in Captain Chandor's presence, "endeavoured to be frank" about their lack of success in reaching a better understanding with their commanding officer. After Lord Balfour's visit several volunteers asked to be sent to Norway, but Captain Chandor's orders, as he understood them, were to keep the unit together at all costs. He took this literally, and on a visit to Helsinki, meeting Atkinson (who had obtained his discharge in Lapua), persuaded him to rejoin the unit as storekeeper. Meanwhile, the Germans formally notified the Finnish government that any volunteers caught in Norway would be court-martialled and shot.

After some six weeks' absence from home Lord Balfour returned to London via Petsamo on the s/s *Argo* (there were two Finnish vessels of this name), and reported to the committee meeting held in London on 17th June. He gave a full account of the situation in Finland, and added that in Savonlinna the only lock-up available to the volunteers was the town gaol, which was "comfortably furnished and the food was good, and the prisoners received attention from the gaoler's daughter." Then, as now, the good people of Savo were noted for making gentle fun of strangers, and someone in Savonlinna must have pulled his Lordship's leg. Kilgour, who delivered rations and messages to the odd volunteer being disciplined in the town's little red-brick gaol said at the time that the bunks were hard, the conditions primitive and damp, and that the place smelled of disinfectant. At the same meeting it was reported that the only "serious trouble" had been from twenty-five Air Force volunteers who had refused to accept lower ranks on being posted back to the unit. This, too, as we have seen, was a fabrication, since the transfer went smoothly, and the "trouble" was really that a number of those volunteers had declined to rejoin the unit. Lord Balfour successfully pressed the Committee to pay the volunteers the extra bonus of 550 marks a month which the Finnish army paid to its own soldiers; and Gibson later noted that thanks to Lord Balfour's "firm but kindly dealing with the men" they had settled down, having been told that they would all be repatriated as soon as possible.

On Wednesday 1st May a special squad of soldiers came from the 3rd company of the 19th Infantry Regiment, under the command of Captain Olavi Salminen, to demonstrate the Finnish infantry technique of advancing over open country. The demonstration took place east of the town, near the suburb of Pääskylä (Swallow Place), and the whole unit marched over the Kyrönsalmi bridge for the day's manœuvres. The demonstration was no smooth parade-ground affair, and it had an air of reality by virtue of the fact that the soldiers taking part in it had experienced the closing stages of the bitter fighting at Taipale on the shores of Lake Ladoga. One of their number, Olavi Järvi, wrote later: "A few weeks after the armistice, while awaiting transfer to the officers' school, I had a stroke of luck. I was one of a number of men detailed to form a demonstration battle-squad consisting of two rifle-sections, which was to give the volunteers a demonstration of Finnish troops in action. We had to dash forward, firing blank ammunition from rifles and machine pistols, to cross an open meadow, and to capture a small hill partly covered by bushes and a thicket of trees, on which there was a machine-gun nest. The British boys were in positions in the area around the small hill. I remember that when in the heat of the action I got into the bushes around it I was only a few yards from a couple of them, who looked at me down the barrels of their rifles. It is difficult to say whether there was any useful lesson for them to learn from our advance. Naturally enough, the Anglo-Finnish battle practice was followed by food. For the previous week, at our quarters in Kerimäki, we had nothing in our mess-tins but the same old sloppy warmed-up pea soup; but now we had delicious food, an appetizing tomato soup."

The following Saturday Captain Chandor produced a new and very intensive training schedule, which the sergeants discussed at tea-time. Francis and Commins, both with long army experience, said that not even in army prisons did men work in such a way as that proposed. Howard had heard that the men were feeling so strongly as a result of rumours that the daily working hours were to be increased that they were contemplating a strike, and that about fifty had signed a pledge not to parade on Monday. Asling said that he, too, had heard of the list, but that in this case, although he had always upheld army discipline, he did not expect the men to obey, and for his part he would not try to force them but would hand in his stripes. Commins and Nicholls said they would do the same; and Asling thought he might be suspected of being the ringleader if he put the matter to Captain Chandor. As none of the sergeants enjoyed their commanding officer's confidence Howard agreed to have a word with him when he went to see him after tea in connection with some machine-gun matters.

Apart from a single diary reference the writer has found no contemporary record or current memory of the fifty-man pledge, and it seems likely that it may never have been compiled. On Sunday 5th May, the day after the sergeants' discussion, Smith M.L. convened a meeting of the volunteers in the barrack-room, with Apostolides as chairman. After passing a vote of no confidence in Captain

Chandor it drew up a petition.* In view of the international situation, it went, the volunteers wished to move to a base "near the proposed point of departure at the earliest date, so that immediate advantage may be taken of any opportunity to return to England, where we may be used to the best advantage of our own country." The signatories would be perfectly prepared to continue their training at a new headquarters, which were evidently intended to be near Petsamo, the only open harbour left in Finland. They requested Captain Chandor to pass the petition to the Finnish authorities at the earliest possible opportunity. The petition bore 116 signatures out of a possible 139, and was given to the sergeant-major for onward transmission. He accepted it somewhat unwillingly, warned his hearers of the consequences of a mutiny, and reminded them that they were still under military discipline. However, he promised to make the men's views known to Captain Chandor. One of the twenty-three men who did not sign the petition was promoted to lance-corporal the following day.

The new training schedule was not nearly as bad as had at first been feared. The enlarged unit was divided into four platoons, and work went ahead. Realising that something had to be seen to be done about hours, food and repatriation, Captain Chandor received a deputation of volunteers before the first parade on Monday, and repeated the warnings of the sergeant-major. This had the desired effect; and strenuous whole-day manœuvres followed. Near Laitaatsilta, a mile or two west of the town, the rifle sections, in turn, advanced along the railway line, through a cutting and round the edges of fields, to surround and capture a machine-gun nest, hidden in a thicket on a hillside on the north side of the railway. To give their position away the machine-gunners fired bursts of blanks from time to time; and for some reason or other there were no trains to interrupt the games. Lunch was a treat. In addition to the army rye-biscuits and cheese there was a delicious confection, liver pie *(maksalaattikko)* , which the volunteers found to be made of rice and minced

---

* see Appendix "C"

liver, baked and served cold with a spoonful of cranberry jam. When the unit returned to barracks later in the afternoon there was an explanation of the day's activities with a sketch-map drawn on a blackboard. However, as no-one had thought of giving a little instruction before the day's exercise on the tactics to be employed, the remarks of Lieut. Joyce, who had been detailed to explain the day's operations, were not fully appreciated.

Training continued both on the square and on the ground, and about this time the unit was taught the Finnish words of command for Halt! *(seis!)* and Advance! *(eteenpäin!)*, but not the word for retreat, since retreat was not in the vocabulary of the III Army Corps. On 9th May the whole unit went to the rifle-range for a day's firing. Matters became somewhat confused when the horse drawing the field-kitchen died suddenly. It was intended that there should be more practice on the range on 14th May, and the unit paraded at a quarter to eight in the morning for the purpose. The machine-guns had actually left in a horse-drawn cart for the range when company orders were changed, and they were fetched back. The officers, including Captain Chandor, then carried out a minute inspection of kit which, in accordance with the then practice in the British army, had to be laid out on its owner's bunk in a particular way. A few surplus articles of clothing were found, as one volunteer noted in his diary, and several others were detained in the guard-room, but the big deficiency in the quartermaster's stores, mainly greatcoats, was not by any means explained. It was in any case too late to start keeping close records after the weeks at Lapua when the stores had been accessible to anyone. The kit inspection lasted until two o'clock; "another day of machine-gun training wasted", as another diarist put it.

Sergeant Vessey's application for leave to go to Helsinki on 16th May was turned down. Captain Chandor told him that the Finns had arranged a big four-day programme for him (Captain Chandor), but that "that stupid petition" had upset it. He added that the Finns no longer thought of the unit as they did before the petition, which he deplored, as it had forced his hand. The first parade on 17th May was as usual at a quarter to eight. Again orders were changed at the last moment, and the machine-gunners were ordered to be back in barracks at a quarter to twelve for a group photograph. Only 131 of the unit, including interpreters and a couple of Finns, were included, and about twenty volunteers managed to be somewhere else when the photographer clicked his shutter. This interruption gave less than three hours' firing practice for the whole of the week, and contrasted strangely with Captain Chandor's earlier remarks that this was the training season and that the final stage was being reached, when time was of the utmost value, and that no leave could consequently be granted. But the keenness of the machine-gunners continued unabated, despite the continual changes in the training programme.

A rift between Captain Chandor and Lieut. Guthrie on the one side and Dr Herford and Lieuts. Joyce, Nurk, Ruck-Keene and Scott on the other, with Captain Miville taking neither part, reached serious proportions on 17th May. The whole affair was due to the fact that Captain Chandor had heard that Dr Herford had spent a convivial hour or two the previous evening in the company of a Finnish officer and three NCOs, and Captain Chandor did not like his officers to be seen hob-nobbing with other ranks in public. He expressed his views somewhat forcibly to Dr Herford, who had sought an interview with him, as he was worried about the lack of communication between his commanding officer and the other officers. In reply to the accusation that Dr Herford had not carried out his wishes, the latter replied that Captain Chandor was under a misapprehension "caused by what the officers on their part felt to be a complete lack of confidence and absence of contact, trust and co-operation." The upshot of a somewhat acrimonious exchange of views was that Captain Chandor threatened to prepare a statement which he would let Dr Herford see before he forwarded it to London. Later the same day Lieut. Joyce, an experienced commander, gave steadying advice, and the promised statement was never prepared.

On 18th May there were the usual barrack-room fatigues,

with two platoons at a time on the square to practise manual signals, which came after a month of field exercises. The sergeant giving the instruction, Taylor H., had just been taken out of the quartermaster's job and had no knowledge of the signals the NCOs had been instructing in, which were from British army manuals. Sergeant Vessey left for Helsinki the following day, with nine men, for three days' leave. Sherry and Smith M.L. preceded them, having taken French leave the day before.

The sergeants and others on the leave party returned from Helsinki on 22nd May, to find the other volunteers anxious for news of any impending departure. "They are again beginning to distrust the announcement that efforts are being made to get us home", wrote one diarist. "The C.O. is so secretive and has such little contact with the unit that the wildest rumours are given currency and discontent begins again." Captain Chandor had no doubt as to the feeling in the unit, since the following day he spoke to the NCOs on the subject, and Sergeants Francis and Taylor H. recommended going north in small parties.

On 24th May there was rapid rifle firing on the range in the morning, and in the afternoon drill in anticipation of the following Sunday's wreath-laying on the grave of the Finnish unknown soldier, at which some unusual movements, such as slow marching and reversing arms, were taught. It turned out later that the wreath-laying ceremony had been held on the previous Sunday, and Captain Chandor was furious that the unit had missed it. Nevertheless, when the unit returned from manœuvres a day or two later a military funeral was heard coming down the main street, so the volunteers were lined up on one side, in single file, turned left to face the street, and presented arms as the cortege passed. For a while the sergeant-major was all smiles and sugar on parade; and he told the volunteers that he was to be commissioned in the West Yorkshire regiment when he got home, and asked how many of them would serve with him.

Someone remembered in time that Friday, 24th May was

Empire Day, so the unit was dismissed at ten in the morning for the day. The following day was taken up with barrack-room fatigues and foot-drill. The sergeant-major had a long and friendly talk with the whole parade, and said he had been sent to Helsinki in connection with the unit's return home, but that the boat which had been coming to fetch it was "no more". He was going down to Helsinki again on Monday to find out more about the unit's departure. "When someone said the men no longer had any faith in their officers", a diarist noted, "the sergeant-major said *he* could get us all home, but it was not fair to expect him to go and tell the officers to pack up and give way to him." The petition had done no end of harm, and but for it the unit would probably have been in England by now, he added.

On the last Sunday in May, when the snow had all gone and the ice in the lakes had melted, a lake-steamer was placed at the disposal of the unit. The volunteers marched down to the quay and went on board, and the ship left. An army band from III Corps provided the music during the trip round the islands to the south-west of the town, and Jarrett conducted it for a while. Lunch-time arrived, and two Lottas, who had volunteered as cooks, produced quantities of rye-bread, butter, beer, and a cauldron of boiled sausages. The sausages were long thin things, quite unlike English ones, and their similarity to something else was not lost on the volunteers, several of whom adorned their trousers with them and walked around the ship looking as if they were seeking a place to relieve themselves. Lunch over, the ship tied up at a little hamlet called Ryhälä, and the unit went ashore for about half an hour. There was little to see, but two families living nearby came down to see the party off. In the evening Sergeant McKay welcomed the volunteers to a party held to celebrate his engagement to a local girl. The wedding took place on 5th July, and Ruck-Keene came all the way from Jyväskylä to be present.

Meanwhile, on 10th May, Ari Kauhanen, a senior official of the Finnish State Police and a German agent, made a report to Captain Nordlund on the state of morale in the unit, two days before the latter was posted from Lapua to

Helsinki. The men were in general satisfied, the report stated, food and billets were regarded as good, but cigarettes were missed. "The men are satisfied with the Finnish officers (there was only one) attached to the unit, as well as with the training led by the Finns. By contrast, they have no confidence in the English officers; on one occasion about forty men refused to obey the order of an English officer to take part in a parade. Chandor is not popular, neither is Miville; the men claim that the latter does not understand the English or their mentality." The men wanted to go home; they came out to fight.

Naturally enough, Kauhanen did not say where his information came from, but it was just the sort of chatter that might have been heard in the company office. The truth of the matter, as we have seen, was slightly different. The cigarette shortage, for instance, chronic in the early days, had been put right in Lapua, and each man, whether smoker or non-smoker, received a ration with his pay each week. As for those who had allegedly refused to go on parade, forty was the number of volunteers who on 16th April had declined to sign an extension of their Agreements of Service but had agreed to stay with the unit until 31st May. Be that as it may, the effect of the report was startling. Word of the "dissatisfaction" reached Vereker's ears and he discussed it with Major Magill, both of whom were probably unaware that its source was an exceedingly unreliable one. By this time the story had become a bit garbled; Major Magill thought that the situation was akin to a revolt whose cause was some unimportant detail connected with the rations. He would, of course, have been aware by this time that Jackson had deserted on 11th May, as he was arranging a passage for him on the ship leaving Petsamo with Lord Balfour, and he may also have heard of the temporary disappearance of Sherry and Smith M.L. His views may have been strengthened when Lieuts. Joyce and Nurk paid him a courtesy call on 24th May.

The three discussed the repatriation of the unit. Major Magill averred that the British Legation had "several hundred" people to arrange for (there were, in fact, 145 volunteers, and forty or fifty civilians who later joined the Legation's homebound party), that eight members of the Legation staff were "hard at it" arranging homebound trips, and that several visits had been made to the North, the gallant Major having been there himself. The Admiralty was sending a boat to Petsamo, and transport of the volunteers to that port could be arranged at a moment's notice. Major Magill wanted any news of their move to reach the volunteers suddenly, so that the Germans could not arrange a surprise. Lieut. Nurk replied that he thought it vital that the volunteers should be allowed to know as clearly and fully as possible what was being done for them, "as they felt there was one eternal muddle, and that to put it crudely they were 'just being buggered about'." He asked for an official statement to be made to them, otherwise, after 31st May, discipline would become almost impossible to maintain.

Convinced now that a mutiny was going to break out, Major Magill dressed himself in his parade uniform, with highly-polished belt and boots and all the trimmings, and travelled up to the seat of the alleged "trouble". First of all he met Captain Chandor and the other officers, and inspected the men's quarters. Then he inspected the officers' and interpreters' quarters in the adjoining hotel. The officers and interpreters lined up in their quarters, Lieut. Nurk standing next to interpreter von Essen. As Major Magill entered the room they came smartly to attention. A French letter fell out of Lieut. Nurk's pocket. Von Essen saw it and took half a pace to the left so that his foot hid the offending object.

Major Magill then appeared on the stage, which served as a canteen and assembly-place, and spoke to the volunteers. His choice of words was not the happiest, and his speech was peppered with expressions which his hearers found highly offensive. Evans S.H., a journalist, took it down in shorthand.* The gist of Major Magill's speech was that the volunteers, whom he referred to as "a fine body of blackguards", were to be demobilised the following day, that

---

* see Appendix "D"

the Finns did not issue demobilisation papers, and that the British Legation in Helsinki wanted nothing to do with the volunteers. His advice that the unit should stick together, since as a whole it had a better chance of getting home than individuals, was clearly not the view of a number of his hearers, who showed in their subsequent attempts to get home via Petsamo that he travels fastest who travels alone. There was also a march-past of the whole unit, down on the quay, at which Major Magill took the salute.

Gibson, who heard about the demoralising effects of Major Magill's speech from Major Chandor and others, and who had probably seen a transcript, noted later in his Report that "a most unfortunate and disgraceful speech" had been delivered by the British Military Attaché to the volunteers. Later in the year Dr Herford asked Vereker to send a letter containing a copy of the speech by diplomatic bag to a medical friend who could pass it on to Lord Dawson of Penn, but Vereker refused, on the ground that Major Magill had his career to consider. So had Vereker.

On 31st May the unit comprised 102 privates, 17 lance-corporals, 8 corporals, 2 lance-sergeants, 8 sergeants, 1 quartermaster-sergeant, one company sergeant-major, and six officers, totalling 146. Of these, only two platoons, totalling 61 officers and men, took part in the last parade on that day, the remainder being either engaged on barrack duties or, in the case of the writer, photographing the parade. The parade took place on the open space by the harbour, where the volunteers were lined up in open order. Colonel Ehrnrooth arrived and greeted Captain Chandor, and then inspected the troops, who presented arms. The unit then re-formed in close order and was led round the town by a military band from III Army Corps, whose overall smartness was marred by the first clarinet, who was wearing lumberjack's boots instead of the regulation army issue of his fellow-musicians. The route lay eastwards from the harbour, past the town sauna, up Tott Street, northwards up School Street to the School, and westwards down Olav's Street, the town's main street, to the barracks. There was some confusion when the first platoon had to halt at the top of the hill in School Street to wait for a gap in the traffic before wheeling left. When the two platoons were properly spaced out again they marched off, with the band and Captain Chandor in the lead. The band played Finnish military marches, which are in a class of their own, and, most appropriately, played "My father was a soldier" *(Mun isä oli sotamies)* as the parade marched down the main street. The day closed with a pay parade, at which the monthly bonus of 550 marks was paid as well.

The parade was the climax of ten weeks' training, which had been divided into two periods. Most of the first four weeks at Lapua had been spent in perfecting foot-drill, rifle-drill and weapon training. On the route marches, march discipline, taking cover from hostile aircraft, and anti-gas measures were practised, with as much time as possible being spent on the rifle-range. The instructors gave elementary explanations or lectures on each subject practised, of a quality which compared very favourably to that later given to the writer and others in the British army. To add to the interest there was some advanced ceremonial drill for the inspections of General Enckell and Field-Marshal Mannerheim, and for the abortive church parade.

In Savonlinna the weekly training programmes were drawn up in consultation with III Army Headquarters. Rapid rifle and heavy machine-gun instruction was given, first in their care, maintenance and mechanics, then in their use on the range with live ammunition, and finally in their tactical use, including mobility and the choice of correct positions, with practice ammunition whose wooden bullets were pulverised in firing. The III Army Corps provided instructors, and by the end of May nearly the whole company had used the rapid rifle and the Suomi-pistol, was trained in the use of the heavy machine-gun, and had fired it on the range, and learned the various functions of each member of the machine-gun team. Field-work, both in open country and in the forests, formed an important part of the training, and such subjects as the use of cover, sending messages, outposts, and the platoon and section in attack and defence, were practised under platoon commanders. Finnish officers provided useful criticism and instruction in these activities. Map-reading practice was unfortunately limited as there were no large-scale maps available, Savonlinna being in a frontier zone, but there were lectures on the use of explosives and on grenade-throwing. But, surprisingly, the volunteers heard nothing about the Red Army.

Copies of two Orders of the Day, in English, were posted in the barracks on 31st May, and a copy was given to each volunteer. Field-Marshal Mannerheim's Order No. 72 was brief and to the point, and is given in full:

> "British Volunteers,
>
> "Now that you are about to leave our country I thank you who with high courage to the aid of Finland in her fight for freedom and independence.
>
> "Though Fate denied you the opportunity of going into action I wish to express to you my gratitude for your courage and enthusiasm in support of our cause.
>
> "We in Finland shall never forget you, who, at a time when your own country was in peril, hastened to our snowclad North, ready to lay down your lives in the cause of freedom.
>
> "May the memories of your service in the Finnish Army be happy ones, and may the future bring success and happiness to your own country."

The III Army Corps Order of the Day, over the signature of Major-General Siilasvuo and Lt-Col. G. Ehrnrooth, covered a great deal of ground. It stressed that from 1st June the volunteers were not to wear uniforms, and that Petsamo was out of bounds to those without a steamer ticket. Food and lodging would be provided for those who stayed with the contingent, and those who wished to live elsewhere were to make up their minds by midnight on 31st May. As civilians the volunteers were asked to make themselves familiar with the laws and customs of Finland.

DEMOBILISATION AND AFTER:

Savonlinna

The volunteers tried out their civilian clothes on 31st May, and changed into them on 1st June, when the contingent began to break up. The first to leave were Captain Miville, who found his own way home to his adopted Ireland, and Volunteers Brooke and Doese, who left for Helsinki on the first available train in search of transport home or work. On demobilisation Captains Chandor and Miville were promoted to the rank of Major, with effect from 28th May, and Lieut. Joyce was promoted to Captain on the same date while on the high seas between Petsamo and home, a berth he had obtained while ostensibly acting as liaison officer in Helsinki. But Dr Herford and Lieuts. Guthrie, Ruck-Keene, Nurk and Scott received no such recognition of their services, though once a civilian again Lieut. Scott resumed his first World War rank and called himself Captain.

Elated by the prospect of going home, now that they were civilians again, many volunteers decided to travel with the minimum of luggage and to dispose of their winter clothing and other surplus items of kit. Selling it would provide funds for the journey, they thought, so a large heap of surplus clothing, some of which may have come from the now unsupervised stores, was made at the entrance to the yard behind the barracks, and was sold piece by piece to passers-by. The trade continued merrily for ten days or so, Ruck-Keene having declined to intervene, and it was finally stopped on Asling's orders just before he left the contingent.

There then arose the possibility that parties of civilians might be able to get a ship at Kirkenes in Norway or Petsamo, which were both open to passenger traffic at the time. Two parties, one for each port, and totalling 35 men, one under Nurk and the other under Captain Cope, who came up to Savonlinna for the purpose, left the town on 7th June. A day later they arrived in Rovaniemi, on the Arctic Circle, only to hear that while they were in transit the Germans had set up a naval patrol at Kirkenes. This enabled them to stop and search all ships leaving Petsamo, and the two parties were accordingly intercepted and ordered to return to Savonlinna. Several volunteers decided to find their own way home, and when the parties returned to Savonlinna on 10th/11th June they were found to be sixteen short. On the journey north by train Dr Herford changed some smaller notes into one £10 note for a military man, only to find when he reached the Middle East early the following year and tried to change it into local currency that it had been demonetised.

As had been expected, discipline crumbled after the departure of the parties for the North. On 8th June those who remained in Savonlinna were, for example, lazing about in bed until nine or ten in the morning, and the barrack-room was in a frightful state. Half the men were lying in their bunks at two in the afternoon, and the volunteer who was supposed to be organising a football-match was just getting into his sleeping-bag, with the remark that they were all too tired. In the evening, however, they amused themselves catapulting potatoes at each other, and the noise up to midnight was appalling.

Back in Savonlinna on 11th June, Captain Cope sought the opinions of the senior NCOs, and was told that in their view, of all the former officers Ruck-Keene was the best of a bad lot (there were only two to choose from, Scott A.H.W. having left and Nurk being anxious to return to Kenya). On 12th June Vereker summoned Major Chandor to Helsinki, the latter leaving Ruck-Keene in charge. Not realising that he was being relieved of his command, he left his kit behind, and it was sent on to him later. Guthrie and Asling were called to Helsinki on 14th June on a similar errand, and on the same day Captain Cope confirmed Ruck-Keene's appointment as commandant. Standing Orders for that day stated that Ruck-Keene was to be Commanding Officer of the contingent, Sergeant Taylor H. was to act as sergeant-major, the other former NCOs were to retain their appointments, and the lance-corporals were to do fatigues with the others. Kyrönsalmi bridge and the land to the east of it were out of bounds, except to go to the sports ground, and then only under an NCO. The Orderly Room was to be open from 8.45 to 4.30, and lights out was at 11. As there was no real darkness that time of year it made very little difference. On 19th June a draft telegram was sent to the British Legation in Helsinki for onward transmission to Gibson: "Owing unsatisfactory discipline Chandor Guthrie Asling have relinquished control", but the message appears to have been held up.

Shortly after leaving Savonlinna the newly-promoted Major Chandor wrote a letter to Lt-Col. Ehrnrooth at III Army Corps headquarters, thanking him for the fruitful co-operation and for all he had done for the volunteers. Acknowledging the letter Lt-Col. Ehrnrooth replied that it had been an honour and a pleasure for him to have had the British volunteers under his command, "and I am convinced that the Unit led by you would have well fulfilled its duties in front of the enemy, if Fate had so decided." He concluded: "Thank you, Major Chandor, for having shown here in a foreign country the national qualities of the English, gentlemanly behaviour and a sense of fair play. With these words I say goodbye to you and wish you all the best."

Gibson noted in his Report that although the volunteers were civilians from 1st June, their affairs had to be administered on military lines, and that when he took over later in the month Mr Ruck-Keene had appointed various acting NCOs, using military titles. This was in flat contradiction to instructions Gibson had sent him (which he probably did not receive) and which in any case could not have reached him before he took over the post of commandant on 14th June. Gibson had foreseen complications which might arise, especially with regard to pay, maintenance, and so forth, and laid it down that men required for special duties should be given civilian titles and should be paid for doing such work. He later repeated his original instructions, and this time Ruck-Keene received them and acted on them. Nevertheless, Gibson wrote that it was to be regretted that Ruck-Keene proved to be incompetent as leader of the party. He could get no answers either to telegrams or to letters, and was "consequently completely in the dark for some time as to what was happening." What he had apparently failed to notice, however, was that following the German occupation of Denmark and Norway communications between England and Finland had become much more difficult, direct postal contact had been suspended, and Foreign Office channels, which were the only ones available to him, were slow and extremely unreliable. Ruck-Keene was doubtless aware of this, and, as the contingent's movements book shows, he spent long periods away from it and was generally to be seen with the volunteers for about one week in every four, sometimes only for a day at a time. He spent the rest of the time with a lady-friend in Helsinki. His absences led the volunteers themselves to appoint a disciplinary committee, with Taylor H. as its first leader, to undertake their absent commandant's responsibilities.

After the return of the two parties from Rovaniemi the thought uppermost in many volunteers' minds was still the need to get home. First to take joint action, on 15th June, were eight who claimed to be Irish citizens, namely Casey, Daly, Kuss, McGee, McMullin, McNally, Moore and Tierney. Lucey and Commins, both Irish-born, did not take part in the exercise, and of the others only Casey had an Irish passport. McGee was born in Scotland but lived in Ireland, and McMullin, born in Ceylon (now Sri Lanka) of Irish parents, was technically a distressed British subject, since he had obtained his discharge in Lapua and rejoined the contingent as a civilian. McNally, whose British passport stated him to have been born in Dublin on 7th October 1910, adopted the name of Mark John McAnaney, born 4th September 1912 in "Bennett Street, Londonderry, Tir Coyyell, Eire". The eight signed a joint letter to the Irish Minister in Berlin, and sent it to the Foreign Ministry in Helsinki with a request to forward it. No reply was ever received.

About this time half a dozen or so volunteers decided to go swimming from a neck of land that stretched out into Lake Haapavesi, north of the town and nearly a mile from the barracks. When everyone was in the water one of their number swam ashore, dried and dressed himself, and slipped back to the barracks carrying all the clothes he could find, but leaving each man with a towel. As might be expected, the bathers failed to see anything funny in having to run up the main street to their quarters clad only in a towel. So when they had found their clothes and dressed themselves again they went in search of the culprit. While four or five of them held him down the sixth, Martin, nicknamed 'The Baron' from his aristocratic bearing, who was a barber by trade, shaved off half his victim's moustache, half his hair, and one eyebrow.

About a week after demobilisation Kilpin caught a cold, and Dr Herford told him not to go swimming. He went swimming nevertheless, and developed bronchitis. Alcohol proved ineffective as a cure, and on admission to the sick-bay on 15th June he was found to be suffering from valvular disease of the heart as well. He failed to respond to treatment with the limited supplies of medicines then available, and on 19th June he was admitted to the civilian hospital in Savonlinna. There he died of bronchial pneumonia at two o'clock in the morning of 20th June. His funeral took place at the cemetery in Savonlinna three days later, a ceremony described in "Savonmaa" (Land of Savo), one of the town's two newspapers, as an especially sad occasion, since the deceased was one of those foreigners who had come to Finland in her hour of need, ready to fight for the country's independence. Volunteers bore the plain white coffin to the grave, and many of the comrades of the deceased who had come specially from Jyväskylä and some of his Finnish acquaintances followed it. The Rev. A.E. Merivirta, vicar of the parish, gave a short funeral oration in Finnish, taking as his text "Greater love hath no man, than he lay down his life for his friend." His words were translated into English by

Miss Eva Mattila, a local school-teacher. The grave was decorated with a spruce cross and wreaths. The District Commander, Lieut. E. Tiainen, brought one wreath, and 2nd Lieut. V. Holopainen brought another on behalf of the Finnish Defence Forces. Major Magill attended the funeral in civilian clothes, as Vereker's representative, and the British army paymaster later tried unsuccessfully to claim his expenses of 513 marks from the Finnish Aid Bureau. As her husband was a civilian at the time of his death Mrs Kilpin was unable to obtain a Finnish pension.

After the contingent had left Savonlinna for its new quarters in Jyväskylä the Hotel Seurahuone admitted having overcharged the officers 935 marks which, after allowing for two unpaid bills totalling 143¾ marks (and dated 20th June) left a balance of 791¼ marks due for payment. However, the Hotel later made a claim of just over 2,000 marks for damage to furniture, and this was referred to the office of the Savonlinna commandant. Whether it was ever paid seems doubtful.

After the unit had been demobilised the spare uniforms were handed over to the Finnish army to supplement a consignment sent out from London early on in the Winter War, and it soon became a common sight in Helsinki to see Finnish soldiers on fatigues in regulation fur or peaked caps and wearing khaki battle-dress. The general opinion of the soldiers was that the uniforms were all right, but as they were mostly of a large size and as the men wearing them were not, the effect was somewhat bizarre.

DEMOBILISATION AND AFTER:

Jyväskylä

On 19th June, under the supervision of von Essen and Corporal Brunow D.C. (brother of Lieut. Stig Brunow), who had joined the contingent from III Army Corps, the volunteers left Savonlinna. They travelled by train to Jyväskylä, about a hundred miles to the west, an important industrial and cultural centre, known as the Athens of Finland, and also the home of the Lahti-Saloranta rapid rifle. The volunteers were quartered there in the Commercial High School, a short distance from the railway station. Former volunteers still mispronounce the town's name as you vascular. There were already some volunteers of other nationalities at the nearby Pedagogic High School when the British arrived. The two groups formed the Jyväskylä Home Guard District, whose commander was Captain P. Västi until August, and then a Colonel Vartiovaara. The volunteers were under the overall supervision of Major E. Haltiavuori, with Corporal Brunow D.C. acting as his adjutant. Ruck-Keene was still in charge of the British contingent, with Corporal Clément, an American Finn, as adjutant. Lieut. Count von der Pahlen, whom we met in Lapua, was in charge of the non-British volunteers from 1st July, with the Finnish Private A. von Heiroth as his assistant.

Jyväskylä lies at the northern end of Lake Päijänne, and its reputation as the centre of an area famed for the illicit distillation of spirits, generically known as pontikka, remains untarnished to this day. This may explain the occasional cases of drunkenness among the volunteers, whose daily pocket-money was insufficient to buy spirits. Spirits could only be bought legally from the State Alcohol Monopoly shop, Alkoholiliike, which was known to the

British as Alcohol I like. One volunteer who was drunk in the first week after arrival found his way back to his quarters without being stopped by police. The first case to come to the notice of the guardians of the law was five weeks later, at the end of July, when a friendly policeman found a volunteer who was drunk and incapable. He took him to the police station and locked him up for the night. The following morning the volunteer returned to his quarters, sober but much bruised. The official report noted that while in gaol he had behaved in such an objectionable manner towards the other drunks that they had taken offence and given him a hiding. Perhaps they did not realise that he was a foreigner.

A few days later the same volunteer received some money from home and decided to go out with some of his friends for a slap-up lunch at one of the town's hotels. After drinking a little more than was good for him he decided that the excellent service given to his party was worthy of special reward. So telling his friends to wait he went out into the town and bought a pair of knickers for the waitress. Even in those far-off days the design of Finnish ladies' underwear was influenced by the frosts of winter; and the knickers were what would now be known as "open crotch". The volunteer returned to the hotel, unwrapped his gift, and, before presenting it to the horrified waitress, held it up for his friends and the others diners to see, with his middle finger protruding through its special central feature.

Last of the recorded drunkenness cases was a volunteer who decided to sleep it off in the Suomi cinema. A policeman found him and took him outside, where, once in the fresh air, he recovered sufficiently to be able to return to the contingent on his own.

During the first fortnight of his supervision of the British volunteers Major Haltiavuori had his illusions rudely shattered, for he was under the impression that the contingent was composed of "gentlemen". A letter over his signature appeared on the notice-board, drafted more in sorrow than in anger, stating that whereas discipline had been good in the first week, in the second week one volunteer had, with permission, left for Helsinki but had been arrested in Savonlinna, and that another had been found in a state of intoxication.

In the middle of July there were 131 British volunteers in Jyväskylä, 19 American Finns, 4 Hungarians, 3 Canadians, 3 Belgians, 2 Norwegians, and one each from Austria, Estonia, Holland, Latvia, Portugal and the U.S.A. In the British contingent the "officers" received 20 marks a day pocket-money, the other ranks 10 marks. There were four British cooks, with Lottas to assist them. The volunteers cleaned their own rooms, and the rules of the place were on display. Breaches of the rules could lead to detention or loss of pay; passes, which had to be shown when leaving or entering the quarters, were valid from 9.15 am. to 11 pm., but the 11 pm. curfew was not applicable to "officers". Dr Herford continued to treat the volunteers. In general the health of the contingent was good, as was discipline, but morale was a trifle depressed as the men could not get home. At the end of the month there was a compulsory medical inspection.

After taking a party of intending lumberjacks to Sotkamo, in the north of Finland, and bringing them back again a week later as no arrangements had been made to feed them, von Essen remained as interpreter to the British contingent until he was demobilised on 10th July with Corporal Clément. Corporal Brunow D.C., their assistant, left twelve days later, and Privates von Heiroth and Närter succeeded him. By this time most of the other foreign volunteers had left, and those remaining, including some Belgians and Latvians, were attached to the British contingent and remained with it for some months. Lieut. Count von der Pahlen was appointed second-in-charge to Ruck-Keene at about the same time. Roome, who had already picked up some Finnish, ran the canteen at a profit to himself; three "sergeants", Commins, Nicholls and Pooke, maintained discipline, and a fourth, Francis, was in charge of the stores. During the time the contingent was in Jyväskylä there were only four "arrests" for indiscipline or for refusing to obey the orders of superiors.

On 9th July the Finnish Aid Bureau sent a cheque for £1,000 to the contingent. It reached Ryder, still in charge of the office, via the British Legation in Helsinki, about three weeks later. Its administration for the purchase of clothing presented some difficulties, since the purpose was to give each volunteer a suit of clothes without putting money in his pocket. Ryder accordingly devised a scheme whereby each volunteer was given a credit card entitling him to buy clothing up to a certain value in specified shops in the town. In preparation for the issue of cards he visited various shop managers, with Lieut. Kaj J. Warras, who had been attached to the contingent as interpreter. Unable to distinguish between one and two r's in a Finnish name, several volunteers who offered their cards to shopkeepers used to say *Varas maksaa* (the thief will pay) instead of *Warras maksaa* (Warras will pay). They laughed when the mistake was pointed out to them, and the phrase went into their slang, along with such monsters as pooker-knife (from *puukko*, the Finnish for a sheath knife), brandy-vin (from the Swedish *brännvin*, spirits), and the mispronunciation of place-names noted elsewhere.

One of the happy features of the contingent's life in Jyväskylä was the football team, which did the British name good service in the district. Its first match, on Friday 28th June, was against Jyväskylä, and was played in army boots with Dr Herford at centre-half. Not unnaturally, the team was soundly beaten, but a crowd of over two thousand people showed full appreciation of the team's difficulties and its sporting spirit. Half the proceeds of the match went to charity, and half to the two teams. Out of its quarter-share the contingent bought football boots. Playing a return match in these boots the volunteers drew 1 – 1, the players being Brabbs, Butler, Butt, Connolly, Evans S.H., Hartman, Dr Herford, Hole, Mallowan, Parker, Patterson, Roome and Tawell, two of whom were reserves. Matches were also played in the surrounding villages, and it was stated semi-officially that the British Legation in Helsinki was arranging matches, but these failed to materialise. In sport generally the contingent distinguished itself, the tennis team creating a mild sensation in the town, while Hicks-Green, runner-up in a pre-war French Open Golf Championship, gave instruction in Jyväskylä and then became a professional at Helsinki Golf Club.

On 6th August the contingent had a visit from Hugh Sladen, the British-born head of the Salvation Army in Finland. He arranged a tea-party for the volunteers and addressed them briefly, saying that he knew that no-one had any money at the moment, but please remember the Salvation Army when you get home. Ten days later another party was arranged thanks to the efforts of a local headmaster named A.V. Laitakari and his assistant Miss Heine. By this time financial arrangements for the contingent had been modified to suit the changed conditions, and were working well. The Finnish Aid Bureau in London remitted a hundred pounds a week through the British Consul in Helsinki, who passed it on to Ruck-Keene's account at a bank in Jyväskylä. Lieut. Scott A.H.W. and Asling were then living away from the contingent at 70 and 50 marks per day respectively.

About this time Captain Waller, who had been serving in Joroinen, and Captain Lace, Lieuts. Armstrong, Elliott and Maund, 2nd Lieut. Taylor H.S. and CSM Walker J.S., who had been stationed at Luonetjärvi, were demobilised, and, with Captain Kenworthy, joined the contingent on 17th August. Later in the month the question arose as to the fate of the arms and military equipment of the volunteers, which had been lodged with the Home Guard in Jyväskylä. Vereker informed Gibson that a decision was needed, for although the Finnish government was willing to store these goods indefinitely it was also willing to transfer them to Sweden and to pay transport charges. Gibson asked the Foreign Office to inform Vereker that the equipment should be left where it was on the clear understanding that it remained the property of the Finnish Aid Bureau or its assignees. "Political difficulties" militated against transferring the arms to Sweden, so Gibson wrote to the War Office informing them of the position and suggesting that as they had already promised to allow the Bureau for any arms or equipment which might be returned in good condition, Gibson should be allowed to nominate the Secretary of State for War as assignee, and that the War Office should refund to the Bureau part of the money paid for the equipment in question. In June 1941 J.S. Somers Cocks, First Secretary at the British Legation in Helsinki, informed Captain Nordlund that the arms, ammunition and equipment were to be stored at the British Legation, though this does not appear to have been done until much later in the year.

DEMOBILISATION AND AFTER:

Korpilahti

The Commercial High School in Jyväskylä was wanted for the autumn term, and so on 7th September the contingent was moved to Korpilahti, a village lying on the western shore of Lake Päijänne some thirteen miles south of the town and known to the volunteers as corpy larty. The contingent was down to only two-fifths of its strength at the time of its move, some thirty members having found forestry jobs, while about the same number were teaching English in various parts of the country. The new quarters were at Tähtiniemi (Star Point), a guest-house built before the first World War and once used as a staging-post or meeting-place for the infant (and then illegal) Home Guard in the days before Finland gained her independence. It lay on a spur of land high above the lake, and was then the property of Mrs Ida Salje. Kirkonsalmi (Church Strait), a narrow strip of water about a hundred yards wide, separated the Tähtiniemi property from the village and its sawmills. The road to the village lay around the head of the bay and was three miles long, so communication with the village was maintained with rowing-boats in summer and on foot across the ice when the lake froze in the winter. As the building had only been built for summer occupation a few alterations had to be made, since the contingent had the prospect of remaining there through the winter. These alterations included converting the water-system to winter use at an estimated cost of 4,000 to 5,000 marks, repairing the sauna at a cost of just under 2,000 marks, and building a barrack-hut in the village for volunteers returning from summer work.

The news of the contingent's move to Korpilahti reached

the Finnish Aid Bureau on 9th September, and the new office opened under Ryder's supervision in one of the Tähtiniemi rooms the following day. Standing Orders included reveille at seven o'clock in the morning, breakfast at eight, dinner at 12.15, tea at 4.15, supper at 7 and lights out at 11. Four volunteers helped in the kitchen, one cleaned the mess-room, two chopped firewood, and one swept the barracks. The volunteers were not allowed to leave the confines of the place without permission, but despite the early restrictions on their movements a cross-country run was organised, in which a number of volunteers took part, including Aitken-Quack, Dr Herford, Kuss, Roberts, Smith S.G.R. and van Beest. Dr Herford won.

The effects of the inflation which followed the Winter War began to make themselves felt at Tähtiniemi, and in the autumn complaints began to be made about the financial situation. It was difficult to go into Jyväskylä to do any shopping, and there were restrictions on the movements of the hard core of volunteers unable or unwilling to find work. After the contingent had been a week in Korpilahti Captain Cope paid it a visit, to make enquiries, at Vereker's instigation. His report to Vereker was circulated, and a copy reached Gibson on 2nd October.

Captain Cope stated in his report, inter alia: "It cannot be pretended that – as a fighting unit – the Contingent has ever had the slightest training in such subjects as Map Reading, Tactics, Gunnery, etc. etc." Gunnery was outside the scope of infantry training in those days, and many of the volunteers had not only had instruction in tactics and map-reading, but were able to read Finnish maps as well. On reading the report Gibson was furious. He immediately wrote to the Foreign Office and to Major Magill, enclosing copies of Captain Cope's report and stating that it was important that all those concerned should have more accurate information about the volunteers. To Major Magill he added: "I have been very surprised to hear from Major Chandor and several of the men who have recently returned home, that you and others at the British Legation have stated that the British Government were always opposed to the despatch of volunteers to Finland, and that therefore the British authorities were not very concerned about their welfare." Gibson stressed that he would not have paid much attention to these statements if they had not been repeated by every man who had recently returned from Finland. "The fact that a few of the men (there were four at the most) have behaved badly ought not to prejudice the British authorities against all the volunteers, the great majority of whom have behaved very well under most trying circumstances, and are all undoubtedly men who can render valuable service to this country if they are given the opportunity." Gibson enclosed copies of letters from Major Chandor and Colonel Ehrnrooth, giving an account of the military training given to the volunteers.

Early in October 1940 it was rumoured among the volunteers that Baxter, Francis and Watkins, who had left the contingent at Jyväskylä to find work in Helsinki, had left for Russia, and that two of them – which two it was not stated – had been shot there. Ari Kauhanen of the State Police investigated the matter, and interviewed Captain Cope, Easton, Haddleton, Punshon and Ruck-Keene, who all happened to be in Helsinki at the time. Haddleton was apparently the last to see Francis before he disappeared, having spoken to him on 29th September at Hietalahti docks. Kauhanen thought the three had left Helsinki for Tallinn, Estonia, either on that day on the Danish s/s *Kabel*, or on 1st October on the Estonian s/s *Kalevipoeg*. According to popular belief at Tähtiniemi they had intended to go to Estonia, and from there on foot to Rumania, a country which was not then at war with Britain, and from thence home. The distance as the crow flies from Tallinn to the Rumanian frontier is some 750 miles, a fact which the trio seems to have overlooked when making its plans.

Various tales circulated among the volunteers about the fate of the three for many months after their disappearance. What had happened was that they set off in a "borrowed" boat in October, but met a storm, and after three days were towed into Tallinn by a Russian coastguard vessel. They were arrested and taken via Leningrad to the Lubianka prison in Moscow, accused of spying. In February 1941 they were transferred to the Butyrka prison, where Francis fell ill and was taken away, and was thought to have died. At the end of August Baxter and Watkins were told they had been sentenced to five years' detention for violating territorial waters, and were transferred separately to a labour camp beyond the Urals, six days' journey from Moscow. In October they were returned to Moscow "for further questioning", but on arrival there they were dumped unceremoniously in the street opposite the British Embassy. At the Embassy the two regained their health, and went to Rhodesia to train in the R.A.F. Baxter was killed in action in a bombing raid on 22nd November 1943 and has no known grave.

Later in October 1940 there was a little light relief at Tähtiniemi, when Punshon received a letter from his wife in Canada, saying that the Finnish Aid Bureau had informed her that between 9th June and 15th August the volunteers were going home. About this time the Finnish authorities supplied a Ford O98T lorry, which had been commandeered from somewhere near Lapua during the Winter War. It was worked by a wood-gas generator and was fitted with wooden seats under a protective hood. Those volunteers who had driving licenses were allowed to take parties into Jyväskylä two or three times a week, and were also allowed to give lifts to the villagers. One volunteer received extra pay as driver.

With Taylor H. now in charge of discipline, the volunteers made concerted efforts in the late summer and early winter to get transit visas for Russia. The idea was sparked off on 27th September, when Haddleton received a letter from one of the homebound party in Stockholm saying that the volunteers there were getting visas and were leaving for Palestine via Russia. Taylor immediately rang up Ruck-Keene, who was in Helsinki on one of his protracted absences, and asked him to make enquiries. Ruck-Keene telegraphed the following day to say that the British Legation in Stockholm knew nothing about the matter. He returned to Tähtiniemi on 1st October with the news that there was a possibility of repatriation via Russia. A week later Captain Cope suggested that the volunteers should visit Helsinki to test the chances of getting Russian visas, so on 17th October Taylor H. went down. In Helsinki he suggested to the British Legation that a telegram be sent to Sir Stafford Cripps, the British Ambassador in Moscow, seeking his assistance in obtaining visas for all the volunteers. He noted in his diary that it was difficult to move the Legation to action, and that he had warned Vereker about Ruck-Keene. On his return to Tähtiniemi Taylor H. formed a "return committee" to deal with repatriation matters (its members were not recorded), and on 2nd November Ruck-Keene, then at Tähtiniemi on a short visit, told Taylor H. that he had had a letter from the Legation in Helsinki to say that they had had an acknowledgement of the message to Sir Stafford Cripps.

Ruck-Keene left for Helsinki again on 12th November, ostensibly to deal with a problem over the passports of four Air Force volunteers whom the Finns had interviewed, but actually to recommend to Vereker that Atkinson, Holliday, Kilgour, Ryder, Summers and van Heteren should be given priority for Russian visas. Before leaving he appointed Taylor H. as Camp Commandant. He returned eight days later with application forms for Russian visas, and left again for Helsinki with Lace on 25th November. Three days before this Atkinson, still in charge of the stores, learned that he had been put on the possibility list for a Russian visa. Ruck-Keene turned up at Tähtiniemi again on 1st December and left the same evening with Atkinson, who had been instructed to go to Stockholm to apply for a Russian visa there. Lace, Lyons and Babbs followed the next day on what was thought to be a similar errand, but Babbs and Lyons obtained jobs at the Legation, the former in the Press Department and the latter as a "consular agent", of which more later. Later Holliday, Dr Herford, Ruck-Keene and Ryder left for Stockholm to apply for Russian visas, Dr Herford having managed it on his own through personal contacts in Finland and Sweden, before the others. Summers and van Heteren also went to Stockholm but did not get visas, while Elliott, a journalist, obtained a Russian visa in Helsinki in November 1940, without Vereker's blessing, and returned to his adopted Australia via Moscow, Vladivostock and Kobe.

In Ruck-Keene's absences from Tähtiniemi things began to go wrong, since Lieut. Count von der Pahlen, although second-in-charge and acting commandant, did not have any formal authority. Nevertheless, he inspected the rooms on 18th December, and his report was displayed on the notice-board. It stated that Rooms 15, 16 and 17 were kept in a state of filth and disorder which could not be tolerated, and that some members of the contingent were found to be asleep in bed as late as eleven in the morning. He suggested that a thorough cleaning be made inside all the buildings on the following Saturday, 21st December, and this was duly done. Ruck-Keene returned to Tähtiniemi the following day with the news that no more applications were to be made for Russian transit visas; and left again for Helsinki the next day. He spent a few days at Tähtiniemi in the New Year, bringing the news that any volunteer who was granted a transit visa would be expected to join the British forces in the Middle East, a condition which the volunteers were eager and willing to accept. Finally, on 13th January, it was revealed that Atkinson, Holliday, Ruck-Keene and Ryder had been granted visas, and that Dr Herford had already left via Russia. Volunteers living away from the camp were not informed.

On demobilisation the volunteers were told that they were not to wear uniform unless it was dyed and badges had been removed. This course was adopted universally, and in the Autumn of 1940 it was a common site to see volunteers on leave in Helsinki wearing black or brown battle-dress or scruffy civilian clothes and dyed army greatcoats. Their general appearance was shabby, and was noted by several lady members of the British colony there. In October 1940 they organised an English-speaking sewing circle, at which they made a collection, and then formed the British Volunteers' Winter Clothing Fund and appealed for money.

The committee of the Fund was under the chairmanship of Mrs L. Tudeer, the British-born wife of a Finnish colonel, and its members included Mrs Vera Birse, whose husband

International or Non-Intervention? The cap badge of the British Volunteers

Crossing the North Sea: Blew-Jones' draft

C.S.M. John Asling, of Kimberworth, near Rotherham; former N.C.O., Grenadier Guards.

Lapua, March 1940.
Route march in snow-cloaks

Lapua, March 1940: British volunteers to right, Hungarian volunteers to left

Savonlinna, April 1940: "Roper's Hole"

Savonlinna, May 1940: Changing the guard

Savonlinna, May 1940: Part of the British Volunteer Company

Savonlinna, May 1940: Captain Chandor

Savonlinna, May 1940: S.H. Evans (later Sir Harold Evans), Baxter, Hicks Green.

Savonlinna, May 1940: "Jock" Chalmers

Savonlinna, May 1940:
McKay

Savonlinna, May 1940:
Purves

Savonlinna, 31.5.1940: Col. Ehrnrooth bids Captain Chandor farewell.

Korpilahti, March 1941: Taking bets for the ski race: Thompson, Glyn

Korpilahti, Summer 1941: gang at Iloniemi sawmill, including Rattigan, Hignell, Butler, Bath, Casey, Daly, and some Finns.

Vilppula Station, June 1941: Count von der Pahlen, Phillips, Captain Nordlund

Korpilahti, June1941: loading ferries before departure. Hugh Taylor extreme right.

Malung, July 1941: The British Coast.

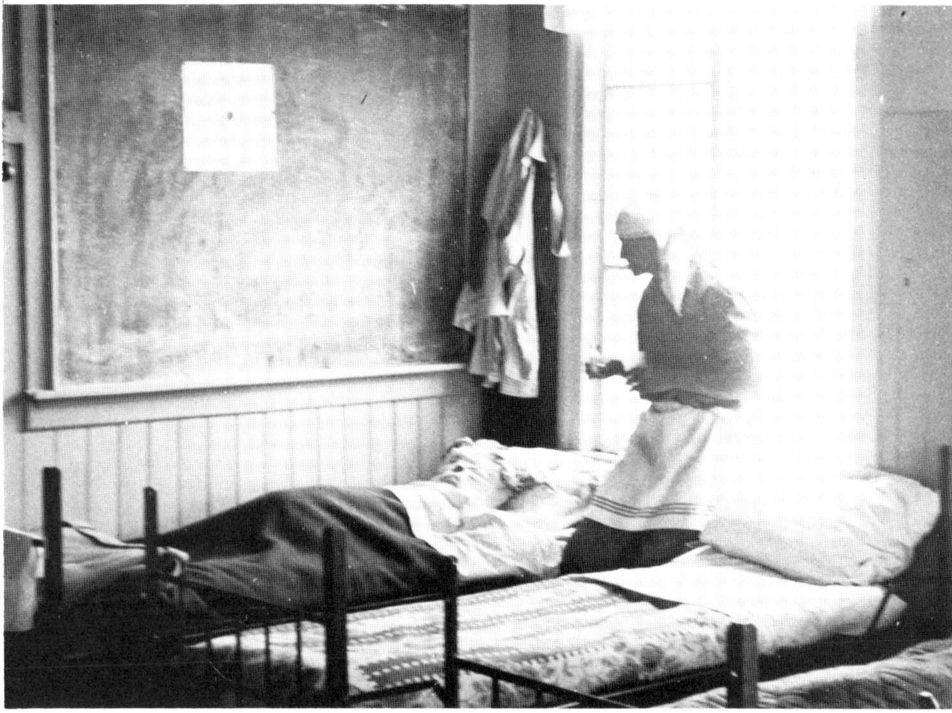

Malung, July 1941, Maternity Hospital Joke: McKay dressed as a nurse

Malung, July 1941: road-mending, McClure (US), Golby

MALUNG, summer 1941: W.D.C. Rattigan

Filipstad, Winter 1941: "Saatana" and one of Van Beest's rabbits

Filipstad, Winter 1941: Ski-ing party: McKibbin L., Graham, Brooke, Herring, Bullen

Filipstad, Winter 1941: McGee's Christmas Card

was a retired businessman, and Mrs May Wolontis, whose husband Peter, an economist, was honorary secretary. Delegate to the Committee, though adviser would be a better word, was Consul Henry McGrady Bell, C.V.O., C.B.E., who had been British consul in Helsinki in 1917-19 during and after the War of Independence. He had subsequently started his own firm, Bell & Sime, which imported Finnish timber into his native Scotland. He came out to Finland early in 1940 to administer British aid, but had been unable to return home when his work was completed. He provided accommodation for the Fund in his suite at the Hotel Seurahuone in Helsinki, and, as he knew all the right people from his consular days, he proved to be a tower of strength, both to the committee and to many individual volunteers.

Gibson was greatly surprised when, on 8th November, he heard through Mr F.H. Benn, of Price & Pierce Limited, that the Finnish-British community in Helsinki had started a clothing fund for the volunteers, and had telegraphed Price & Pierce Limited to ask if the Finnish Aid Bureau would contribute to it, adding that the appeal had Vereker's approval. As already noted, the Bureau had already sent £1,000 to Finland for additional clothing, and it was Gibson's intention that Ryder should administer the sum and that Ruck-Keene should notify the Bureau when it was exhausted, but no notification was ever received. Gibson therefore consulted with the Foreign Office, and then telegraphed Vereker asking who had organised the appeal and stating that such an appeal was very undesirable and totally unnecessary, as the Finnish Aid Bureau was responsible for clothing the volunteers. Vereker replied that the President of Finland (Kyösti Kallio) had contributed 25,000 marks and Field-Marshal Mannerheim 10,000 marks. Gibson then saw Sir Orme Sargent at the Foreign Office, who agreed with him that the appeal should never have been made and that it was most unfortunate that these two prominent people should have been asked to subscribe. The two decided that the appeal should be stopped immediately, and that the contributions from the President and the Field-Marshal should be returned to them with an appropriate letter of thanks and explanation. Another telegram was sent to Vereker, and Gibson wrote two personal letters to the distinguished donors. In addition, on 22nd November, he transferred £1,300 to Vereker through the Foreign Office, which held it up for over three weeks, and then wrote to as many donors to the appeal fund as possible. But as the money raised in Finland had been spent long before Vereker finally received the clothing cheque from Gibson, he was left with a balance in hand of about £900 – and a mild rebuke from the Foreign Office, who thought that he should have let Gibson know when the first £1,000 clothing cheque had been spent. The £900 was soon absorbed in sending each volunteer to the dentist, and in providing a spare pair of spectacles for those who wore them, including the writer.

In spite of the hostility of Gibson and Sir Orme Sargent and Vereker's co-operation, however, the gentlemen were unable to stop the machine which the ladies had set in motion with such enthusiasm. The Report made on the winding-up of the Fund shows that among the donors were Lady Ryti, wife of the Prime Minister Sir Risto Ryti, who gave 25,000 marks. A variety performance held in Balders Lokal, now a theatrical museum, raised 10,089.30 marks net of expenses. Mrs Atkinson and Mrs Adsbøl organised a bridge party at the Verekers' residence and, with Mrs Vereker's support and encouragement, raised 10,285 marks. The Helsinki Finnish-British Society held a Christmas party and raised 1,033.75 marks, Colonel Serlachius gave 1,000 marks, a Miss Astrid Salmela made a collection in her office and produced another 1,000 marks, and the Finnish-British Society Discussion Club raised another 193.25 marks.

The sums raised were sufficient to provide 117 pairs of ski-boots, 300 pairs of socks, 27 sweaters, 29 ski or working sweaters, 48 pairs of ski-trousers, and 51 overcoats. Mrs Sylvia Jansson raised 2,450 marks towards a wireless-set, and, with a further 700 marks from the Fund a six-valve Phillips set was bought for 3,150 marks. In mid-December 1940 Consul Bell and the fund's secretary travelled up to Tähtiniemi to hand out the clothing and other items, some of which had been obtained from the Finnish army and through the Finnish Ministry of Supply. The Fund's final accounts were prepared early in 1941 prior to the winding-up of the Clothing Fund Committee on 18th February. They showed that contributions totalled 61,749.05 marks, which included 157.75 marks bank interest. After the items listed had been paid for and administrative costs of 8,315 marks had been met, there remained a credit balance of 542.65 marks, which was applied towards a set of false teeth for an un-named volunteer. The result of the Committee's activities was that each man at Tähtiniemi was properly protected against the coming winter's cold. Those living elsewhere were enabled to get a new suit of clothes and an overcoat from Finnish Aid Bureau funds. Meanwhile, back at Tähtiniemi, Daly and Summers busied themselves converting blankets into ski-jackets, for which there was a keen demand.

Unaware of the efforts being made in Helsinki on their behalf, a couple of volunteers living at Tähtiniemi came down to Helsinki in November 1940, with a long report on the conditions there, which they intended to send home. The report recorded that on the advice of the Finnish Aid Bureau volunteers had travelled to Finland in their oldest clothes, and that a number of them had disposed of their civilian clothes at Lapua on going into uniform. The monthly bonus of 550 marks paid to the volunteers still in the unit on demobilisation had been stopped at the end of June (though not paid for that month to those who had left the contingent to seek work), and at the end of August the Finnish Aid Bureau had sent every man a notice to the effect that pocket-money would be cut to 10 marks a day. Certain "Officers and NCOs" whose work had proved unsatisfactory had been replaced, and one of them was receiving 170 marks a week pay and 40 marks a day billeting allowance, or 450 marks a week in all, which was unfair. A grant for clothing of 1,100 marks per man had been made in August, but had not been made known to those living away from the contingent.

Stressing that Tähtiniemi was only suitable for summer occupation, and that most of the inmates were only clad for summer weather, the report recommended an immediate grant of 3,000 marks per man for winter clothing. This would be 1,000 marks for a fur-lined winter overcoat, the same for a suit of warm clothes, 400 marks for a pair of ski-boots and 600 marks for shirts, underclothing, etc., some of which could be provided from the contingent's stores. In furtherance of these recommendations the report suggested that an official Finnish government cable be sent to the Foreign Office or War Office in London, asking them to persuade the Finnish Aid Bureau to send out 3,000 marks per man, plus a permanent weekly extra for billeting of not less than 250 marks per man. Alternatively, it was recommended that funds be remitted to Finland and that the British Consul in Helsinki should be persuaded to help. The sale of surplus army stores at Tähtiniemi was also recommended, to provide the funds for buying clothing, and the Finnish Aid Bureau was asked to transfer itself to Finland, where independent persons could administer its funds. The ten marks a day pocket-money paid to volunteers in Finland, the report added, compared unfavourably with the equivalent of about 19 marks paid to volunteers in Sweden, who also received 609.90 marks a week for board and lodging.

In November only 44 volunteers remained at Tähtiniemi, 82 were away working, and 14 were on leave or official business, making a total of 140, to which had been temporarily added nine miscellaneous foreigners, five of whom were away working. Five local Lottas took turns to do the cooking, and the food was found to be particularly good and varied when the writer visited the place the weekend before he typed the report. The report appears to have been circulated in Finland as well as being sent home.

Four volunteers who shall be nameless were an intermittent source of trouble both at Jyväskylä and Korpilahti during the autumn and early winter of 1940. The disciplinary committee discussed their behaviour, and early in December suggested the removal to another place of the three who had been convicted of theft. Taylor H., the head of the committee and effectively second-in-charge at

Tähtiniemi at the time, wrote a confidential report on the offenders for Lieut. Count von der Pahlen, analysing each man's behaviour. The report was passed to Captain Nordlund at the Headquarters Volunteer Office, who warmly congratulated its author and discussed it with two departmental chiefs at the Finnish General Staff and then with Major Magill. On the grounds that their crimes and behaviour made them a bad example to the other volunteers and had a predictable influence on discipline, which had been comparatively good apart from some "borrowing" of boats to get back to Tähtiniemi from the village, Captain Nordlund formally requested the State Police to take them temporarily into protective custody. The necessary steps were taken, and at the request of the Chief of Police, Korpilahti district, the three volunteers were taken to a safe place pending their extradition under the Law of 1st April 1938, paragraph 26, with a proviso that after expulsion they should not return to Finland within five years. Ari Kauhanen, evidently under the impression that all the volunteers were just as bad, and who had been a party to these negotiations, wrote that it occurred to him that from the point of view of discipline it might be advantageous to let the other volunteers at Tähtiniemi know as soon as the three volunteers were in custody. Such news would clearly make them consider that it would be best to behave themselves. Word soon went round the volunteers living away from the contingent that Kauhanen was a man to be avoided.

The three volunteers spent some months at the central gaol in Helsinki, where in February the fourth joined them to serve seven months for larceny. The volunteers at Tähtiniemi were so incensed at this last slur on their good name that, in a commendable display of esprit de corps, they asked Lieut. Count von der Pahlen to have the fourth offender expelled from the contingent under Clause 10 of the Agreement of Service. Gibson considered the request, but in April turned it down on the grounds that the Agreement had terminated on 31st May the previous year, though he promised to reconsider the matter when the sentences had been completed. After about three months it became evident that it would not be possible to get rid of the first three offenders, and Captain Nordlund recommended that they be released, if only conditionally. They were accordingly let out in mid-March, and were sent for a short time to work for Lieut. Lerche on his property on Nauvo island. They returned to Tähtiniemi with the fourth man in time for the departure of the contingent for Sweden.

An outward mail route via Russia and Iran was opened in the autumn of 1940, and a different kind of complaint was heard at home in December, when some volunteers managed to send letters to their friends or families, stating that they were starving and that their clothes were so ragged that they could not go out. The politicians got hold of the story, and a question was asked in Parliament about these complaints. As Gibson was quite certain there was no truth in them, he consulted with Gripenberg, who telegraphed Field-Marshal Mannerheim to tell him of the complaints and asking him to appoint a committee of enquiry which could send an official report to London as soon as possible. On making enquiries it was soon discovered that the men who had complained most were living in good hotels in Helsinki, on money remitted from home, and that their lack of clothing was nothing more than having no dinner-jackets to wear at the dinners and bridge-parties to which they were invited. One of the letters of complaint was traced to a member of what, while in uniform, had been known as The Mayfair Gang, and who, although he had worked for some time at the British Legation in Helsinki, was not included in the Legation party when it travelled home through Germany, France and Spain.

The earlier arrangements for paying pocket-money to the volunteers and cash for the contingent's running expenses continued at Korpilahti, and in January 1941 the British Consul in Helsinki was still passing the £100 a week from the Finnish Aid Bureau to Ruck-Keene's bank in Jyväskylä. Volunteers at Tähtiniemi were paid cash on Thursday, and those employed away from there had a credit sent to their account, also on Thursdays. Those absent on leave did not get the ten marks a day, but received a return rail pass from Jyväskylä to Helsinki and 170 marks. Where a volunteer's address was not known his pocket-money was calculated and paid to him when he returned to Tähtiniemi. In addition to the normal ten marks a day, volunteers employed on camp duties received the following: Paymaster 50 marks, "sergeants" 40 marks, two medical orderlies 20 marks, orderly-room clerk 20 marks, "quartermaster-sergeant" 15 marks, kitchen orderly 15 marks, carpenter 15 marks, two stokers 12½ marks, sanitary orderly 10 marks, wood-hauler 10 marks, and the commandant 100 marks, making a total of 420 marks a day as at 31st December.

On 15th January 1941, not knowing of Ruck-Keene's impending departure, Gibson wrote to him to say that all payments made to the volunteers after 31st May 1940 had been ex gratia and would not have been made but for Lord Nuffield's generosity. Each man should have had a letter on that day, informing him that his contract with the Finnish government and the Finnish Aid Bureau had been terminated. Meanwhile, the British Legation in Helsinki informed Gibson that the £100 weekly credit to the contingent was being passed to the Headquarters Volunteer Office.

In anticipation of the visit of Field-Marshal Mannerheim's committee of inspection, the Tähtiniemi disciplinary committee made its own report in January 1941. It recorded that since Lieut. Count von der Pahlen had taken sole charge (officially on 13th January, but in practice about five weeks earlier) most of the complaints had been put right, including issues of soap, toothpaste and cigarettes, and the granting of leave-passes. Those which still awaited settlement including the raising of the daily pocket-money from ten marks, overcrowding, the lack of mail from home, and the making of an effort to enable volunteers to go to Stockholm to apply for transit visas through Russia. Also, the majority of the volunteers wanted work. The committee added:

"We are under the impression that had Thorney House

appointed experienced officers to command the unit, few, if any, of the complaints would have had to be made, and the unit would have been back in British territory long since."

The report was signed by Graham J.M., Demore, Glyn, van Heteren, and Philips, who then formed the disciplinary committee, and copies of it and possibly of the November 1940 report were made available to the Field-Marshal's committee.

The Field-Marshal's committee was composed of Mrs Ruth Serlachius, the British Vice-Consul in Vaasa Viktor Bruun, a Jyväskylä engineer named Sohlberg, and Captain Nordlund. It made its inspection at the end of January and reported early in February that the volunteers were generally satisfied. However, the ten marks a day was unanimously agreed to be too low, even for modest Finnish conditions, particularly as the cost of living in Finland had risen considerably since the spring of 1940. That ten marks a day was a modest sum is shown by the fact that at the time Pooke had a job as a fitter (viilari) in Helsinki and received nine marks an hour, while an English teacher in the same city could expect 20 to 25 marks an hour for private lessons. The committee also recommended that the Tähtiniemi sauna should be refurbished, at the expense of the Jyväskylä Home Guard.

As a result of the committee's recommendations, the Finnish authorities most generously decided to make a special grant of an extra ten marks a day to each volunteer, so that each man would receive twenty marks a day. Those living away from Tähtiniemi then began to receive fortnightly payments from Finnish sources as well as the weekly payment from the Finnish Aid Bureau. Payment was generally to a savings bank account opened for the recipient the previous November, when all volunteers began to receive ten marks a day from the Finnish Aid Bureau. When the news of the increase reached the volunteers, on 5th February, they immediately sent a telegram in the names of the disciplinary committee to Field-Marshal Mannerheim:

"We are deeply touched by your personal effort in making possible the greatly-needed and generous addition to our pay unexpectedly announced today, and wish to express to you our most sincere thanks for the constant interest you have taken in our welfare. We assure you that your efforts and those of our Finnish officers will long be remembered by us all."

A copy of the report of the Field-Marshal's committee was telegraphed to Gibson, who in turn sent copies to members of both Houses of Parliament, to relatives and friends of the men who had complained, and to other interested parties. On hearing of the generous Finnish grant Gibson then ruled that the shilling (11 marks) a day credited to each volunteer's account in London would definitely cease on 31st March, since the Bureau did not have unlimited funds. He pointed out to the Foreign Office and to Lieut. Count von der Pahlen that if the credit were continued the volunteers would almost be better off than serving British soldiers. A recruit's pay in the British army was then two shillings a day.

In August 1940 the Finnish authorities struck a medal for all those who had been in the country's defence forces at the time of the armistice. The reverse of the medal issued to Finnish subjects bore a Finnish swastika (quite different and of greater antiquity than the Nazi one), and the inscription *Kunnia, isänmaa* (Honour, Fatherland), while those issued to volunteers from other countries bore the inscription *Summo in periculo fautoribus adiutoribus Finlandia memor* (Finland remembers those who helped her in her hour of danger). The ribbon was black with two narrow vertical red stripes in the centre, and had a bar bearing the word *Kotijoukot* (Home Forces). On 1st February 1941 a medal and a certificate of entitlement to wear it were given to each volunteer. Those working away from Tähtiniemi were able to obtain theirs from the Headquarters Volunteer Office in Helsinki, while the three in protective custody in that city received theirs through the post via the governor's office. In Tähtiniemi Commander Hollming of the Finnish General Staff, who came up from Helsinki specially for the purpose, presented the medals at a simple ceremony on behalf of Field-Marshal Mannerheim.

"Finland", he said in a speech to the volunteers, "feels greatly indebted to you who, leaving your homes of your own free will and offering your lives, volunteered to defend the eastern boundary of civilisation and the highest values of life. As a mark of this appreciation I have the honour to hand you these decorations in the name of our Field-Marshal. Bear them with the firm conviction that courage and chivalry will never disappear from our world, and may they also be a reminder to you of your enforced stay in our country."

As Ruck-Keene, Ryder, Atkinson and Holliday had already left the country, Captain Nordlund forwarded their medals and certificates to Somers Cocks at the British Legation in Helsinki, with a polite request that they be sent to their recipients through the British diplomatic bag. They were returned the following day with a curt note to the effect that British subjects were not supposed to accept foreign decorations without the permission of His Majesty the King having been obtained. Captain Nordlund promptly forwarded them through the Finnish diplomatic bag to the Finnish Aid Bureau. Captain Cope ignored Somers Cocks' ruling, which was in any case wrong, and accepted his medal gratefully. In the summer of 1941, H.M. King George VI graciously granted permission for the volunteers to wear their medal. Permission was suspended, however, between 6th December 1941 and 19th September 1944, while Britain and Finland were at war. "Paper war", as one Finnish provincial newspaper editor remarked to the writer in 1949, for the only warlike action against Finland on Britain's part was to drop a few bombs in Petsamo fjord. So little was known of Finland in Britain at the time that the writer was asked by several senior officers in 1942-43 why the devil he was not wearing his Finnish medal ribbon on his uniform.

The members of the homebound party which left Lapua on 23rd March 1940 were also entitled to the medal, but it seems doubtful whether more than a handful of them heard about it or received it. Ironically enough, one of the last volunteers to claim his medal was Major Chandor, who received his in 1964. There are still a few volunteers who have not claimed them.

In February 1941 Gibson wrote to relatives of the volunteers to disprove the rumours going about to the effect that the 130-odd left in Finland were being treated rather badly. Investigations on the spot, he wrote, had shown that improvements had been made following Captain Cope's visit to Tähtiniemi, that Field-Marshal Mannerheim's inspection committee had reported that ten marks a day pocket-money was insufficient, and that the Finnish authorities had agreed to pay an additional ten marks a day. The misrepresentations about the volunteers, he continued, had not only been offensive to the Finns, but also to the British Legation in Helsinki. He had recently found that some of the Finnish Aid Bureau's messages to the volunteers, sent via the British Legation in Helsinki, had never reached their destination, and this might account for some of the mis-statements. Now that the volunteers were under the direct care of Captain Nordlund it was certain that all messages he received for the contingent would reach it. Complaints brought to Gibson's personal notice had all been traced to volunteers living away from Tähtiniemi, and he had a strong suspicion that some of them had been inspired by foreign agents striving to impair Anglo-Finnish relationships.

Belatedly following the example of the Irish, in mid-February 1941 nine volunteers claiming Canadian nationality drafted a telegram to the Canadian Prime Minister, Mackenzie King. They handed it in at the Headquarters Volunteer Office in Helsinki, with a spare copy for Captain Nordlund, who forwarded the original to the British Legation for onward transmission. It is doubtful whether it was ever sent, since no reply from Somers Cocks was filed. The telegram sought assistance in obtaining transit visas through Russia, as several volunteers had recently left for home that way, and its signatories stated they wanted no financial aid. They obligingly gave their passport numbers, showing that the best claims to Canadian citizenship were those of Hall, Walker J.S., and Waller, who held Canadian passports, and of Punshon, whose wife and daughter lived in Toronto. Of the others Holtom was born in Bath but resident in Canada, McKibbin R. was born in Bexhill-on-Sea (his brother McKibbin L.G. was born in Bradford and took no part in the exercise), Graham E.M. was born in St Petersburg (now Leningrad), and Millington-Hogg in London, Ontario, though he had two passports. Read and Demore, the one born on Vancouver Island and the other in the Channel Islands but having a Montreal address, made no claim to Canadian citizenship, while Taylor H.S., a Canadian, was teaching English in Kouvola at the time and did not hear about the telegram.

A question in the British parliament in March 1941 elicited the reply that there were about 130 former volunteers still in Finland. This was reported in a leading Helsinki newspaper, which added politely that the British Minister there "works energetically" for the benefit of these volunteers. Somers Cocks, elated by this unsolicited testimonial, cut out the news item and sent it to Captain Nordlund, who filed it, having underlined the words "works energetically" and added "!?" in his own hand.

One of the several Scots volunteers, not surprisingly nicknamed Jock, walked over the frozen lake from Tähtiniemi to Korpilahti village one winter's evening in twenty degrees of frost, and spent a convivial evening with some locals who plied him with drink. He returned to his quarters late at night, singing, as was his wont on such occasions, snatches of "Annie Laurie". His room-mates put him to bed, and hid his trousers to prevent him from wandering round outside in the cold. But after a while Jock decided that he would like to go back to his friends in the village, so he slipped out of the building and walked over the ice in his shirt and underpants. He felt a little drowsy as he neared the village, and was found asleep in a snowdrift by some late revellers on their way home. They carried him back to Tähtiniemi, none the worse for his little outing.

Sanitation was one of the problems at Tähtiniemi. The

single water-closet in the building was insufficient for the winter use of a hundred and more well-fed men, so a primitive addition was built in a shed a short distance from the main building. The construction was simple: inside the door was a flight of steps leading up to a long wooden bar which served as a seat. The solid and liquid matter dropped into boxes placed on a sledge below, and these, when nearly full, were hauled away with a horse to the dump, and emptied. At least, that was what was intended. Winter came, and the contents of the boxes froze solid. The mountains grew higher and higher, until finally they nearly reached the bar, and were too high to be taken away, as there was only a low door in the end wall of the shed, just high enough for the boxes on the sledge. Something had to be done, so the volunteers held an election. With 87 votes for and only one single vote against, Read was elected to the job of solving the problem, for which he received 50 marks. He borrowed a saw, cut off the tops of the mountains, harnessed the horse, and hauled away load after load of odourless frozen solids.

Meanwhile, in the middle of January, Vice-Consul Viktor Bruun sent two pairs of skis to Tähtiniemi for the use of the volunteers. These were followed a few days later by a further eleven pairs from a private source and 25 pairs on loan from the Finnish army. By this time the volunteers had made numerous friends in the village, and, with their help, began to acquire the rudimentary skills of skiing. An unexpected result of the interest shown in this sport was the start of a news-sheet called *The Tähtiniemi Courier*, with Barton and Gooderham as joint editors. The first number was dated 12th March and was typewritten in several copies by Gooderham, who was a clerk in the contingent office. In addition to Nos. 1 to 5, which appeared between 12th and 17th March, a Special Edition appeared on 13th March, consisting of a single sheet with a cartoon of Budd and Brown on a kick-sledge, which they had crashed on a run downhill from Tähtiniemi to the lake. A Sports Edition was dated 15th March, and a Sports Special came out on 22nd March. A post-Easter number was dated 16th April. From its un-numbered and undated issue of about 22nd March the

Courier was duplicated. In that number its editors wrote that henceforth it would be published on Fridays.

A few days after the first number appeared the British Legation in Helsinki recruited Barton as a "consular agent" and sent him to Sodankylä on the Arctic highway north of Rovaniemi to observe German troop movements. His successor as editor was McGee, a journalist by profession and an artist of some skill, who used horse-racing terminology to enliven the accounts of the various ski-races. Thompson was in charge of distribution, and posted copies to volunteers living away from Tähtiniemi. If the Courier is to be believed, he sent a copy to the volunteers' former Commander-in-Chief, for the paper recorded that "Reports from reliable sources state that the Field-Marshal was greatly aided in his recovery from an attack of influenza by reading the *Courier*." The paper ceased publication before the contingent left for Sweden.

In its own sarcastic style, which owed something to the Society columns in British newspapers, the *Courier* recorded faithfully all the local events involving volunteers. It had a tactful turn of phrase for everyone. The return of a volunteer from protective custody was described by the editor himself, who found himself "greeting 'Legs', the popular hooch hi-jacker, who has spent some time away from us investigating penitentiary conditions in Finland." When, a day or two later, "Legs" was arrested in Jyväskylä for some minor misdeed, the *Courier* remarked that "he had spent the night at his customary Jyväskylä hotel, where he has a room permanently reserved." On another occasion reference was made to two volunteers who had indulged in an alcoholic orgy involving unprintable army songs as having been seen (and heard) "chanting the Soldiers' Song over the foaming mehu of the Lotta Kahvila". Mehu is non-alcoholic fruit juice, and the Kahvila was a café run by the local Lottas. And a volunteer who got a black eye in a scuffle was said to have had "a recurrence of an eye infection."

The *Courier* was assiduous in recording nicknames. Thus Casey was referred to as Box, Bath as Sauna, Weaver as Red (though whether from the colour of his hair or his politics the writer did not say), and Law, who had been in the Army Dental Corps, as Molar. Phelps, who stood nearly six foot two, was known from his early days as Lofty, Smith S.C.R., who would buy and sell anything, was known as Trader Smith or Trader Hound, and Parker, whose home was in Lincolnshire, was known as Boston. Stuart-Menteth, who ate frequently between meals, was called Biscuit, and several others were given honorary military titles, such as Major Humphries of the Camel Corps, Captain Jock Graham, Admiral Patterson, General Commins, Colonel Bradley, and Squadron-Leader Mackie. Only Lord Bobbie Waugh and the Hon. Bernard Carrick were elevated to the nobility, and Professor van Heteren was the only one to receive academic status.

After two or three numbers of the *Courier* had appeared, the editor took the opportunity to ask Mr and Mrs Salje their opinion of it. The former replied in Finnish "I have never heard of it", while his wife said "Thank you very much" in English. The Finnish Corporal Fahler, the assistant adjutant, described it as "full of louzes", while the lady who brought the milk was reported to have said it was the most wonderful thing that had happened in Korpilahti since she was a girl.

The first ski-race recorded in the *Courier* was the (Great) Tähtiniemi Handicap, in which fifteen volunteers took part: Alexander, Casey, Ford, Hall, Hartman, Hole, Lyons, Kilgour, McKibbin R., Parker, Patterson, Phelps, Purves, Stuart-Menteth and Taylor H.S. Glyn and Thompson took bets on the competition; and Hole was the winner. The second race was the Jyväskylä Gallop, and like the first was over a six and a quarter mile course. Three of the contestants, Alexander, Phelps and Weaver, got lost while trying to take a short cut. Hole won again, with Patterson second and Lyons third, and earned himself a pair of skis as a prize.

The Ragtime Derby followed, for those who had not taken part in either of the other races, and was over a course of a mile and a quarter. This was won by McMullin, to the great amusement of the Finns who had come to watch, and was commemorated in a McKibbin L.R. cartoon. Then came the Serlachius Stakes Handicap, in which the runners were nearly the same as those in the Tähtiniemi Handicap. Hole won yet again, with Patterson second and Lyons third. Having won two pairs of skis Hole offered one pair as first prize in the next race, which was run over a slightly different six and a quarter mile course. This time Ford won, in 60.66 minutes, plus 5 minutes handicap, with Roper second and Weaver third.

Following these races the skiers were invited to try their skills against those of the people of Korpilahti. Another handicap race against a team of local under-16 boys, described as the International Ski Contest, was the next to take place, and was won by the Korpilahti team. Presenting the prizes for the race Captain Nordlund, who had come up from Helsinki for the occasion, prefaced his remarks with the observation that this was the first international race ever held in the village. He congratulated the boys on their victory and the losers on their sportsmanlike behaviour throughout. It is a matter of some surprise that in 1983 the race was reported in Korpilahti as never having taken place, though diaries show that the Korpilahti boys issued their challenge on 10th March, the day after the Tähtiniemi Handicap.

On 22nd March a 5 x 3¼ mile handicap relay race was run against a team of the five Korpilahti girls who took turns, as Lottas, to help in the Tähtiniemi kitchen, the misses Lempi (or Lyyli) Ahonen, Kirsti Helander, Sinikka Mutila, Iris Reivilä, and Hilkka Reivinen. The event was described in the *Courier* as The Great Anti-Girl Handicap. The first couple to start were Parker and "Madame Lucia" (probably Miss Mutila), and the paper noted: "Eve soon outstripped her adversary, and from thence on it was a repeat of the age-old story – male chasing female – to the joy of the female and the eternal frustration of the male." The paper also noted that on the same day the local policeman, senior constable Väinö Häkkinen, who had aided and abetted the Finnish girls' team, had skied a total of nearly sixteen miles with ease, "and we advise any intending absconders to wait for the snow to thaw before attempting a speedy getaway." The girls completed the course in 2 hours 17 minutes 42 seconds, and the volunteers in 2 hours 40 minutes 20 seconds, losing by 12 minutes 38 seconds.

The prize for the race, a cup inscribed "British Contingent 22.3.1941, 5 x 5 km. Team First Prize" (if ever it existed outside the *Courier's* columns), was presented to the Finnish girls' team at a ball held in the Home Guard Hall in Korpilahti. A number of local guests were invited, including the policeman, the baker Mr Luume, and the local Home Guard chief J. Punamäki. Of the event the *Courier* observed: "We are not familiar enough with the history of Korpilahti to know if there have been similar scenes. Possibly the Civil War period (1917-18) may have provided them. In short, our dance was a riot – in fact it was several riots and a couple of disagreements." The band on this occasion was The Carelian Boys *(Karjalan Pojat)*.

Presenting the prizes for the race, Lieut. Count von der Pahlen spoke to the Korpilahti girls and said: "I think that the statement made in your challenge to the volunteers is quite true – that you have helped them very much to master the difficult art of skiing." After presenting the prizes for the Ragtime Derby he invested Budd with the Order of the Falling Star, for his frequent contacts with the snow during the race. Budd, not to be outdone, offered Lieut. Count von der Pahlen the Order of the Rising Star, symbolising the ever-rising esteem in which the Count was held among the volunteers.

The dance had an unexpected sequel. One of the tunes which The Carelian Boys played was a popular waltz from the Winter War, When Our Road to the Battlefield Lay (*Taistoihin tiemme kun toi*). Its catchy tune set the volunteers thinking, and after some deliberation some fresh words emerged whenever the tune was played on the Tähtiniemi wireless:

> But he laughed when she told him to *pois*,

For he knew that she meant every word.
He could tell by the sound of her voice
That she thought that he was a turd . . .

Pois is the Finnish for go away; and the rest of the song was unprintable.

The need to get home was not forgotten amid the festivities, and a few days after the dance twenty-three volunteers telegraphed Mr (later Sir) Winston Churchill, then Prime Minister, asking for an effort to be made to repatriate them. Mr Churchill replied that every effort was being made but that the difficulties so far were insuperable. Meanwhile, in Korpilahti the weather was becoming warmer, and as the ice in the lake began to melt the volunteers spent a couple of days building a temporary causeway over the frozen arm of the lake between their quarters and the village. It consisted of planks laid lengthways on short cross-logs, which floated just above the surface of the water when the ice had melted, much wire being used in its construction so that the logs could be used again.

Together with Captain Nordlund, Colonel Serlachius visited Tähtiniemi on Sunday 30th March to deliver the Christmas fare, largely chocolate and cigarettes, which had been sent out from the Finnish Aid Bureau. There was a laughter when Lieut. Count von der Pahlen introduced the Colonel to the volunteers as a member of the Finnish Aid Bureau on this side. The delay in their transport from the s/s *Ergo,* which had arrived in Petsamo on 30th December, was probably due to the fact that the goods were not in the "urgent" category, though Colonel Serlachius mentioned that the ship had had to wait five or six weeks for its turn at the quay. Under the heading "Gibson Grants Guineas Grudgingly" the Tähtiniemi *Courier* reported that Colonel Serlachius had also told the volunteers that Thorney House had ordered that as they had been demobilised on 31st May last the shilling per day per man previously credited in London had been discontinued after 30th June, but that after a long exchange of cables Gibson had granted an extension of the London credits to 31st March 1941. Colonel Serlachius added that in his view once the contract had been signed pay should have continued until the volunteers returned home to England, a view with which the volunteers agreed to a man.

Gooderham went to Helsinki early in April to collect the Christmas gifts which had been sent out for Thorney House in addition to the foodstuffs. Colonel Serlachius handed them over to him at a party held at the Officers' Club, in the presence of members of the English colony, including Mrs Tallberg, Mrs Tudeer, Mr and Mrs Wolontis, Mrs Birse, Mrs Åkerman, Consul Bell and his secretary Miss Westlin, Colonel Hannula, Mrs Tötterman, Mr Cooke of Price Waterhouse (the internationally known chartered accountants), Somers Cocks (representing the British Legation), and numerous volunteers, including Budd, Hill, Lenox-Conyngham, Mallowan (who was credited with a new unorthodox and highly successful method of teaching English), Pearce, Read (who was recorded as giving English lessons at cut prices), Summers, Tawell, and Woodburn. The writer was absent owing to chicken-pox. Budd read a speech of thanks written for him in Finnish, and managed to get round all the difficult words including the Finnish for pit-props (propsipuita), one of the commodities in which Colonel Serlachius had interests.

At the end of April a report appeared in *Helsingin Sanomat*, the leading (and pro-British) Finnish daily newspaper, saying that the Russians had refused 150 volunteers transit visas, on the grounds that they had fought against them on the Finnish side, and that the Russians had asked the British government to repatriate 400 Baltic seamen, which had been refused. Field-Marshal Mannerheim cabled this information to Gripenberg.

A list of the 128 members of the contingent, prepared in May 1941, gave a good indication of the overall situation. Of the total, 44 were unemployed and living at Tähtiniemi, where a further eight were on the camp staff. Another 34 were engaged in different types of work in various parts of the country, and of these 22, of whom two were rather deaf, were in Helsinki and elsewhere teaching English. A further five performed the same function for the British Council in the larger provincial towns. The British Legation in Helsinki employed seven, as doorkeepers, cipher clerks and Press Department assistants, plus six "consular agents" stationed in Petsamo, Ivalo, Sodankylä, Kemi, Ylivieska and other strategic places where the movements of German troops and equipment could be observed. The Ivalo man, Carrick, was a trifle careless one day, and a German officer who saw him openly observing an army column offered, in excellent English, to lend him a pencil. Those not teaching or watching exercised a wide range of skills, including those of barber, carpenter, caterer, driver, gardener, gymnastics instructor and labourer. In the Helsinki area, where, as might be expected, there was a concentration of volunteers, Aitken-Quack was working for Price Waterhouse, Bullen, Daly, Pooke and Prince were working as fitters in the wood-gas generator department of Hietalahti Dry Dock and Engineering Works, Herring was working as a ladies' hairdresser at Salon New York, Hicks Green was a golf professional at the Helsinki Golf Club, McNeil was at Tilgmann's printing-works, Montague was working as a production manager at Ford, Sherry was working at Kone engineering plant as a draughtsman (he later joined the British Legation), Smith M.L. was at a market-garden on Vuosaari, an island to the north-east of the city, White was working at the Swedish Theatre, and Zipfel was selling gramophone records at Music Fazer, the country's top music shop.

Among those living away from Tähtiniemi whose occupations were not noted, one man, a kleptomaniac, was serving a seven-month sentence for larceny, and another was in hospital. By June all the contingent except a hard core of about twenty (whose pay Vereker and Somers Cocks were trying to stop) had had some form of employment or other since demobilisation, some, like the writer, having been working the whole time. Two of the volunteers employed at the British Legation in Helsinki were doorkeepers, and the Foreign Office asked Gibson to provide uniforms for them, but Gibson replied that he could see no reason for granting special concessions to the two men who were presumably the most fortunate of the lot.

At the invitation of Colonel Serlachius the volunteers put together a football team to play a game at Mänttä, against a local team one suspects was largely composed of the Colonel's employees, on 10th June. The teams were as follows:

British: Bradley, Glyn, Hole, McKibbin R., Parker (captain), Purves, Thompson and four others;

Finnish: P. Aro, H. Haikka, Hj. Kelin, A. Kentonen, A. Lampinen, R. Lehtola, V Mäcklin, B. Orden, A. Puhakka, P. Väitänen and O. Selänpää, with Aarne Eloranta as referee. The local paper noted that England, from as far away as its Dominions of India, South Africa and Canada, had put up a team of volunteers who had come to Finland during the Winter War. A large crowd of onlookers followed the game, which was a clean, rapid and friendly one. In the visitors' team were many good players, but there was a lack of co-operation between them, and also a lack of accuracy when trying to score. In the second half their style improved, and Mänttä's 4 - 0 lead at half-time became 5 - 2 at the close.

The events leading up to the volunteers' departure from Finland can be said to have started in the autumn of 1940, when Germany asked for permission to bring equipment and troops through Finland in transit from Germany to northern Norway. Finland was powerless to say no, and granted Germany's request. Shortly afterwards the first consignment of men and materials came through Vaasa, where it was put on a train for Rovaniemi. From there lorries carried it up to the Norwegian frontier and beyond. The following spring there was a build-up of German forces at their staging-post on the Arctic Circle near Rovaniemi, and on 9th June 1941 Field-Marshal Mannerheim, hearing that the Germans were concentrating their forces in Lapland and not sending them on to Norway, decided that they were up to no good. Several groups of reservists, mainly defence and anti-aircraft units, were then called up for general manœuvres. This was plainly to be seen in the streets of Helsinki and other large towns, where suddenly great numbers of men appeared in new military uniforms, with new sheath-knifes. Several volunteers who were working in Helsinki at this time noticed the increased activity, and rightly concluded that it might be the prelude to fresh hostilities between Finland and Soviet Russia. Remembering why they had come to Finland they made enquiries as to whether they could volunteer again for the Finnish armed forces. The reply which one of them received, from General Staff Headquarters, was exceedingly polite: we thank you, but the answer is no. However, you may enrol at the Red Cross Hospital as a blood donor.

On 13th June, Gibson received a telegram from Finland informing him of the increased German activity there and suggesting that it would be best to send the volunteers to Sweden for their own safety. He discussed the matter with Gripenberg, and the two proposed to the Finnish authorities that Field-Marshal Mannerheim should rely on his own judgement as to whether or not to send the volunteers away. Fearing that Finland might undertake some form of military co-operation with the Germans, the British government informed the Finnish government on 14th June that it would blockade the port of Petsamo. Three days later the Finnish Ministry of Defence ordered general manœuvres. This was, in fact, a general mobilisation, since it involved about 630,000 people, or one-sixth of the country's population.

The German High Command issued an Order to its troops on 18th June, stating that it was no longer necessary to conceal their country's intentions any longer. Germany attacked Russia the following day on all fronts, including the Finnish Lapland front, and the German government officially notified the Finnish government of its intentions in Finland on the evening of 21st June. Meanwhile, the decision to send the volunteers to Sweden had already been taken – the volunteers were told at the time that Field-

Marshal Mannerheim had arranged matters personally – and on 19th June those living away from Tähtiniemi were given train passes to Jyväskylä and told to report to Lieut. Count von der Pahlen. A number of volunteers living in Helsinki received a telephoned order from Ari Kauhanen of the State Police to report to the Headquarters Volunteer Office. They left the city on 20th June, when it was already clear that the general mobilisation was taking place, as the trains were full and it was a case of standing-room only.

The weather was hot and sultry, and it was with some discomfort that the volunteers from Helsinki made the train journey to Jyväskylä via Tampere and Haapamäki. Several of the party decided to get something to eat at the station restaurant at the last-named place, and one nearly missed the train. However, he managed, sandwich in hand, to catch it as it pulled out of the station, and travelled to the next stop standing on the buffers of the last coach. After spending the night in the town the party continued to its destination by bus.

On arrival in the village one of the Tähtiniemi staff met the party and directed it to an army hut in the village. On reporting to the camp office several asked whether there was any work to be had in the district. It turned out that the sawmill at Iloniemi required labour to replace the eight men who had just been called up. So eight men hired bicycles and rode the two miles to the sawmills, where, in pairs, they knocked up wooden sections for army huts. Bath, the only proper carpenter, was at 34 the oldest in the party. Brooke, 21, the youngest, was made foreman-interpreter, as he was the only one who could speak Finnish sufficiently well. The others in the party were Casey, Daly, Hignell, Ilbury, Butler and Rattigan. They soon discovered that by stacking the ready-cut parts for the sections in a different way the output could be considerably increased. This point was not lost on the manager, who invited the other men in the sawmill to come and watch those mad Englishmen, whose daily work-norm was set at sixteen sections, and who had found out how to produce twenty to twenty-three. When the time came for the party to leave, on 27th June, the manager paid everyone at the standard piecework rate and said how sorry he was to see the volunteers go.

The order that the volunteers should leave Tähtiniemi for Sweden was received in the evening of Thursday 26th June and was communicated to them the following day. Announcing this Lieut. Count von der Pahlen stressed that the success of the journey depended entirely on the volunteers' own discipline and forbearance. Those who, against the wishes of the authorities, refused to join the party would do so at their own risk, and would lose the protection of the Finnish authorities and of the British Legation and Consulate; and the State Police would immediately take care of them. Before the main party left Korpilahti three volunteers declared their intention to remain in Finland. McKay and Asling had recently married Finnish girls and had good reason for staying, while Rattigan had been toying with the idea of taking Finnish nationality to facilitate his departure from the country. Rattigan and McKay were ordered to report to the State Police in Jyväskylä, while Asling was ordered to Lapua. Three others, Neumark, McMullin, and Taylor H.S. (the last-named had recently married a Jyväskylä girl), were given permission to go to Helsinki to report to the State Police, with a view to joining the Finnish army. With their slight knowledge of Finnish this proved impossible, and they rejoined the contingent in Sweden in July, together with Smith M.L., who claimed U.S. citizenship and who had been trying to get out of Finland via Petsamo. In addition to these, nine men remained on the staff of the British Legation in Helsinki, five were working at the British Legation in Stockholm, Gordon was unaccounted for, and three others, Pershke, Prince (who came as far as Vilppula) and Sherry were presumed to be somewhere in Finland. Sherry, in fact, was employed at the British Legation in Helsinki at the time. Last of all came Davey, who liked Finland so much that he decided to settle down somewhere near Korpilahti. His absence from the contingent was noticed at Mänttä, and the Finnish police picked him up a few days later. They took him to the Swedish frontier and handed him over to the police, who in turn delivered him to the contingent. After he had refused to co-operate with the Swedish authorities he was transferred to the Långmora internment camp at Långshyttan, near Falun, where he was awaiting repatriation in May 1942.

Saturday morning, 28th June, was occupied in packing. Those of the volunteers living in the army hut in the village took their luggage to the lakeside, or rather, rolled it down the hill to a small creek, ferried it over to Tähtiniemi, and dragged it up the hill to the main building, where it was loaded into a lorry. Count von der Pahlen, now in civilian clothes, was in overall charge, and the Finnish corporals, L. Wahlhelm and H. Fahler, accompanied the party as far as the train. Taylor H. and van Heteren were in charge of discipline, Roberts C.D. was in charge of the stores, and Gooderham acted as clerk and checker. The rest of the volunteers were divided into nine groups, each under its own leader, and containing ten to twelve men. The leaders were Demore, Graham J.M., Holtom, Lace, McKibbin R., Tawell, Vessey, Walker J.S. and Woodburn, with Law in charge of two patients from the sick-bay, making a total of 106 volunteers.

While the lorry was being loaded with luggage and stores, the question arose as to the fate of the stocks belonging to the canteen. It was clear that they could not be packed up and taken away, and after a hurried conference it was decided to give them to the widowed mother of the two Korpilahti boys who had run the ferry. With other surplus equipment the gift came to two ferry-boat loads, much to the surprise of the volunteers and the delight of the recipient.

The buses left the village at a quarter to five in the afternoon. As they were heavily laden and driven on wood-gas, which gave little power at slow speeds, they stopped at the bottom of the long steep hill just west of the village. Here the passengers alighted and walked up the hill, rejoining them at the top of the downward slope. Supper was at Mänttä, where Captain Nordlund met the party. After supper the journey continued to Vilppula railway-station, where a special military train, No. 4177, was waiting, and where seven volunteer firemen joined it. Captain Nordlund saw the party off, and the train left just after half past nine. As it was near midsummer there was little darkness to complicate matters, though Prince managed to disappear and arrived in Sweden a week later.

The train spent half an hour at Ruukki station the following morning, when eighteen Poles under a Mr Tokarski joined it, making with the Jyväskylä Poles, who had joined the train separately, a party of 26, plus 14 of other nationalities. The whole party then comprised 153 men. The trip continued from Ruukki without stopping at the larger stations and junctions. At twenty past two in the morning of 30th June it arrived in Tornio, where a Captain Tollett from Headquarters met it. After a short stay, during which "various foreigners" signed an undertaking sent up from Headquarters, the train continued to Haparanda, on the Swedish side of the frontier, where it arrived at half past three Finnish time. Here a difficulty arose. As only the British contingent and one Pole had entry permits for Sweden, the Swedish immigration authorities insisted that those without entry permits should return to Finland to await their visas, so Count von der Pahlen took them back to Tornio and reported by telephone to Captain Nordlund. He then rejoined the British contingent, whose train had been waiting at Karungi, some distance north-west of Haparanda. Food on the journey consisted of Finnish hard bread, butter and cheese, with water and lemonade where available. Count von der Pahlen noted in his report on the journey: "It must be acknowledged that all the volunteers left Finland with sorrow, and unwillingly, and expressed continually, despite the changed conditions, their sympathy for the country to which they had all come as volunteers."

The last letter from Korpilahti reached Gibson on 27th June. Taylor H. drafted it, and Lieut. Count von der Pahlen signed it. It reported that everything possible had been done to secure the comfort and contentment of the volunteers, and that there was no reasonable ground for any complaint. In circulating the letter Gibson remarked that "many letters have since been received from the men expressing their gratitude for the arrangements made for their welfare." Coming at a time when the only direct postal communications between the two countries were through diplomatic channels, it seems likely that Lieut. Count von der Pahlen received the letters, not Gibson.

On 28th June Gripenberg received a telegram from Field-Marshal Mannerheim stating that the volunteers were leaving Finland, and on 30th June a further telegram arrived to say that all the volunteers except two employed at the British Legation in Helsinki (reference here was intended to Stockholm) had arrived safely in Malung, in charge of Count von der Pahlen, an event which did not take place until the following day. The volunteers were then placed under the care and supervision of the British Consul in Stockholm, who also had charge of those volunteers who had been in Sweden since April 1940.

In the second part of his Report Gibson noted that between the beginning of October 1940 and September 1941, the general behaviour of the volunteers had been good, with only a few cases of drunkenness and insubordination, and only one criminal punishment of seven months for larceny. Lieut. Count von der Pahlen had reported that the Lottas spoke well of the volunteers and had generally complimented them on their chivalry towards women. The great majority of volunteers had lived within their means, though the worst offenders in incurring debts were the airmen, despite the fact that they had received more money than the others. Lord Carlow helped some of them out of their difficulties, and the Finnish Aid Bureau refunded him the sums he had advanced.

HELSINKI AND LONDON

At this point it is appropriate to consider the efforts made in London and Helsinki to repatriate the volunteers, and the interference in the contingent's affairs on the part of the British Legation in Helsinki. As we have seen, the Legation obligingly arranged the passages home of Lord Balfour and Jackson, who left together at the end of May or early in June 1940 on the s/s *Argo*, and of Captain Joyce, who left on 1st June on the s/s *Regulus*. Major Chandor, whom the Legation subsequently denied helping but who may have asked for a steamer-ticket as the price of relinquishing his command, left Petsamo early in July, shortly before the port was closed to normal passenger traffic.

On 27th July it was reported that the s/s *American Legion* was on her way to Petsamo to pick up American subjects, including American and Canadian volunteers from Finland. The United States had not yet joined in the war against Germany, and on hearing the news Gripenberg at once called on the American Ambassador in London to ask that the British volunteers in Finland might be included, but Washington declared this to be impracticable. In July, as noted, Gibson obtained War Office approval for a scheme to send all the volunteers willing to join the British forces in the Middle East to go there via Russia, and a telegram was sent to Sir Stafford Cripps in Moscow, asking him to try to obtain the necessary visas. Similar telegrams were also sent to Mallet in Stockholm and Vereker in Helsinki, at Gibson's request, on 23rd July. Vereker made a few half-hearted efforts to comply with the terms of his telegram, but prevented those volunteers of whom he did not approve personally from applying for visas for Russia, which were not granted until Turkish and Syrian visas, only obtainable in Stockholm, had been secured. Visas were also needed for visits to Sweden. Meanwhile, attempts to get the volunteers included with British troops being exchanged for German troops interned in Sweden proved fruitless, as there were not enough Germans for the purpose.

Major Chandor returned home on 7th August, at which time only 45 of the 227 volunteers had managed to get out of Finland, and of these only about thirty had reached London. He reported to the Committee a fortnight later that naval officers in Iceland had said it would be a simple matter to send a ship to Petsamo to collect the volunteers, provided permission could be obtained. The scheme came to nothing, since the Germans had already warned the Finnish government that their naval patrol based at Kirkenes in Northern Norway would search all ships leaving Petsamo, and that any infringement of normal traffic would result in the closure of that port, which at the time was Finland's only maritime connection with the outside world. Then the Bureau tried the Air Ministry, who were not in favour of flying the volunteers home as it was too risky.

In a long written statement which he presented to the Committee, Major Chandor laid stress on the importance of Ryder, who as a sergeant and later as a civilian had charge of the unit's and contingent's books and who had had to work under very difficult conditions. "He worked literally night and day for weeks on end. He had the whole responsibility of the finance of the Unit – the books to open and keep – he had nobody to help him, and I cannot speak too highly of him and of his work and devotion to duty. Without his efficiency I do not know what I should have done, as I could not have found anybody to take his place." He hoped that the Committee might find it possible to recognise at the proper time the great service he had done. At the same time he told the Committee that he had written to the Prime Minister to urge that some immediate steps might be taken to repatriate the volunteers formerly under his command. "I said they were trained troops, many of them potential officers, eating their hearts out to get home". He added that in his opinion they would prove of great value to any commander.

In the first part of his Report, written in September 1940, Gibson noted that when the Finnish Aid Bureau was set up the Prime Minister at that time (Mr. Neville Chamberlain), Mr Winston Churchill and Lord Halifax had each assured Colonel Roosevelt that they were anxious that the Volunteer Force should be a great success, and the Committee and many other distinguished men worked hard to that end. "This fact seems to have been lost sight of by some people, including some British officials in Finland and Sweden, and there is now a tendency to enlarge on the misbehaviour of a few volunteers and to forget that, small as the effort was, it met the increasing public demand in this country and made a considerable impression for good both in Finland and in America." It was true, the Report continued, that a few volunteers had behaved badly, but it should be remembered that they arrived in Finland at the time of the armistice, which was always a most difficult time to maintain discipline in any military organisation. There was no doubt that if the men had been called upon to fight they would have given a good account of themselves, and the noteworthy fact was not that a few of them had behaved badly but that the great majority of them had behaved so well in the most trying circumstances. It would surely have been most unfortunate if, in Field Marshal Mannerheim's Order of the Day of 24th March, when he thanked the various countries who had come to Finland's aid in response to the appeal of the League of Nations, there had been no mention of Great Britain. "May it not be that some day the fact that we did so will be of some advantage both to this country and to Finland?" he concluded.

At the end of September 1940, 30 volunteers had reached home, three were on their way home via the U.S.A., three had gone from Sweden via Russia to Palestine to join the British forces there, and one had gone from Finland via Russia to Kenya to join the East African forces, seven had left the contingent, eleven were prisoners in Germany, one had died, 138 were still in Finland, and 33 were in Sweden, making a total of 227. Gibson's Report, giving these figures, noted that whatever the legal liability of the Committee might have been at this time under the Agreement of Service, it seemed clear that it was still responsible for the repatriation of the volunteers unless it was forced to plead frustration, a view reversed in November, when Gibson was advised that the Committee was not responsible.

The position was not much improved in November, when there were still 136 volunteers in Finland, 28 in Sweden, 13 in Germany, 8 in Palestine, 1 in Canada who had joined the army, 1 in Kenya, 1 married and settled down in Sweden, 3 foreigners returned to their own countries, 3 disappeared in Russia, 1 died, and 32 returned home, the last two having stowed away in a Finnish ship in Petsamo. Of those still in Finland 60 had found work in forestry and other occupations, 12 were teaching English, and a number of others were living away from the contingent in various jobs. At this time Vereker wrote that he had decided to make all the volunteers apply for transit visas for Russia, though evidently not those who were working, and that Mallet had agreed to support applications made in Stockholm for a number of picked volunteers. Vereker recorded a visit to the Soviet Minister in Helsinki to intercede for eight of the anti-aircraft specialists.

The interference of the British Legation in Helsinki in the affairs of the volunteers began at the end of May with Major Magill's speech, and continued when Vereker dismissed Major Chandor, Lieut. Guthrie, and sergeant-major Asling. Major Chandor's movements were kept so secret that, not knowing that he was on his way home, Gibson telegraphed to him on 5th July to instruct him, with effect from 31st May, to pay only ten marks a day pocket-money to each volunteer, but not the 550 marks monthly bonus they had received as soldiers. The telegram was sent via the Foreign Office to the British Legation in Helsinki, where it was held up until 3rd August. On that day Captain Cope wrote to Ruck-Keene to say that the gist of a Foreign Office telegram to Vereker was that ten marks a day was to be paid to all volunteers.

On 17th October Gibson received through the Foreign Office a copy of a printed circular which Vereker had sent to every volunteer, setting out the new conditions and rates of pay which would take effect from 1st September, and which noted that from that date the Finnish Aid Bureau would not pay the ten marks a day to those living away from the contingent and not in work of which the commanding officer approved. All those not living with the contingent were instructed to get in touch with the commanding officer at Jyväskylä. The circular, a foolscap sheet in three English type-faces currently in use in Finland, was prepared and printed in Helsinki. It was probably drafted by Somers Cocks, and was an accurate statement of Gibson's proposals, including that of additional pay for volunteers employed on contingent duties. However, the continuation of the credit of a shilling a day in London was not in accordance with Gibson's wishes. Having called the attention of the Foreign Office to this and corresponded with Vereker, Ruck-Keene and Colonel Serlachius, Gibson finally decided that as the shilling had been promised it should be credited up to 31st March 1941. He sent another telegram on 8th October, presuming that Ruck-Keene was paying the ten marks a day as instructed. The latter, meanwhile, asked permission to pay extra money to those employed on special duties within and for the contingent, and that the pocket-money be increased to twenty marks a day. Gibson agreed to the employment pay but refused the extra pocket-money. Further correspondence followed, and resulted in the writer and other volunteers living away from the contingent and working being paid ten marks a day from 1st June, with an extra 70 marks just before Christmas. This, as noted, was in most cases paid, with the ten marks a day from Finnish sources from February 1941, direct to a savings account opened in a conveniently situated bank for each volunteer, and continued to 13th June 1941, a week before the contingent assembled in Korpilahti for the journey to Sweden. A further ten marks a day was paid in cash for the period 13th-28th June.

On 3rd December 1940 Vereker asked Gibson if the Bureau would pay for the repatriation of the volunteers via Vladivostock and the U.S.A. , at a cost of £200 to £250 per head. Gibson replied he was afraid the volunteers might give a lot of trouble both in Russia and America while making such long railway journeys, and that the cost was much heavier than the fare to Cairo. He added that if Russian transit visas could be obtained for the journey to Vladivostock they could be obtained for the journey of Odessa, and these men would be useful if they could be got to Cairo. If, however, when most of the men had left Finland for the Middle East or elsewhere there were a few left who could not join the Forces, then the Bureau would consider bringing them home via Vladivostock. In January 1941 Vereker informed the Foreign Office of his intention to exert strong moral pressure on all volunteers fit for military service to join the Forces in the Middle East. His intention was never carried into effect; and a scheme to send the contingent through Russia in a sealed train proved impossible.

On 22nd February 1941 Gibson sent a telegram to the contingent ordering that no volunteer should leave Finland without reference to Vereker. This may seem odd, but it reflects Gibson's growing exasperation, and brings us to the case of Ryder. As we have seen, Ryder had been paymaster-sergeant from March 1940 and had a fuller knowledge than anyone else of all that concerned the contingent, its individual members, and its finances. In furtherance of his policy of depriving the contingent of its management Vereker summoned Ryder to Helsinki on 5th December 1940 and told him he was to go to the Middle East via Russia. Ryder replied that although he would like to leave for personal reasons he thought it was his duty to remain with the contingent until the last, and when Vereker nevertheless insisted on his departure Ryder lodged a very strong and emphatic protest. He then went to Stockholm, to apply at the Soviet and other consulates for visas, and returned to the contingent on 17th December.

Meanwhile, although Lieut. Count von der Pahlen had in effect been commandant at Tähtiniemi since the previous September, his appointment as such was not confirmed until Ruck-Keene obtained his Russian visa early in January

1941. On 12th January, apparently on Vereker's instructions, Ryder wrote a memorandum to Nordlund, with Ruck-Keene's counter-signature, suggesting that the Finnish authorities should take over the care and administration of the British volunteers. The next day Vereker informed the Foreign Office in London that Atkinson, Dr. Herford (who had left early in January), Holliday, Ruck-Keene and Ryder had obtained transit visas for Russia, and that as there would, after their departure, be no suitable man left among the volunteers to take charge of the contingent (how he reached his conclusion remains a mystery), it should be handed over for "disciplinary and financial administration" to the Finnish Headquarters Volunteer Office. He added that the proposal had the approval of Field-Marshal Mannerheim. On the same day Vereker asked Captain Nordlund that the Headquarters Volunteer Office should take over the liquidation (this was the word he used) of the British contingent, with effect from 15th January, adding that the Field-Marshal had agreed to this as well, though not the Finnish Aid Bureau. Captain Nordlund replied that the contingent would need a commanding officer at 100 marks a day, a paymaster at 80 marks a day, a book-keeper and typist, and a quartermaster at 30 marks a day. This compared with 100 marks being paid to Lieut. Count von der Pahlen, 50 marks to the paymaster, 30 to his assistant, 20 to the orderly-room clerk and 15 to the quartermaster, with 10 marks a day to other volunteers doing part-time work for the contingent. In a letter to Gibson at this time Captain Nordlund took the opportunity to say how happy and proud he was to be associated with the British volunteers.

After consulting with the Foreign Office Gibson replied that the Finnish Aid Bureau had no authority to place British civilians in Finland under Finnish military discipline, and thought the men might object. He added that the man in charge of those remaining in Finland should be the last to leave the country, otherwise the men would feel that they had been deserted by those in charge of them and that Russian visas had been obtained by favouritism. He accordingly asked Gripenberg to obtain fuller information about the proposals. Enquiries made through the Finnish Foreign Ministry showed that it had been proposed that the contingent should come under the overall control of Captain Nordlund, their former commanding officer at Lapua and head of the Headquarters Volunteer Office; that Lieut. Count von der Pahlen, formerly second-in-charge at Jyväskylä and nominally in charge at Tähtiniemi would be the resident officer in charge, and that otherwise the administration would be very much the same as hitherto. It appeared, however, that although Field-Marshal Mannerheim had approved the proposals in principle, he would have preferred the existing arrangements to be continued. Gibson accordingly advised the Foreign Office that if it or Vereker would take full responsibility for placing British civilians under Finnish military control, which transfer Vereker thought was necessary, he would agree, but that Ryder or Ruck-Keene must remain with the contingent. Vereker ignored this, and on 3rd February telegraphed the Foreign Office to say that Ryder, Ruck-Keene and the others had left, and that on his own responsibility he had already placed the volunteers under the control of the Finnish Headquarters Volunteer Office. Two days later Gibson received a telegram from Field-Marshal Mannerheim approving the arrangement.

Ryder left Finland with his companions on 31st January and reached Cairo in mid-February. Here he telegraphed to Gibson to say that he resented being removed from the contingent and that he wanted to come home to report. Through the Foreign Office Gibson sent a message to the British Consul in Cairo, asking him to send Ryder home by the quickest possible route. But instead of seeking an air passage through the British Headquarters in Cairo the consul put Ryder on a light aircraft which flew him to Lagos in West Africa. Here he had to wait nearly two months for a ship, which brought him to Liverpool in the middle of a heavy air-raid, and it was not until 6th May that Ryder reached London.

On reporting to Gibson at the Finnish Aid Bureau Ryder made it quite clear that many of the difficulties and misunderstandings which had arisen were due to the fact that the volunteers had lost confidence in the Bureau and had never had any confidence in the British Legation in Helsinki. The loss of confidence in the Bureau was largely the result of bad communications, since, as we have seen, some of Gibson's letters and telegrams never reached the contingent. Other messages which the contingent had received were in a form different from the original, and there was no satisfactory explanation as to how this had occurred. Those that were sent via the Foreign Office and the British Legation in Helsinki were being delayed and garbled, and were passing into hands other than those for whom they were intended. Similarly, many of Lieut. Count von der Pahlen's communications sent through British channels had never reached Gibson.

From all that Ryder told him, Gibson concluded that in fairness to the volunteers, and for the future smooth working within the contingent, it was essential to send each member a full explanation of all the difficulties which troubled them. At Ryder's suggestion he sent a long letter to Lieut. Count von der Pahlen, with instructions to give every man a copy. It was dated 26th May, but did not reach its recipients until July, in Sweden, as it, too, was held up at the British Legation in Helsinki, which took exception to one paragraph, as noted below.

Stressing that the Prime Minister was much concerned about the repatriation of the volunteers, Gibson's letter stated that the Foreign Office, the Admiralty and the War Office had done all they possibly could do, and that the Finnish Aid Bureau had seized on every possible chance and tried it to the utmost. At first the Bureau had hoped to get the contingent home by sea, subject to life-saving apparatus being available. There was no truth in the story that a ship had been chartered and later cancelled because of the expense. Sea trips had been frustrated through enemy action, and plans to repatriate the volunteers in civilian aircraft "had to be abandoned", though the necessary pilots had been found. An exchange scheme with the Germans had failed because the numbers could not be balanced. "Of the Russian transit visa scheme you know and I need not say anything about it except to assure you that the British Minister in Helsinki has done and is still doing all that possibly can be done to obtain visas." The order in which visas were applied for was determined by the British Minister, who was guided by each man's qualifications. No volunteer should think of going to Russia without a visa, and nothing should be done which would injure Finnish neutrality or Finnish interests. But whereas Gibson's advice was good, his information was quite clearly wrong, for Vereker was not seeking visas.

As regards officers, Gibson continued, if the armistice had not been signed Colonel Roosevelt would have arrived in Finland, together with "seven regular officers of first-class ability, a second-in-command, an adjutant, four company commanders and a quartermaster." These were the men who were to have trained and led the unit, with the assistance of officers and NCOs to be selected from the unit. News of General Winter's illness did not reach the Bureau in London until several (actually two) weeks later, when General Enckell telegraphed Gibson asking him to appoint Chandor as commander. This Gibson accepted, because he knew that Chandor had served with distinction in the first World War, had commanded a Bombing School for two years, and had the recommendation of Field-Marshal the Earl of Cavan.

The most interesting and revealing paragraph, and the one which the British Legation in Helsinki insisted be deleted before copies of the letter were circulated to the volunteers, read: "I hear that there is a feeling among you that your officers have got away themselves and left you in the lurch. In fairness to Chandor and Ryder I must tell you that they were taken away from the unit by the British Authorities in Helsinki, against their own wishes. I cabled instructions to the British Legation in Helsinki to the effect that Ryder should remain until the last, but my instructions were not followed, and Ryder left under protest." This was an accurate statement – Ryder himself has confirmed it – and had it been made public the results for Vereker and Somers Cocks would have been disastrous. The reason that the British Legation in Helsinki ordered the deletion of the paragraph in question was that Vereker had already told the Foreign Office in London that Ryder was prepared to stay if he, Vereker, instructed him categorically to do so, but that as the unit was under Finnish administration it would no longer be possible for Ryder to return to it. Furthermore, as Ryder was "thirty-seven years old and not physically robust", Vereker had not felt justified in preventing his departure. Yet Ryder lived to the age of eighty-three.

As a consolation to those still in Finland, Gibson added that most of the men who had come back home had been commissioned in the Forces, "so they cannot be as hopeless as some of you thought." The physically unfit men sent out had been intended for duties at the base, which they were fully competent to perform; and hundreds of others had been rejected on medical grounds.

Ryder mentioned to Gibson the resentment which he in common with all the volunteers felt when someone in Finland (probably a British diplomat) referred to the contingent as "a lot of jail-birds". On hearing this Gibson immediately sent an indignant protest to the Foreign Office, the War Office, and the British Legation in Helsinki. It was true that one or two had been guilty of some minor offence years ago, but Gibson had refused to enlist anyone with a seriously bad record. "Indeed, some of the interviewing officers thought I was too strict, and used to remind me that I was sending out fighting men, and not a Sunday School class." Six volunteers, or under 2 2/3% of the total had criminal records for such minor offences as bigamy, petty larceny and false pretences, and the two cases of theft which had led to prison sentences. Details of one theft were passed in confidence to the Finnish police, who were investigating a burglary.

Within six days of the Headquarters Volunteer Office taking over the administration of the contingent the ever-efficient Captain Nordlund provided a list of all the men who had come under his supervision. It was already evident that the new arrangements were working well; Lieut. Count von der Pahlen was popular among the volunteers and did much to improve the conditions of life at Tähtiniemi. He was, in fact, so popular that Ford and Millington-Hogg exchanged his office door with that of the Tähtiniemi lavatory. The Count took it as a good joke. Another result of the change was that for the first time Gibson was able to say that his communications were being answered promptly and fully, though that was because they were reaching him through Finnish diplomatic channels.

On 21st February 1941 the London *Evening News* reported that efforts were being made to get transit visas through Russia for 129 volunteers in Finland. *The Daily Telegraph* added that about 130 of the British volunteers who went to fight for Finland against Russia and who became prisoners when the Finns were overwhelmed were still detained in Finland. Efforts were being made to secure their repatriation, and most of those who became prisoners had returned home following negotiations. Gibson's denial of these reports appeared in the latter paper six days later. He stated that they had conveyed an entirely wrong impression, "especially to the relatives of the British volunteers who are still in Finland and the English people who still feel an affectionate admiration for the Finnish people." Except via Russia, for which only fifteen volunteers had obtained visas, there was no present safe exit for the volunteers still in Finland, who were not, and never had been, "prisoners". Since demobilisation in May the previous year they had settled down to live in Finland until they could be repatriated, and despite the language difficulty many of them had found employment.

Gibson found that Vereker took a very long time indeed to answer specific enquiries, and repeated requests for information about the volunteers' health, whereabouts and employment after demobilisation were not even granted the courtesy of an acknowledgement. Much of the information Vereker sent Gibson of his own accord was inaccurate, and Gibson imagined that he relied too much on Major Magill and Captain Cope, neither of whom were likely to get accurate information. So in May 1941 he wrote to S.G.

Allchin at the Foreign Office, asking him to obtain the information sought. Allchin immediately telegraphed Vereker, on 10th May, and eleven days later Vereker forwarded a list prepared at the Headquarters Volunteer Office, containing all the information required.

Somewhat surprisingly, at the end of May Somers Cocks, who had had some correspondence on the subject with Captain Nordlund, wrote to say that the German government had agreed to the repatriation of fifteen named volunteers, who were unfit for military service. How they had been selected is by no means clear, but the choice, on paper, was a good one. As luck would have it, the increasing German activity in transporting troops and equipment through and into Finland and the departure of the contingent for Sweden rendered these arrangements abortive. None of those on the list were told of its existence, and they accompanied the rest of the contingent to Sweden at the end of June. However, it is worth noting that one volunteer on the list, who joined the homebound Legation party from Helsinki, subsequently obtained a commission in the R.A.F., that another, who was repatriated on the diplomatic plane from Stockholm, became a rear-gunner in the same service, and that a third, an Irishman, saw service in the army in France after D-Day.

In June 1941 Sir Stafford Cripps, still British Ambassador in Moscow, came to London. Gibson approached him through the Foreign Office to discuss the question of Russian transit visas. Sir Stafford had been trying to get them for a long time, but again took up the matter with the Soviet authorities on his return to Moscow. Unfortunately the visas arrived in Finland too late for them to be exercised, as the Russian frontier with Finland had already been closed. No-one thought of sending the contingent to Russia via Sweden. However, while the volunteers were being collected together at Tähtiniemi Vereker applied to the Swedish Legation in Helsinki for entry permits into Sweden for 119 volunteers and eight volunteer firemen, and on 25th June received a reply that entry permits for the 127 had been granted.

Having got rid of any responsibility it might have felt for the volunteers, the British Legation in Helsinki took steps to record its afterthoughts. In July a letter with the typewritten signature "Chancery" (which indicated that Somers Cocks was its author) was sent to the Northern Department of the Foreign Office. It stated that the policy of the Legation in fixing the priority for the departure of the volunteers via Russia was their potential utility to the British war effort and *not* their utility to the contingent. How their potential was decided we may never know, but there are three possibilities. One is that Vereker was using a list obligingly provided by Gibson in the summer of 1940. Another is that one of Vereker's staff had gone through the box of files from Tähtiniemi which was deposited at the Legation for safe-keeping in January 1941 when the Headquarters Volunteer Office took over the administration of the contingent, which papers have since been lost. The third and most likely possibility is that the choice was made from Vereker's own knowledge and from the few application forms filled in at Tähtiniemi after being distributed to some selected volunteers but not to the whole contingent. None of these three possibilities would give an up-to-date picture of each man's capabilities, particularly as regards his educational and professional qualifications and his proficiency in languages. Whichever solution is right, the writing of the "Chancery" letter shows that Vereker and Somers Cocks were well aware that they were not carrying out Foreign Office instructions to apply for Russian visas for all the volunteers, only four of whom obtained them on the Legation's initiative, and that they were anxious to protect themselves against having to reply to uncomfortable questions to which an honest answer would be incriminating.

This being so, any account of the attempts to repatriate the volunteers would be incomplete without a summary of the extraordinary conduct of Vereker in his capacity of British Minister in Helsinki. An Old Etonian like Major Magill, whom he had known since the latter's boyhood, he had served in the Grenadier Guards in the first World War and shared Major Magill's dislike of the volunteers. Former members of Vereker's staff describe him as a charming and well-educated person; but the volunteers found him an unpleasant pompous bully. Before he came to Helsinki at the end of February 1940 he had been Counsellor at the British Embassy in Moscow for a couple of years, before which he had been First Secretary at the British Legation in Stockholm, in 1937-38. He was first of all responsible for replacing the original volunteer unit's commanding officer, adjutant and sergeant-major, without authority. Later, while employing volunteers at his Legation, he interfered in the contingent's pay arrangements, and deprived it of its new commander, its accountant and its store-keeper, the three men responsible for its administration, all without prior reference to or authority from Gibson. This left the way clear for him to ask the Finnish military authorities, at very short notice, to take over the running of the contingent, and successfully removed the risk of having a hundred and twenty distressed British subjects on his hands.

As Head of Mission Vereker exercised absolute control over the messages from the Finnish Aid Bureau to the contingent. These had to be sent as official messages through the Foreign Office and his Legation. As we have seen, under his authority, his Legation mishandled messages from London to the contingent and vice versa. His staff distinguished themselves for boorish behaviour; on one occasion Somers Cocks so incensed Smith M.L. that the latter gave him a black eye. Taylor H., who visited the Legation several times on contingent business as the head of the Disciplinary Committee and spokesman for the volunteers at Tähtiniemi, noted in his diary that his receptions there had been anything but friendly, and that Somers Cocks and other diplomats had treated him with a marked lack of courtesy. When, for instance, he telephoned the Legation in mid-December 1940 he was told that all the diplomatic staff were out except the Minister, who was furious at being called. He also noted early in June 1941 that when he finally managed to get a personal interview with Vereker the latter forbade him to discuss the question of transit visas for Russia with Field-Marshal Mannerheim, with whom Taylor

H. also had an appointment. And in public members of the Legation staff snubbed Gooderham, who had succeeded Ryder as clerk and accountant at Tähtiniemi, while Ryder was once prevented by force from entering the Legation. Undaunted, he went to see Hugh Sladen at Salvation Army Headquarters, who gave him an introduction to Mrs Tudeer, who in turn gave him an introduction direct to Vereker and enabled Ryder to avoid any further unpleasantness.

In defence of Vereker it should be remembered that he was one of many Ministers chosen more for their social background (he was the younger brother of Lord Gort) than for their knowledge of Finland, or, indeed of world affairs and of his fellow-countrymen. Lacking channels through which he could obtain accurate information about the volunteers, he had to rely on his staff, who seem to have shared his propensity for presenting opinions as facts. As an example of the misinformation fed to him in May 1940, he wrote: "In view of the notoriously bad state of discipline in the British unit, I am apprehensive lest . . . many more of them may desert and become distressed British subjects, or otherwise a source of yet further embarrassment to the Finnish military authorities, who yesterday reported to General Enckell, head of the Volunteer Bureau of the Finnish General Staff, that discipline among the British volunteers is so bad that they fear serious disorders unless the whole contingent is disbanded immediately." Had such developments actually taken place Lieut. Stig Brunow would have reported them; and it seems likely that Vereker's information was based on nothing more than a report of the pro-German Ari Kauhanen, already mentioned.

The news of the conduct of Vereker and his staff soon leaked out, and it is little wonder that Finns, both officials and private citizens, started asking the volunteers (the writer included) uncomfortable questions about this foreign envoy who was so openly hostile to his fellow-countrymen. Vereker himself had the reputation of being ignorant of Finnish conditions, such as the existence of two official languages, Finnish and Swedish, and had very little contact with the Finns, whose capital city he always referred to as

Helsingfors (the Swedish for Helsinki). He seems to have had little contact with his subordinates, too, or influence over them, and was unaware of the conduct of some of his diplomatic staff towards the volunteers until Dr Herford (and Gibson before him) obligingly put him in the picture early in December 1940. But he did nothing to put things right. Vereker, however, should not be seen in isolation, for he was one of numerous second-rate officials sent to Finland, a country which the Foreign Office seems to have regarded at the time as of little importance, despite its then reputation as a centre for international espionage. His predecessor Snow, for instance, was recalled to London in disgrace just after the outbreak of the Winter War, and Sir Andrew Noble, one of his post-war successors, was so arrogant, so incompetent and so unpopular that, to use a Foreign Office expression, he was remembered in the prayers of his staff. As might be expected, one or two good Ministers were appointed, notably Sir Oswald Scott, but it was not until the post-war reforms in the Foreign Office bore fruit that Britain's representatives in Finland were consistently of a standard which both countries deserved.

Gibson drafted the second and final section of his Report in September 1941. Taking the kindest view that he could, for he knew that it would be read in the Foreign Office, he wrote that he thought that the lack of confidence in the British authorities in Finland on the part of the volunteers was due to the fact that the attitude of the British Minister in Helsinki and of his Military Attaché was "we can do nothing for you because you came out here to fight the Russians, with whom the British government are in friendly relations." But that friendly relationship did not develop until some time after the German attack on her Soviet Russian ally in June 1941. During the Winter War, as Gibson would have known, Maisky, the Soviet ambassador in London, was ignored in diplomatic circles and was barely persona grata at the Foreign Office. More remarkable is the fact that the Legation's hostility towards the volunteers continued during the period when it knew that discussions were taking place between the Foreign Office and the

Finnish Aid Bureau prior to the former taking over the responsibilities of the latter. That hostility continued after the volunteers had left Finland, satisfied in their own minds that the Legation in Helsinki had done its very best to avoid its responsibilities towards them. With the benefit of hindsight readers may be forgiven if, in the context of the nineteen-eighties, they conclude that Vereker's actions were those of a weak man whose sympathies lay more with the Russians than with his own countrymen, and that his policy towards the volunteers did not have the approval of the Foreign Office.

What of Anglo-Finnish relations at this time? We have seen that the British government's warning to Finland not to co-operate militarily with the Germans was to announce a blockade of Petsamo in June 1941. How this was managed with the Germans in effectual control of the Norwegian and Finnish arctic coasts is not clear. The Finnish government replied by requesting the withdrawal of the British "consular agents" from the northern part of the country, six of whom, and possibly more, were former volunteers. A month later, when it had become evident that Finland had joined in the attack on Soviet Russia, with a view to re-occupying the territories ceded after the Winter War, the question arose as to the continuation of normal diplomatic relations between Finland and Britain. In a letter dated 19th July to President Ryti Hitler demanded that in order to prevent espionage in Finland for Russia's benefit Finland must break off relations with Britain. On 20th July the Finnish cabinet passed the matter to the Foreign Minister, Witting, with instructions either to discontinue British commercial and military representation in Finland, or, if the situation demanded it, to stop their "detrimental activities."

In dealing with the matter in this way the Finnish government was evidently trying to conceal its embarrassment at having to treat an old and valued friend in such a manner, for Britain was second after France among the great powers to recognise the newly-emergent Republic of Finland after the War of Independence of 1917-18. As Vereker did not want to close his Legation, Witting waited until a week had passed and then informed him that as Germany's fellow-fighter (this is a literal translation of the Finnish word used officially) Finland found it difficult to maintain diplomatic relations with Britain. For this reason she intended to close her Legation in London for the time being, anticipating that Vereker would take similar steps in Helsinki. Vereker passed the message on to the Foreign Office. The British government replied on 1st August that the fulfilment of Finland's intentions compelled it to recall its Legation from Helsinki, and the formal breaking-off of diplomatic relations between the two countries followed immediately afterwards. But on 4th August, when Germany invited Finland to join the Axis or Rome-Berlin-Tokyo Agreement, the Finnish government stoutly rejected the offer.

Before we leave Finland a few special words of thanks are due to the Finnish General Staff, who rightly anticipated that after the armistice it would take a little time before the last of the foreign volunteers could be repatriated and their affairs be wound up. The Headquarters Volunteer Office therefore continued its existence after hostilities had ceased, and until September 1940, when the last Finnish-American volunteers had left through Petsamo, there was an American-Finnish Demobilisation Office in Helsinki. The Headquarters Volunteer Office, which dealt with foreigners of other nationalities had two other addresses before settling down at Kasarminkatu 28, 3rd floor, in July 1940. Here Captain Nordlund was assisted during the autumn by a former American volunteer named W. Sullivan who for a short time had been attached to the British contingent in Jyväskylä at 10 marks a day. Corporal A. Clemström, a Finn, succeeded him in the early winter.

Captain Nordlund's office was conveniently situated within a minute's walk of the Headquarters of the Finnish General Staff, and, with customary Finnish thoroughness, looked after the interests of the volunteers of all nationalities remaining in Finland. As far as the British were concerned, it looked after them in much the same way as a British consulate in a foreign country would have looked after British subjects in normal times. Captain Nordlund became a guide, philosopher and friend to the numerous volunteers who called on him, and during the autumn of 1940 issued a formation badge to each one as a souvenir of his service. If the volunteer had been in uniform, the badge would have been worn on the left-hand pocket of the battle-dress blouse, but as they were civilians it was worn on ski or sports jackets. Shaped in the form of a cross, with a green border, it was made of copper, and bore in its centre the black, white and orange Osasto Sisu formation sign, which contained a large letter *S* and the word Sisu. Around this was a chain of 26 links, representing each of the nations which had sent volunteers to Finland, and in the bars of the cross were the year, 19 – 40, and the letters D – E, standing for Détachement Étranger. The badges were made in Helsinki by Veljekset Sundquist, but to whose order and at whose cost it had not been possible to ascertain, since the manufacturers lost their records in a fire in 1944. Enquiries in Helsinki have shown that neither the General Staff, the War Museum, nor the War Archives, have any record of the badge, whilst one of the country's leading authorities on military insignia confessed himself baffled, as until 1981, when the writer visited him, he had never seen one. As the badges were only issued to the volunteers left in Finland in the autumn of 1940 it is likely that only about 150 were made, and that they were made privately to Captain Nordlund's order. Had they been made on the instructions of Field-Marshal Mannerheim or of any senior-ranking officer their history would undoubtedly have been recorded. Captain (later Major) Nordlund was a modest man; and Osasto Sisu was his particular "baby".

After orders had gone out summoning the British volunteers to Tähtiniemi prior to their departure for Sweden there was no further need for the Headquarters Volunteer Office, and on 23rd June Lieut. Kaj J. Warras, now Captain Nordlund's assistant, wrote to Somers Cocks at the British Legation, to say that the Office was closing on that day, and to enclose receipts totalling 8,037.65 marks, the cost of repatriating Butt and Nightingale, who had stowed away aboard the s/s *Delaware* at Petsamo the previous summer.

Back in London, meanwhile, the staff of the Finnish Aid Bureau had been rapidly reduced after the armistice, and by 20th April 1940 it consisted only of Gibson, Edmunds (who was now both paymaster and accountant), and a secretary. The latter left, and her replacement was a junior clerk whose salary was paid by Price & Pierce Limited. Thorney House suffered bomb damage on several occasions during the summer, until at last, on 31st October, the damage was so serious that it became necessary to vacate the building. The skeleton staff still remaining was transferred to Flat 16, Marsham Court, S.W.1., and moved in on 18th November. As the office was immediately opposite the temporary Finnish Legation, the Legation also having suffered a bomb in the first week of September, liaison was made easy, and overheads were saved amounting to £250 per annum.

The possibility of transferring the work of the Bureau to the Foreign Office was discussed at a Committee meeting on 20th November 1940, Amery having both made the proposal and suggested that it should be subject to Lord Nuffield's agreement. Lord Nuffield concurred, and Gibson prepared a memorandum stating the case. However, as Anthony (later Sir Anthony) Eden, the Foreign Secretary, was about to leave for the Middle East, he instructed his officials to deal with the matter. Unfortunately those officials had no concept of time, and discussions continued at a leisurely pace until the end of February 1941. Then Gibson became impatient, and sought an interview with R.A. (later Lord) Butler, Eden's deputy. Early in March the Foreign Office stated that if the British government was to take over the responsibility for the volunteers, it thought that the Treasury would insist on their being treated as distressed British subjects. Gibson pointed out that in the opinion of the Committee it would be unfair to treat the volunteers in that way, and stressed that it would mean that they would lose the very considerable help in lodging, food and pocket-money which the Finnish government was generously providing, and also the extra food, clothing and pocket-money which the Bureau gave, because no distressed British subject would be allowed to receive such help.

Finally, at the end of March 1941, Butler agreed to see Gibson and Needham. He promised to discuss the matter with the Treasury, and at the end of April the Chancellor of the Exchequer agreed in principle that the Treasury should take over part of the Bureau's financial liability. He suggested that a basis of settlement should be worked out by representatives of the Treasury, the Foreign Office, and the Bureau, and be submitted for approval. Three days later the parties met and agreed that the details of a clear-cut settlement should be worked out when the British government had agreed to assume responsibility. It was further agreed that the volunteers should not become distressed British subjects, but that they should be maintained at their existing standard of living. It was also agreed to inform the British Ministers in Helsinki and Stockholm (this was done early in April), and that all concerned should work with a view to the Foreign Office taking over from the Bureau on 30th June, and ten days later the Foreign Office took over. The maintenance and repatriation of the volunteers then became the responsibility of the British government. For the Foreign Office it was a happy coincidence that the volunteers were on their way from Finland to Sweden on the day it took over.

There was still the matter of the credits which had been building up in London during the volunteers' absence. With Lord Balfour's assistance Gibson arranged with the District Bank to hold the balances, a liability which the Treasury could not very well have undertaken to discharge. The Bank agreed to act as Trustee for the money, and opened an account for each man. On returning to London each volunteer had to report to the Foreign Office to collect a note of identification to present to the Bank, on which the Bank paid out the balance due.

The final closure of the Bureau took place on 16th July, when Gibson handed over to the Foreign Office the personal files of the 166 volunteers still overseas. Of this number 116 were in Malung in Sweden, 13 were interned in Germany, 3 had disappeared in Russia, two had disappeared in Sweden, and the remaining 32 included those either employed at the British Legations in Helsinki and Stockholm, or were in camps or institutions in Sweden away from the contingent. The closure of the Bureau neatly absolved Gibson and his colleagues from having to account personally to the Finnish authorities, or to any volunteer for the sums standing to his credit at the District Bank, or for any other sums or legal liabilities.

The work of the Bureau in London, Finland and Sweden was paid for out of gifts amounting to £6,414, which were received in February and March 1940, and from Gripenberg's special fighting fund, which may also have received assistance from the Finnish government. When Gibson's fund was exhausted Gripenberg made grants to him from time to time, amounting in all to £16,500. These combined sums were sufficient to pay the Bureau's expenses in London, all current expenses, and the Bureau's share of the maintenance of the contingent in Finland, which came to £100 per week. However, bills for the equipment supplied from War Office sources, totalling £4,283, were not settled until the terms of the transfer of the work of the Bureau to the Foreign Office had been agreed. At this time it was possible to estimate fairly accurately the amount required from Lord Nuffield's guarantee to balance the accounts. Gibson asked Lord Nuffield for £14,000, which was the maximum sum that would be needed, and agreed to refund any surplus remaining after the liabilities had been settled.

Gibson's Report makes no mention of the immense expenses which the Finnish tax-payer bore on account of the volunteers, since he had no means of ascertaining their size. As we have seen, between March 1940 and the summer of 1942 these included accommodation and food, and from February to June 1941 pocket-money as well. There was also half the medical expenses (the Finnish Aid Bureau paid the other half), which included treatment at the military hospital in Helsinki for a number of volunteers, and the expenses of keeping four volunteers at the Central Gaol in Helsinki in protective custody. The total of these sums may never be known, but it was undoubtedly large, since, even by modern standards and after allowing for over forty years of inflation, the amounts collected in Britain through public and voluntary appeals and paid to the Finnish Aid Bureau, were relatively modest. That Gibson was nevertheless aware of the Finnish contribution is shown in a comment in the second part of his Report:

"One of the outstanding features of the whole adventure is the completeness with which the Finnish government has fulfilled its part of the original agreement and the generosity with which it has at all times treated the volunteers."

SWEDEN AND HOME:

Malung and Filipstad

We now rejoin the volunteers, whom we left in the train in Sweden. After nearly three days in transit the 127-man party arrived on 1st July at Grimsåker Halt, Malung, in Dalarna, about 200 miles north-west of Stockholm. The halt was only a few hundred yards from the contingent's new quarters in the old building of the People's High School, which lay not far from the church and south-east of the town. It settled in without incident. Reporting a few days later to Captain Nordlund, Count von der Pahlen wrote that the behaviour of the party, and its discipline during the journey, had been exemplary: the train had stopped at nearly every station in Sweden opposite trains carrying German troops in the opposite direction.

E.M. Nielsen, until 20th June British Consul at Petsamo, was serving at the British Legation Consular Department in Stockholm on 4th July, when he prepared a report on the camp at Malung for the volunteers from Finland. He probably saw the place before the volunteers arrived, for he only recorded sleeping capacity for 117 men. However, he noted that the People's High School was a wooden building of three storeys, which had been used to house Norwegian civilian refugees the previous year. On the ground floor were two dining-rooms capable of taking all the men at one sitting, a large kitchen, two rooms taking a total of 13 men, and rooms for use as a sick-bay and for recreation. On the first floor were two large rooms holding thirty men each, two smaller rooms for ten each, and a recreation room. On the top floor were two smaller rooms holding six and and eight men. Beds and double-decker bunks were installed before the contingent arrived, and there were washing facilities and a sauna in the new building across the road. On the subject of camp administration Nielsen, repeating what the British Legation in Helsinki had told him, stated that there was no suitable candidate within the ranks of the contingent for the post of commandant. This statement was simply not true, for there were several, some of whom were ex-officers, including Kenworthy, Lace, Scott A.H.W., Grant, Reynolds (who had come over to Stockholm some months earlier), and Taylor H., all of whom enjoyed the volunteers' respect.

Nielsen's report contained an alphabetical list giving each volunteer's name, home address, and personal details, including those of one allegedly born in 1930. There was a separate list of volunteers who had reported to the British Consulate in Stockholm, who were described as self-supporting. They included six former Ministry of Economic Warfare Inspectors, in Finland known as "consular agents", Barton, Burch, Carrick, Dixon R., Kilgour and Lyons, and six others who had been employed at the British Legation in Helsinki and who, with the exception of Prince, were given jobs at the Legation in Stockholm: Hopkinson T.G., Pershke, Rankin, Reynolds and Seyler. Rolf August Hellenius, born in Finland and a naturalised Canadian, who had been British Vice-Consul in Rovaniemi (he was selected in preference to Howard), was also on the list. Jones S., a member of the party which left Lapua on 23rd March 1940, later obtained the post of doorkeeper at the Legation, and held the job for a quarter of a century.

The fact that the volunteers were now under the general supervision of the British Consul in Stockholm, who had been given the job of attending to their board, lodging, clothing and general welfare, was not apparent, and the only noticeable change in their way of life was a payment of five kronor or a little over five shillings, pending arrangements for weekly pocket-money of four kronor. With the help of Seth Andersson, the chief of the local fire-brigade and the representative of the Swedish Evacuation Commission (*Utrymningskommission*), Count von der Pahlen continued to manage the contingent's day-to-day affairs just as he had in Finland. For the first fortnight the volunteers were in quarantine, and the area around the school was put out of bounds to the local population, while the volunteers were forbidden to visit the town. Notices were put up near the buildings to the effect that they were out of bounds, but, owing to the vagaries of the Swedish language (the notices said *Fridlyst Område,* Protected Area), they suggested that something rare was being preserved. Perhaps it was!

During the period of quarantine permission was given to the volunteers to bathe in the nearby *Västra Dalälven* or West Valley river. The path to the river lay from the school, over the railway-line at the halt, across the end of a field of potatoes, and past the church to the bathing-place on the sandy bank on a bend in the river. On going past the field one day a party of volunteers found a shapely young lady in a bathing-dress weeding the potatoes. Several tried to speak to her in the rudimentary Swedish they had picked up in Finland, but it soon became apparent that she spoke some English, and she became known as The Potato Queen. The writer believes her name was Åsa. The bathing-place was also out of bounds to the locals, who promptly dubbed it *Den brittiska kysten* (the British coast).

The volunteers lost no time in settling down in their new surroundings, and in getting themselves organised. One outbuilding served as the contingent's office and another next to it became the sick-bay, where Law and Glyn continued to provide medical attention. The old village lock-up nearby was sometimes used to house recalcitrants and to store personal property, and its key was kept in the office, where Gooderham continued to act as clerk and typist and Roberts as storekeeper (and later as paymaster). Apostolides was interpreter, and spoke Swedish with a strong Vaasa accent, to the great amusement of visitors to the camp. Nicholls and Pooke started a laundry in the basement of the new school building, the upper part of which was out of bounds to the volunteers, and in the next room Martin opened a barber's shop. Bradley ran the canteen in the old building, and McKibbin R. offered a service massaging stiff joints. And for those interested in learning

Swedish, or improving their knowledge of it, Gilkison, the head of the volunteer firemen, ran informal open-air classes. Meanwhile, many volunteers, few of whom had acquired more than a smattering of Finnish, wanted to let their friends in Finland know where they were, and a brisk demand arose for someone who could translate their letters into Finnish and the replies into English. The two with the best qualification, Kuss and Brooke, realising that they had a monopoly, agreed to make a standard charge of one krona per letter translated, irrespective of length or language. To their credit it should be recorded that they never compared cases or broke confidences, though they occasionally sought each other's guidance over dialect phrases and borrowed each other's dictionaries. One of the most energetic letter-writers was Smith S.G.R., whose wedding to a Finnish girl had been put off on account of his sudden departure for Sweden, and who used each translator in turn. Thanks to their joint efforts his fiancée was able to join him in Malung, where they were married early in December.

A few days after the train carrying the contingent to Malung had passed through the rail junction at Krylbo, near Ludvika (where Captain Blew-Jones' draft had had supper on 16th March 1940), an ammunition train blew up there. Whether the train was German or Swedish was not stated in the Swedish wireless news bulletin, but just to make sure that the British were in the clear a couple of policemen called at the People's High School a day or two after the incident and had a long chat with Count von der Pahlen, who assured them that none of his boys had as much as got out of the train anywhere near the scene of the explosion.

A pleasant surprise in the week after the volunteers arrived in Malung was the announcement that arrangements had been made for them to transfer their bank balances from Finland and to convert them into Swedish kronor. Members of the contingent had also brought some 200,000 marks, some £900, in Finnish notes with them, and these, too, were converted into kronor, despite Finland's desperate shortage of foreign currency. Both exchanges were made thanks to Captain Nordlund having made an application to the Bank of Finland at the appropriate time.

During July four of the remaining seventeen members of the party which had left Lapua in March 1940, and who were still awaiting repatriation, rejoined the contingent. These were Dunne, Jones W.C., Green W., and Le Mee-Power. About the same time Asling, Davey, Neumark, McKay, Taylor H.S. and Rattigan arrived from Finland and Prince from Stockholm.

A book of punishments was kept in the camp office, and showed that between 24th July and 8th August 22 men were disciplined for minor breaches of camp rules, such as staying out after hours or causing a disturbance. Punishments varied from two to five days helping in the kitchen to chopping firewood. Only one serious incident occurred, if serious it can be called, on 24th July, when nine men were recorded as having caused a disturbance late in the evening. Whether this was due to drink or high spirits was not stated, but it was just as much a reflection of the informal nature of the administration as it was on the "trouble-makers", whom the Swedish Foreign Office thought were the cause of it. Suffice it to say that punishments fell off rapidly in number, and that after mid-August no further entries were made in the book.

It did not take the Germans long to discover that the volunteers were on their way to Sweden. On 28th June, following representations from the German Minister in Stockholm, the Head of the Political Department of the Swedish Foreign Ministry reported to the Prime Minister that his attention had been called to the fact that many of the volunteers had worked in the British intelligence service while in Finland (a gross exaggeration), and that from the German point of view it was extremely desirable that during their stay in Sweden they should not have the opportunity to continue such activities. He therefore submitted that during the whole of their stay in Sweden they should be interned under secure conditions. As the six who had acted as "consular agents" had been kept separate, and were at the time at the British Legation in Stockholm, there was no need to take the wishes of the Germans too seriously. So four weeks later the Swedish Foreign Ministry informed its Berlin envoy that there were about 130 British volunteers living at Malung, of whom five were living in the town away from the People's High School, and three were temporarily employed at the British Legation in Stockholm.

In the first week of August Vice-Consul Aird came up to Malung from Stockholm to inspect the volunteers' quarters. He told the contingent that residential permits were not being granted for Stockholm or Gothenburg, and reported to his superiors, who passed on the information, that the Swedish authorities had not returned the passports of about a third of the volunteers who had applied for permission to live away from the People's High School. He also recorded that of the contingent of 117 volunteers and seven volunteer firemen, about fifty had already got jobs. Later in the month Captains Grip and Bussler from the Swedish General Staff came to inspect the contingent's quarters and were apparently satisfied as they made no comment.

On 12th August came the sad news that Count von der Pahlen had been called home to Finland. Before his departure the following day he gave each man a bottle of the local beer, and the whole contingent assembled to drink his health. To show their appreciation of his work on their behalf the volunteers made a collection and bought a silver cigarette-box for him as a parting present, which they sent to the Finnish Legation in Stockholm for onward transmission. With it went a letter from Medlicott, saying on behalf of the volunteers how sorry they were that they could not present it in person. "This small gift", he wrote, "carries with it our gratitude for all that you have done for us in the past, and our very best wishes for the future, and will, we hope, be a useful souvenir of your days as our commanding officer."

Count von der Pahlen's replacement, who represented the British Consul in Stockholm, turned out to have been selected with considerable care. He was Frederick A.L. Charlesworth, a Londoner who spoke Swedish as a result of having spent several years as English lecturer at Uppsala university, and who had become nationally known in Sweden for his English by Radio courses. He had a great sense of humour and understood accountancy, and his approach to the volunteers was as informal as that of his predecessor. He took no time at all to slip into the routine of the camp, and kept things going in much the same way as they had been before.

Shortly after Charlesworth's appointment Kamrer Frank, of the Swedish Evacuation Commission, spent two days at Malung inspecting the quarters and acquainting himself with conditions. He found the rooms at the People's High School well-swept and tidy, and the conditions of the accommodation satisfactory. He reported to the Swedish Foreign Ministry, who in turn recommended that the camp be placed under a Swedish superintendent, as Charlesworth was unpopular. The truth of the matter, however, was somewhat different. Because few of the volunteers could understand the finer points of Swedish there was a general distrust of Andersson (whom the writer found to be a pleasant man), but they understood enough to realise that relations between him and Charlesworth had become somewhat strained. This was due to the fact that, despite soap being rationed in Sweden at the time, Andersson knew someone in the local subsidiary of Unilever, the Sunlight Soap company, who produced some unrationed soap for the volunteers. It was a little caustic, and harsh on the skin, but nevertheless welcome. Charlesworth had insisted that he should sign the letter of thanks, as he was Camp Commandant. Andersson thought that *he* should sign it, as he had obtained the gift. Eventually the two men made it up, and worked happily together until early in 1942, when Charlesworth returned to Stockholm to resume teaching.

In London, meanwhile, Gibson recorded that in the fourth week of August the breakdown of volunteers was as follows: In Sweden 147 (including two men at the British Legation in Stockholm), at the British Legation in Helsinki 2, prisoners of war in Germany 13, joined H.M. forces in the Middle East 10, gone to various countries at their own request and discharged from the contingent 10, resident in Haifa 1, missing in Russia 3, dead 1, and returned to England 40, making a total of 227.

When the restrictions on their movements were removed, many of the volunteers enquired about the possibilities of finding work. Unemployment in the district was high at the time, and the only jobs open to foreigners without a special permit, they were told, were in forestry and road-mending. A dozen or so decided to try forestry. The first lumberjacks worked in a forest on a steeply-sloping hillside above the main road about a mile down the valley from the People's High School, and were employed to thin out the forest and to cut the thinnings into poles thirteen feet long. They set to work with a will, those with experience from Finland teaching those without, and in a few days the job was finished. Then it was announced that permission would be granted to forestry workers to live away from the camp, and the group split up. Only two opted for road-mending: Golby and an American seaman named Jesse Curzon McClure, born 23.12.1895, who had been sent to the contingent pending repatriation.

Several of the forestry gang then went to the local employment exchange, where a patient and friendly lady instructed Brooke and Rattigan to report to a local farmer, Hemmansägare Nilsson, of Holarna. He took them to a piece of forest near the hamlet of Backselen, some seven miles from the town, where they spent some weeks cutting and stacking firewood in cubic metres, for each of which they received 3.25 kronor or about 3s. 3d. Mr Nilsson provided a one-room log-cabin with a fireplace and a cooking-pot in one corner, two rough beds, and a table, and the two soon found that by cutting three or four cubic metres a day they had sufficient for the necessities of life and could go to Malung twice a week on hired bicycles to obtain supplies. Taylor H.S. joined them after a week or two, but left early in September, so the two worked on until the end of the month when Rattigan got a job in a Malung factory making fur coats for the Swedish army. After a week or two Brooke returned to the People's High School and got a job splitting firewood at a private house in Malung. Ultimately about forty of the contingent obtained forestry jobs in the district. Some of the most successful had done similar work in Finland and went to work for Mats Döhlmark of Torrberg, Yttermalung. These were Babbs, Lucey, Montague, Smith M.L., Tawell and two others, with Hole as cook. Another party followed the first to Backselen, comprising Bullen, Casey and Dixon A.H.F., with Alexander as cook, while in Arvselen, a little further away from Malung, were Cooper, Humphries and Maund.

For several centuries Malung has been the centre of the Swedish leather industry, and a few volunteers were able to get jobs in the local factories and workshops making leather goods. White, who had picked up a good deal of Swedish while working at the Swedish Theatre in Helsinki, got a job with the local printer (and took part in the town's Spring Revue), and numerous others obtained part-time jobs splitting firewood at various houses in the town.

Two Swedish ladies and a girl assistant ably managed the kitchen at the People's High School, and the volunteers took turns to help them with the washing-up. One day, in seeking a little variety, Mackie offered to help make the pudding, and produced a splendid plum duff. It was a great success, and its weight and solidity earned it the nickname of Stuka Pudding, after the well-known German dive-bomber. Stuka pudding became a regular feature, and on a later occasion Mackie made a batch of it the day a volunteer was discharged from the sick-bay after being on a starvation diet for a week. Determined to make up for lost time he tucked into the Stuka pudding. While on his third helping Lucey, an Irishman of gentle disposition and large appetite, was persuaded to challenge the invalid to an eating contest. As there were plenty to witness the contest, Thompson and Glyn took bets on it, and numerous sums were laid. The ex-patient won, seven helpings to six, and as he was not the favourite the bookies made a large profit and suitably rewarded the winner. The latter admitted afterwards that he had woken up in the middle of the night with the feeling that he had swallowed a sack of cement.

Towards the end of July Asling received the news that his Finnish wife, then awaiting their first child, was to join him in Malung. Not unnaturally, he communicated the news to the ex-sergeants who shared a room with him, and to everyone else. McKay, who was renowned for his horse-play, waited until Asling had gone into Malung to do some shopping, and then turned the ex-sergeants' room into a maternity ward, with a dummy pregnant woman in Asling's bed. Then he dressed himself up as a nurse, holding a bottle in one hand and a spoon in the other, and posed nearby. The volunteers who had cameras were then summoned to the scene to take pictures. What Asling said on his return from Malung is not recorded, perhaps fortunately, though one of the contingent who had met her in Finland was deputed a few days later to welcome the charming Mrs Asling on her arrival at the People's High School. Thompson and Glyn promptly started taking bets on the gender of the Aslings' first-born, who, despite the bulk of the money being placed on a girl, turned out to be a boy. He was christened John Charles Gustav at Malung church early in September.

Like its Helsinki counterpart, the British Legation in Stockholm was some what unhelpful to the volunteers, though it was not openly hostile, and its mistakes were largely errors of judgement which arose through following Vereker's advice. In mid-August the first party of six whom it selected for repatriation by the diplomatic plane left for Stockholm, and a short while later a further ten left. The choice was unfortunate, to say the least, for after the departure of the second party several months went by before any more left for home. This was widely thought to be due to the authorities in London believing that the rest of the volunteers were equally unsuitable for military service. The two parties included, for instance, the volunteer with the artificial leg, two elderly volunteers one of whose "nerve was shattered" (but who had an aristocratic background), and one with a stiff leg. At best only two had pilots' licenses and were in any way suitable for active service, as was the qualified engineer who accompanied them and who ended the war running a factory in Bristol.

On Saturday 6th September Humphries and Maund got on their bicycles and rode away from Arvselen, about eight miles from Malung. Where they went to nobody knows, but as Humphries had earlier made no secret of his desire to go to Norway and steal a boat in which to sail home, it seems possible that Norway was their next stop. The news of their disappearance reached the Swedish Foreign Ministry on 10th September, and the official Swedish view, as noted in various documents, was that they had disappeared from their place of work and had presumably gone to Norway. Rumours current in the People's High School, where Humphries had been seen some time earlier cleaning an automatic pistol, suggested that a Norwegian had joined or even led the two missing volunteers, and had promised to act as their guide. Where they went to is shrouded in mystery, since the Norwegian authorities and organisations whom the writer has approached have no traces of them. They were presumed dead many years ago, and their families collected the sums standing to their credit in London.

Meanwhile, in Finland the Germans refused safe conduct from Sweden by air to the staff of the British Legation in Helsinki. In the middle of August, however, they granted permission for the party to travel in a special train through Germany, France and Spain to neutral Portugal. On 18th August the *Daily Telegraph* reported that travel arrangements had been made, and that Consul Bell, "probably the most influential Englishman in Scandinavia", would accompany the party. He did. On 8th September the party, which had arrived in Sweden a day or two earlier, departed from Kalmar for Lübeck in the Finnish s/s *Oihonna*. From there the train took them through Germany as agreed, and on to Lisbon. The diplomatic staff and their families were repatriated immediately, but the others were delayed in Lisbon as distressed British subjects, and did not reach home until just before Christmas. A number of volunteers who had worked for the British Legation and the British Council in Finland were included, as well as three of the fifteen volunteers whom it had been agreed with the

Germans in May were unfit for military service. It is a sad reflection that had someone told Humphries and Maund, who disappeared only two days before the ship sailed from Kalmar, they, too, might have been repatriated with the Legation party, since the former was one of the fifteen unfit volunteers and the latter had worked for the British Council. The reason the other eleven unfit men were not taken is not clear, but it seems likely that the size of the party was limited by the accommodation on board ship, and that the independent English teachers from Helsinki, who lacked any special status, took their berths. The volunteers in the Legation party were: the six "consular agents", Apostolides, Babbs, Evans S.H., Grant, Mallowan, Medlicott, Neumark, Punshon, Pryse, Seyler, Sherry, Taylor H.S. with his Finnish wife, the British Vice-Consul in Oulu, Trevor Cash, and possibly Phillips and Stead. Three firemen, Bramwell, Cory and Tatchell, were also in the party. While waiting in Lisbon Sherry met with an accident with a Portuguese gas water-heater, but recovered sufficiently in time to return home with the others, albeit partially incapacitated.

In September the senior partner of Theodore Goddard & Company, the London solicitors, approached the Foreign Office on behalf of Mrs Woodburn, whose husband was a volunteer. As his contact in the Foreign Office was a Parliamentary Secretary who wielded considerable influence his client was granted the privilege of sending one postcard a month to her husband through the diplomatic bag, and Woodburn, then working as a lumberjack, was granted the same facility. Correspondence showed the interesting fact that repatriation by air had been explored on behalf of the Foreign Office as early as January 1941, and that in October there was "some ground for hoping that it may be possible to get the men home gradually by air", using the diplomatic plane from Stockholm.

In the third week of October it was announced that the People's High School was needed for the winter term, and so on the 20th of the month, in pouring rain, the contingent left by train. Fresh quarters had been found in Filipstad in Värmland, about a hundred miles to the south as the crow flies but much further by train, a town whose prosperity in past centuries had been based on iron mining and smelting. Its interests now lay in engineering and in factories producing a wide range of products from ink to rye-biscuits, and there was (and still is) an old-established and flourishing School of Mines and a working mine as well.

At Filipstad buses took the contingent out to Kalhyttan, an old wooden building dating from the last century, which took its name from an ironworks. It lay a little over a kilometre west of the town on the Karlstad road, at the foot of a low range of hills. Some years earlier the Swedish Society for the Promotion of Skiing (*Skidfrämjandet*) had bought the building and turned it into a compact and slightly austere guest-house. Single-storey dormitory blocks erected behind the main building formed three sides of a square, and were allotted to the volunteers. While they were in residence the lady manager, Miss Maj Hallén, supervised the kitchen and outdoor staff, while discipline and supplies were the concern of Charlesworth and Andersson, who had rooms in the main building.

Once again the contingent organised itself. Summers resumed his tailoring activities, and when the electric iron was not needed for pressing jackets and trousers it was put upside-down in a specially-adapted tin, and used as a hot-plate for boiling water for tea. Others explored the countryside within the boundaries permitted, at first on foot, then on hired bicycles, and, when the snow came, on skis. And in the evenings Read, who had acquired a roulette wheel with a view to earning a little money, provided an interesting but to himself unprofitable alternative to poker games.

It did not take the volunteers long to discover that in the basement of one of the buildings at the back of Kalhyttan was a fine steam bath, and permission was obtained from Miss Hallén to heat it up. Swedish steam-baths, although heated by stoves similar to those found in Finnish saunas, are more like Turkish baths, for their heat is a dry heat, and the Swedes do not enjoy the steam and high temperatures which are a feature of saunas in Finland. The former inmates of Tähtiniemi knew all about saunas and, like the Finns, enjoyed them hot. So they heated this one up to somewhere near boiling-point, and began throwing water on the stove to make steam which would enable them to enjoy the heat. A few minutes later Miss Hallén's half-witted assistant opened the door of the sauna to see how the volunteers were getting on. He peered through the steam at the thermometer, gave a loud yell, and fled back to the main building, where he told his employer that those mad Englishmen had set the place on fire and were boiling themselves to death. Later in the winter, when there was snow on the ground, the volunteers, unable to roll in it after a sauna (a Finnish custom they had picked up), as there was no suitable secluded place, took buckets of snow into the sauna and rubbed themselves with handfuls of it.

Shortly after Finnish Independence Day, 6th December 1941, when Great Britain declared war on Finland, Kuss and Brooke were exploring Filipstad and stopped to examine the goods in a tailor's window. "*Voi jumalauta* (crikey!), said Kuss in Finnish, "what prices!" Behind them a small voice repeated in Finnish "*Voi jumalauta!* " The two turned round to find a couple of six-year-old Finnish refugee children. A few questions in their own language revealed that there were about twenty such children in the district. Kuss, being Irish and therefore not at war with Finland, made a collection among the volunteers at Kalhyttan and organised a Christmas party for the Finnish children, one of whom was fetched in a taxi from a farm over twelve miles away. The party was a great success, and, not to be outdone, the other Irishmen in the contingent sent a Christmas greetings telegram to Field-Marshal Mannerheim, comparing Ireland's fate with that of Finland.

An attempt to arouse the politicians to action over the volunteers was made just before Christmas 1941, when Brown, an Australian, discovered that it was still possible, though very expensive, to send telegrams to London through civilian channels. So he sent a telegram to D.N. Pritt, K.C., M.P., at the House of Commons, stating that in view of Mr Pritt's interest in the former British volunteers in Finland he was informing him that no efforts were seemingly being made to repatriate the volunteers, unlike other British subjects in Sweden, and that nothing but glib evasions had come from the authorities there. Even the notorious "Lord Haw-Haw", the renegade Englishman who spoke on the German wireless, had stated that the volunteers were stranded and ignored. Pritt was the Member of Parliament for North Hammersmith, and he had written a book, "Light on Moscow", whose fourth edition contained a chapter on Finland. Being on the extreme left wing of the Labour party he not unnaturally took sides with the Soviet Union during the Winter War, and his interest in the volunteers had been shown a couple of years earlier when he asked a question in Parliament about their recruiting, which had led to press publicity of the very kind he had hoped to avoid. Pritt sent Brown's telegram to Sir Anthony Eden at the Foreign Office, with a note to the effect that while he indignantly resented the suggestion that he had ever taken the slightest interest in British volunteers for Finland, he passed on the telegram in case anything could be done "to repatriate these gentlemen, even if you have to intern them as Fascists when they arrive."

As already noted, it was widely believed among the volunteers that the reason for the long delay in their repatriation was that the War Office thought they were all "category men", of poor physical standards and consequently unfit for military service. To correct this impression McGee, who had a puckish sense of humour and who was more resourceful than most, produced a "Merry Christmas" poster. In a circle in the centre was a volunteer asleep in bed, surrounded by pictures of battles, death and destruction, bombs exploding, aircraft crashing and tanks firing, with the inscription *Pax in Terra – Hominibus Bonae Voluntatis* or "Wake Me When It's All Over!" Smith M.L. photographed it and had a few dozen enlargements made which he sold to his friends. One copy was posted to the British Minister in Stockholm. Very soon afterwards it was announced that eight men would leave for home each week on the diplomatic plane, which had been making regular night flights home and back since the early summer of 1940, on three different routes. Apart from Rankin, who had been working at the Legation in Stockholm and who was sent home at the end of February 1942, regular flights for the Kalhyttan contingent began in the second half of March.

At the end of December the Filipstad Slalom Club held its annual dinner and dance at the Stadshotel. Several volunteers who were proficient skiers and who had joined both the Ski and Slalom Clubs when the snow came, decided to attend. During dinner song-sheets were handed round, containing verses referring to the events of the year and to various local worthies. This was much to the amusement of the volunteers, who joined in singing an old Swedish folk-song with modern words about themselves. Roughly translated, it went like this:

> Now Kalhyttan is chock-a-block with Britons,
> From bitter games of war they came last week.
> Our Chairman Bernhard thinks they're worse than kittens
> Because they're not aware of ski-technique.
> They just wander in the snow,
> All bareheaded as they go,
> And the slalom-hill out west, it simply bores them.

"Bernhard" was Bernhard H. Bergström, an engineer.

Volunteers took the opportunity to improve their skiing skills, and in February a very successful skiing competition took place when the local paper noted that the Englishmen had an opportunity of showing their newly-acquired proficiency. The course consisted of two circuits of a trail, totalling 3 miles 220 yards. There were thirteen starters, and the result was Tierney 25 mins. 48 seconds, Smith 26 minutes and Van Beest 27 minutes. At about this time Brooke took part in the national cross-country ski-race called the Vasa Run, and covered 12½ miles in 1 hour 46 minutes.

In January 1942, after assisting as an interpreter in a court case in Malung, in which a volunteer was involved, Charlesworth returned to Stockholm, and his replacement was welcomed at Kalhyttan. Named Major Johnstone, he had seen service in the first World War, though how he came to be living at Tumba, near the city, was never really explained. He remained with Andersson at Kalhyttan until the last of the volunteers had been repatriated.

Fifteen men made a spectacular attempt to get home in the early spring of 1942. They volunteered to join twelve Norwegian ships in an attempt to break through the German blockade of the Swedish coast. Signing on as supernumeraries at one krona a month, the members of the party included some ex-seamen and some who had seen service in the first World War, as well as some of the more optimistic and enterprising inmates of Kalhyttan. Once on board the ships in Gothenburg harbour they were trained below decks in great secrecy to fire machine-guns whose parts and ammunition had been smuggled on board. The ships had been in Swedish waters when the Germans occupied Norway in April 1940, and the British government had chartered them from the Swedish representatives of the owners. It had been intended to take them out at night during the late winter, but the Germans, who had got wind of what was going to happen, brought a court case, and the clearance of the ships from Gothenburg was delayed. Finally, about ten o'clock at night on 31st March the ships put to sea. They left Swedish territorial waters and scattered, and a German naval patrol vessel spotted them early the following morning. Despite a lack of proper air cover some of the ships managed to reach British ports, the crew and volunteers aboard the one which was torpedoed being saved. Those who reached home in this way were Bradley, Hill M.C.A.T, Pearce, Reynolds and Taylor H. Those taken prisoner and interned in a German camp for seamen were Bishop, Brabbs, Henley, Hole, Lace, Lenox-Conyngham, Mackie, Tawell and Tillbrook. Seven of these were on the s/s *Skytteren,* formerly the White Star liner *Suevic,* which had been sold to the Norwegians and converted to a whaler after running aground on the Maenheere Reef, off the Lizard, in March 1907. Commins, the only volunteer on his ship, landed in Sweden again when it returned to Gothenburg.

As most of the ships had been laden with ball-bearings, the Iron and Steel Control, under Sir George Binney, naturally took an interest in the welfare of the nine interned volunteers. On their return home after the war each received £250 from official sources and one-ninth of the residue of the Iron and Steel Tobacco and Cigarette Fund. Sir George, who had arranged welfare and payments, wrote in August 1945: "The Finnish Volunteers were most grateful for the generous settlement, and any bitterness which they may have felt on their return from Germany is now completely dissipated. They feel that they have been fairly and squarely compensated by His Majesty's Government."

The man who chose the candidates for repatriation by the diplomatic plane, which flew between Stockholm and Leuchars in Fife, seems likely to have used the misinformation which the British Legation in Helsinki had supplied. He gave preference to the older men above military age and left almost to the last those who were fit and of the right age to serve in the Forces and those who were living away from Kalhyttan on money remitted from home. A considerable number of the latter managed in a relatively short time to acquire a good working knowledge of Swedish. However, so successful was the diplomatic plane that by 10th April 1942 there were only 36 men awaiting repatriation, excluding one who was in an asylum and another who had been transferred to Smedsbo internment camp on account of a number of irregularities. Brooke, who was due to be called up the week after he left London, was one of the last to go, and left Sweden late at night on 26th April, together with Graham J.M., Green W., Holtom, Ilbury, Jarrett, Stewart-Menteth and Zipfel.

The last nine volunteers left Kalhyttan in May: Keen, Kuss, Le Mee-Power, McGee, Martin, Moore, Rattigan, Roberts and Sinclair-Lockhart. Six of them were under thirty years of age and fit for military service. The last few volunteers living privately in Filipstad and Malung, including one "shacked up" with a local business-woman (who still remembers him with affection) left during the spring and early summer. Kuss, meanwhile, obtained a job at the British Legation in Stockholm, reading Finnish newspapers, and several others, mostly manual workers, were given temporary work there pending repatriation, largely, one suspects, decorating the offices, though Haddleton was employed at Bromma airport to guard the diplomatic plane.

Seth Andersson wrote to "Dear Pahlen" in June 1942 to say that the last volunteers had left Kalhyttan. This is where the line can be drawn, for by then the contingent had ceased to exist.

ENVOI

Life is full of surprises, and in the succeeding years volunteers have met in odd places. Brown met Roberts on the top of a bus in London during the war, and Roberts found Casey running a pub in West London shortly after. On leave in 1944 he ran into Asling, and in uniform bumped into Martin. Dr Herford met Moore one night on a landing-craft on its way to the Normandy beaches in the summer of 1944. Dunlop met Golby in Durban at about the same time, and after peace had broken out met Read in Naples. Apostolides ran into Brooke in London during the war, and Herring met Brooke on Kolding airfield, Denmark, in February 1946. After he had obtained the post of assistant press attaché at the re-opened British Legation in Helsinki later the same year Brooke met Major Nordlund, who was then aide de camp to President Paasikivi. He ran into von Essen in the street, and subsequently met Count von der Pahlen. Roper and Byrne visited him in the summer of 1948 when they made a prolonged stay in the country and saw Brooke again in 1950, as did Read. In the latter year Captain Scott A.H.W. visited Finland and met Brooke by accident on a coastal pleasure-boat. Back in London in the 1950s Brooke met Commins, working as a doorkeeper at the Waldorf Hotel, and Major Chandor and Lieut. Guthrie when the latter was being filmed for a *This is Your Life* television programme. On Finland's Independence Day in 1965 the Finnish Ambassador in London invited volunteers to the official reception to celebrate the 25th anniversary of the end of the Winter War, and those that turned up included, in addition to the writer, Major Chandor, Lieut. Guthrie, Dr Herford, Thompson, and Lieut. Stig Brunow, who happened to be in London on business. A couple of years later Brooke met Jones S. at the British Embassy in Stockholm.

And what of the places where the volunteers were

stationed? Lapua has grown, and now lies a short way west of the new highway to the North. One side of the main street was pulled down after the war and rebuilt to a new line to permit the construction of a wider thoroughfare, as befits a town of its importance. The Workers' House was unfortunately burnt down some years ago, and its site is now occupied by a neat row of shops with flats above them. The local newspaper, *Lapuan Sanomat,* has its editorial offices roughly on the site of the barrack-room. Savonlinna has almost doubled in size, and many of the places where the volunteers learned the rudiments of infantry tactics and forest fighting have disappeared under new housing estates or factories. The site of the rifle-range is now part of a smart suburb of the town. The road to the east now crosses Kyrönsalmi on a new bridge north of the old road and rail bridge. The Hotel Seurahuone, where the officers were billetted, was accidentally burned down a few years after the war, but a local consortium which included the family of the late Mrs McKay, rebuilt it in a more permanent style. At about the same time the theatre and ballroom on the main street, in which the volunteers were quartered, was pulled down to make way for a supermarket. Roper's Hole was filled with putty after the war, but is still clearly visible, and the level place near the harbour where the volunteers were drilled has been grassed over.

In 1949 the writer visited Kilpin's grave, to find it unmarked. The British Consul in Helsinki told him that he had no official funds with which to erect a gravestone, and the grave remained unmarked until 1963, when Kuss visited it and brought the matter to the notice of the cemetery's administrator. In the autumn of that year a headstone was prepared at Kuss' expense, by mistake dated 19th May instead of 20th June 1940, and erected about two metres west of the actual place of burial. When the writer, armed with a photograph he had taken of the grave a few weeks after the funeral, pointed out the exact location to the man in charge at the cemetery, in the summer of 1964, the reply was that his predecessor, who was responsible for the error, had not kept a proper map. "But isn't it comforting to know that your friend is somewhere near?" he added cheerfully.

In Jyväskylä the wooden building which housed the Commercial High School has been pulled down to make way for the new bus station. In Korpilahti Tähtiniemi is a tourist-home again, just as it was before the volunteers arrived. A mock well has been put in the yard in front of the main building and the trees have grown considerably but still retain their original features. The army hut in the village where the volunteers from Helsinki were housed was removed some years ago to make space for a supermarket, and on the other side of the street are some fine new buildings which have replaced the pre-war wooden ones. The village has grown very considerably, and a new main highway skirts it and keeps heavy long-distance traffic away from the main street. Iloniemi sawmill, despite a fire in 1941, continued to work until a few years ago, but now only the brick buildings, the chimney and some houses remain; and in summer the site is a mass of willow-herb.

Malung has seen many changes, and the old wooden People's High School was pulled down some years ago to make room for a car-park, while the road across the railway to the church has been diverted away from the modern People's High School. Most of the old outbuildings remain. The town has grown considerably, but its prosperity is still based on leather. A big new highway runs up the valley east of the town, and there are many new buildings and factories. There are still numerous people there who remember the volunteers, and quite a number of them have kept in touch with their volunteer friends since the war. One or two volunteers, including Dixon A.H.F., Daly, and the writer, have since re-visited the place, and have been made warmly welcome. That a stay of only a few months should have created such a fund of goodwill is, perhaps, the contingent's most surprising achievement.

Kalhyttan, near Filipstad, is in different hands, but still caters for visitors. Filipstad town, too, has seen many changes. The centre is hardly recognisable, since most of the old wooden buildings have been pulled down and replaced with modern ones, and the general impression is of an uneasy compromise between the nineteenth and twentieth centuries. The volunteers, who had little contact with the townspeople, are long since forgotten, and an appeal in the local paper to anyone who could remember them to come forward brought no reply.

And what of the volunteers themselves? Time has taken its toll, and many have died, some, like Hall, Hill F., McKibbin L.G., Smith M.L. and Taylor H.S. on active service, others, like Sir G.D.P. Sinclair-Lockhart, Carwithen and Pearce, in far-flung corners of the Empire, and McKay at home in Savonlinna; and numerous others at home in Britain. During the war Dr Herford played a leading part in organising the medical services at Arnhem, for which he was awarded the D.S.O. Lieut-Commander Brian Reynolds, R.N., led a flotilla of fast motor-boats back and forth through the German blockade of Sweden, bringing home valuable cargoes of ball-bearings, for which he was awarded the M.B.E. and D.S.C., only to be blown up by a stray German mine while on his way to Gothenburg after peace broke out. And after his service in Finland, where he was a competent and popular officer, Lieut. Nurk obtained his own visas and returned to Kenya via Russia and the Middle East. He was given an emergency commission in June 1941, and by October, when he was gazetted a Captain in the East African Intelligence Corps, he had already won the Military Cross. From there he transferred to the Special Air Services, and saw action behind the German lines in Italy, where as a company commander he distinguished himself in action, firing a 75 mm. field-gun over open sights. After the war he served as Military Attaché at British Embassies in Sofia, Athens and Addis Ababa and in the Congo. He died in 1976. Meanwhile, Watkins commanded a bomber squadron in the R.A.F., and on demobilisation became a senior civil airline pilot; he died in 1984.

When the District Bank agreed to hold the volunteers' money Gibson suggested that any unclaimed balances should in course of time revert to the Bank as some small return for its work and trouble. But the Bank refused to accept this, and in the 1960s asked Ryder to trace and arrange payments to the last sixteen volunteers or their heirs. This was an immense task, for Humphries and Maund were missing presumed dead, McKay had died in Savonlinna, two others had no fixed abode, and one had been Her Majesty's guest in various places up and down the country. The first claimant was Dr Herford.

Several of the volunteers' Finnish friends are still most fortunately alive, and the writer has been in touch with them during the preparation of this book. They include Major-General Gustav Ehrnrooth, the two Brunows, Dr Kaj J. Warras and von Essen. Of the others, Major Norlund, Count von der Pahlen and Bror-Leo Lerche have died, as has von Essen in 1984.

After the war, when Harold Macmillan was Prime Minister, Evans S.H. acted as his press secretary for eight years, and was awarded the C.M.G. and the O.B.E. He was later knighted, as Sir Harold Evans, 1st Baronet. Lieut. Guthrie founded Action Research for the Crippled Child, a multi-million pound charity which provides funds for research into crippling diseases. At home in Ireland Kuss became an author, and several of his books have been translated into Finnish and Swedish, while Way recently wrote *The Garden of my Beloved,* an allegory which was translated, inter alia, into Finnish. Other volunteers have made their mark in a wide range of professions, including the arts, aviation, banking, the Civil Service, the Diplomatic Service, education, factory management, historical research, insurance, journalism, the law, medicine, sport and stockbroking, to name but a few. Many of the others have disappeared or retired into obscurity, and the writer has been unable to locate them. But if the eleven per cent sample of those he has managed to contact, both at home and overseas, is a representative one, and he has every reason to believe that it is, it is pleasant to record that the volunteers' sympathies still lie where they lay fifty years ago.

BIBLIOGRAPHY

ALLAN, James: *No Citation* (Angus & Robertson, 1955)

ARCHIVES: Public Record Office, London; War Archives, Helsinki; State Archives, Stockholm; Sir George Binney; H.H. Chandor; H. Gibson; Hon. H.J. Howard, Count N. von der Pahlen; H. Taylor.

BARKER, Ralph: *The Blockade Busters* (Chatto & Windus, 1976)

BELL, Henry McGrady: *Land of Lakes – Memories Keep Me Company* (Robert Hale, 1976)

BRITISH RED CROSS SOCIETY AND ORDER OF ST JOHN: *Official History of the War Organisation, 1939-47.*

CITRINE, Sir Walter (later Lord): *My Finnish Diary* (Robert Hale, 1940)

DAVIES, A. Tegla: *The Friends' Ambulance Unit* (George Allen & Unwin, 1947)

EVANS, Sir Harold: *Downing Street Diary* (Macmillan, 1980)

FAGERSTRÖM, Birger, Hannula J.O. and Sandberg, Börje: *Suomi taistelee (Finland Fights) (Suomen Kirja, Helsinki, 1940)*

FINNISH FOREIGN MINISTRY: *Statement concerning Finnish-Russian Relations and the circumstances leading to the Invasion of Finland by the U.S.S.R. on November 30, 1939* (Simpkin Marshall, 1939)

HENRY DOUBLEDAY RESEARCH ASSOCIATION: Newsletter No. 87, 1981-82

JACKSON, Peter: *The Sky Tramps* (Souvenir Press, 1965)

KORHONEN, Arvi (editor): *Suomen Historian Käsikirja* (A Handbook of Finnish History) (Werner Söderström, Helsinki, 1949)

LAPPALAINEN, Matti: *Taivisodan historia* (The History of the Winter War) (Werner Söderström, Helsinki, 1980)

LEIVISKÄ, *Iivari, and Levämäki, Lauri:* Guide to Finland (Suomen Kirja, Helsinki, 1938)

MAGILL, J.H.: *Tasavalta tulikokeessa* (A Republic Tried by Fire) (Weilin & Göös, Helsinki, 1981)

NEVAKIVI, Professor: *Apu jota ei pyydetty* (The Help Which Was Not Asked For) (Tammi, Helsinki, 1972); *Ystävistä vihollisiksi* (Friends Became Enemies) (Tammi, Helsinki, 1976)

NEWSPAPERS: *Finland*: *Helsingin Sanomat; Itä-Savo; Keskisuomalainen; Kuorevesi-Mänttä-Vilppula; Savonmaa; Sisä-Suomi; Uusi Suomi; Vaasa. Sweden: Värmlands Tidning; Dala Demokraten. U.K.: Aero Pictorial; Daily Express; Daily Mirror; Daily Sketch; Daily Telegraph; Daily Worker; Manchester Guardian; Mining World; News Chronicle; Northern Echo; Scottish Daily Express; The Times; Yorkshire Post*

NORTHERN UNION BANK (PYP), Helsinki: Savings Account Book No. 37187 (1941-42)

PRITT, D.N.: *Light on Moscow* (Penguin Books, 1940)

RISLAKKI, Jukka: *Erittäin salainen* (Top Secret) *(Love Kirjat, Helsinki, 1982)*

WALZEL, Illo von: *Möte i Lappo* (Meeting in Lapua) (Werner Söderström, Helsinki, 1941)

ACKNOWLEDGEMENTS

The writer's sincerest thanks are due to the following people and organisations, who have provided him with information, documents, diaries, photographs and recollections. The locations of those outside the U.K. are given in parentheses:

ACCIDENT RECORD OFFICE (Tapaturmavirasto) (Finland)

ANGLO-FINNISH SOCIETY OF LONDON

ASLING, Mrs. E.

ATKINSON, G.A.S.

BABBS, T.E.H.

BARHAM, Simon

BARKER, Ralph

BECK, J.C. (Finland)

BOSLEY, Rex

BOSWELL, R.W.D.

BRIDGEMAN, Brian

BROOKS, Mrs Naomi (Spain)

BRUNOW, Dage Collin (Finland)

BRUNOW, Stig (Finland)

CHANDOR, Martin

COOKE, Edward (Canada)

DE BURGH-THOMAS, H.P. (Australia)

DEPARTMENT OF INTERNAL AFFAIRS (South Africa)

DIXON, A.H.F.

DUNLOP, J.B.

EARL, Bryan

EDIT STRENG'S BOOKSHOP (Finland)

EHRNROOTH, Major-General Gustav (Finland)
ELLIS, C.A.P.
ENQUIST, Professor Nils Erik (Finland)
von ESSEN, Göran Mauritz ("George") (Finland)
EVANS, Sir S.H., Bart.
EVANS, Dr William
FINNISH-BRITISH SOCIETY (Finland)
FINNISH CHURCH GUILD
FINNISH GENERAL STAFF
FINNISH FOREIGN MINISTRY
FINNISH MINISTRY OF MARINE
GALITZINE, Prince George
GASTER, B.H.
GEE, H.V.
GENERAL MEDICAL COUNCIL
GIBSON, Mrs Carol
GILKISON, C.A.
GLYN, Dr J. St G. (South Africa)
GREENLEAVES, Harold, M.A.
GUSTAFSSON, Hugo (Sweden)
GUTHRIE, D.D.
HANCOCK, William (Sweden)
HEINOLA, Juhani (Finland)
HENRY NIELSEN LTD. (Finland)
HERFORD, Dr M.E.M., M.D., D.S.O.
HILL, Stephen Paull Jewill
HOLLIDAY, W.C.
HOLTOM, R.F. (Canada)
HOWARD, Hon H.J. (Italy)
HUMPHRIES, Derek
HUNTER, Dr Alastair

JOHNSON, J.W.E.

JÄRVI, Olavi (Spain)

KELLY, Mrs Sonia (Ireland)

KENKKÄINEN, Pauli (New Zealand)

KETONEN, Arne (Finland)

KEYWORTH, Lance, M.A. (Finland)

KOTAMO, Oiti (Finland)

KUSS, Mr and Mrs G.V. (Ireland)

LAZARUS, A.A.

LIBRARIES: London Guildhall; University of Helsinki (Finland)

LINTON, Rev. Sidney

LOIKKANEN, Ilta Elena née Ruuskanen (Finland)

LONDON TRANSPORT

McMULLIN, M.A. (Ireland)

MALLOWAN, Mr and Mrs C.G.H.

MATTHEWS, Rev. Gerald

MEAD, Professor William Richard

MILLINGTON-HOGG, G.W. (Canada)

MONTAGUE, J.C. (Canada)

MUSEUMS: Imperial War Museum; War Museum (Finland); Norwegian Home Front Museum (Norway)

MÄKI, Tenho (Finland)

NAISH, Miss Marjorie

NATIONAL WESTMINSTER BANK

NELSON, Neville C.

NEUMARK, O.W.

NOEL-BAKER, Lord Philip

OLD BOYS' ASSOCIATIONS: Ampleforth Abbey; Bedales; Bryanston; Downside Abbey; Eton College; Harrow School

von der PAHLEN, Count Peter (Finland)

PARSONS-SMITH, Dr Gerald

PHELPS, J.G.

PHOTOGRAPHERS: Olavi (Finland); Pettersson (Sweden); Rattigan

POLICE ADDRESS OFFICE (Finland)

PRICE WATERHOUSE & CO.

QUETTON, Hugh (Canada)

RANTALA, Vesa (Finland)

RATTIGAN, W.D.C.

REIVILÄ, Iris (Finland)

RELIGIOUS SOCIETY OF FRIENDS

RISLAKKI, Jukka (Finland)

ROBBINS, Mrs Peggy née Harrison (Canada)

ROBERTS, C.D. (Canada)

RUUSKANEN, Captain Pentti Ilmari, 7th Infantry Regiment (Finland)

RYDER, R.D.

SECCOMBE, P.J.

SERLACHIUS LTD. (Finland)

SKID-OCH FRILUFTSFRÄMJANDET (Ski and Open Air Society) (Sweden)

SOTATIETEEN LAITOS (Institute of War Studies) (Finland)

SPECIAL FORCES CLUB

SPRING, Derek W.

STRACHEY-HAWDON, Mrs H.

SYLWAN, Bertil (Sweden)

TAYLOR, Mrs Mary

THOMPSON, L.R.

THOROUGHBRED BREEDERS' ASSOCIATION

THURSTAN, Mrs Marion

TIITU, Kustaa (Finland)

TOLKKI, Aarne (Finland)

TOSH, Mrs W.H.

WAR MUSEUM (Sotamuseo) (Finland)

WARRAS, Dr Kaj J. (Finland)

WATKINS, H.

WAY, R.E.

VESSEY, R.

WOMENS' TRANSPORT SERVICES (F.A.N.Y.)

WOOD, Miss Kathleen Amelia

and several people and organisations who have asked to remain anonymous or who have failed to answer letters.

APPENDIX "A"

List of Volunteers

1. **Enlisted in London and reached Finland** (227)

AITKEN-QUACK, Richard Welford, accountant	1913 Harrogate
ALEXANDER, Robert, miner	1909 South Shields
APOSTOLIDES, John Graham, teacher	1917 Calcutta
ARCHER-SHEE, Richard Martin	1907 London
ARMSTRONG, Kenneth, laundry manager	1915 Hull
ARTER, Douglas William, gunsmith	1920 London
ASLING, John, soldier	1905 Yorkshire
ATKINSON, George Arnold Stanley, architect	1906 Chiselhurst
AVERILL, Charles Rochford, paint chemist	1915 Morden
BABBS, Thomas Edward Harvey, salesman	1922 Birmingham
BARTON, David, engineer	1903 London
BATH, Charles Percival ("Sauna"), carpenter	1907 Exeter
BAXTER, Montague Frank	1915 Wandsworth
van BEEST, Vivian Henry, cook	1921 Barry
BISHOP, Victor Charles, labourer	1906 London
BLEW-JONES, Douglas Holden, soldier	1894 London
BODDAM-WHETHAM, Hugh Alexander	1890 Wrexham
BOSELLI, Emanuele L.	1915 Italy
BOSWELL, Robert William Douglas, colliery agent	1912 Edinburgh
BOWHAY-SANDERS, Leonard George, outfitter	1913 Broadstairs
BOWMAN, Jake	1898 Fremantle
BRABBS, James, clerk	1920 Streethouse
BRADLEY, Albert George, packer	1902 Walworth
BRISTOW, Harry Corby	1907 Stockport

BROAD, Peter James, valet	1918 Deal
BROOKE, Justin ("Gus"), undergraduate	1920 Churchill
BROWN, Eric Heywood, pilot	1916 Melbourne
BUDD, Frederick George, solicitor's clerk	1909 London
BUDDEN, Ronald Charles, clerk	1909 Southampton
BULLEN, Charles John Stephen, labourer	1909 London
BURCH, Russell Ward, electrical engineer	1908 Stowmarket
BUTLER, Alexander Hugh Ormonde, student	1920 South India
BUTT, Montague Robert, farmer	1915 Puddington
BYRNE, Thomas William, clerk	1915 London
CARRICK, Bernhard Frederick, car salesman	1908 Camberwell
CARWITHEN, George Edward Terry	1908 Edinburgh
CASEY, John, baker	1912 Waterville, Eire
CHALLENGER, Andrew Latimer, masseur	1907 Darlington
CHALMERS, Edward Costello ("Jock"), seaman	1906 Stirling
CHANDOR, Hugo Henry, farmer	1895 Woldingham
CLARK, Edwin Alfred, gardener	1911 Gosport
COMMINS, Patrick Francis ("Paddy"), telephone engineer	1897 Dublin
CONNOLLY, Henry ("Harry", "Aitchie"), miner	1913 Maltby
COOK, Walter W. Charles	1888 Peckham
COOPER, Peter John ("Wolf"), motor mechanic	1916 Reading
COUGHLAN, James, motor driver	1911 Tullamore, Eire
CUMBERLEGE, Francis Charles Ray, motor cyclist	1898 Sevenoaks
d'ABO, Terence Darwin Nicolai, stockbroker's clerk	1916 London
DALTON, Denis Neale, trainee pilot	1918 Southport
DALY, Liam Proinsios, pipe fitter	1915 Clonmellon, Eire
DAVEY, John, kitchen hand	1909 South Wales
DAVIDSEN, S.A., interpreter	
DE BURGH-THOMAS, Hubert Patrick, soldier	1916 Southsea

de LIGUORI, Prince Alfonso	1896 Venice
DEMORE, Roland Raymond, metal machinist	1911 St Peter Port
DIXON, Alfred Herbert Fryer, farmer	1909 Bristol
DIXON, Raymond, pilot	1914 Monkseaton
DOESE, Donald William, bank cashier	1909 London
DUNLOP, John Bonar, sculptor	1916 Dunedin, N.Z.
DUNNE, John Brendan, independent	1917 Ireland
DUPREZ, Charles Edward Manhattan	1917 London
DUTSON, Fred, machinist	1913 Oswaldtwistle
EASTON, Arthur Leonard, boxer	1916 London
ELLIOTT, John, journalist	1901 London
ELLIS, Charles Alfred Pascoe	1914 East Ham
EVANS, Esmond Victor, gardener	1900 Sutton Coldfield
EVANS, H(oward) G. ("Shitty")	
EVANS, Sidney Harold, journalist	1911 Brierly Hill
FARRAGUT, Peter Maclister	1913 Cork
FITZGERALD, Desmond Maurice Bingham, actor	1914 Southsea
FLEMING, John	1908 Port Glasgow
FORBES, Alastair Cameron, writer	1912 Limpsfield
FORD, George, barman	1918 London
FORD, John Henry	1913 Birmingham
FRANCIS, Frederick Robert	1895 Croydon
FRASER, Arthur Herbert	1898 Inverness
GEDDES, Jack Fitzgerald, naval officer (rtd.)	1916 Woking
GEE, Howard Valentine	1913 London
GILHESPIE, George	1906 Newcastle on Tyne
GLYN, John St George, medical student	1916 Johannesburg
GOLBY, Jack Reginald ("Popeye"), builder	1903 Cheltenham
GOODERHAM, Gordon, civil servant	1912 London
GORDON, Vincent Anthony	1913 London
GRAHAM, Edward Manuel	1914 St Petersburg
GRAHAM, John Murray, mining engineer	1895 Scotland

GRANT, Charles John Patrick , rtd. soldier	1880 Calcutta
GREEN, Bernard Cyril Hicks ("Hicks Green"), professional golfer	1915 Bristol
GREEN, Walter	1905 London
GRIFFIN, James Arthur	1907 Wingate
GUTHRIE, Duncan Dunbar, actor	1911 London
HADDLETON, Stanley Cyril Joseph, aircraft fitter	1906 Birmingham
HALLETT, Arthur Walter, tiler	1910 Reading
HARRISON, Montague Philip Everson, soldier	1898 Belfast
HARTMAN, John Victor, publicity manager	1910 Sheffield
HAYWOOD, Ronald Edward ("Spit"), coachbuilder	1914 Dudley
HENDERSON, Arthur	1912 Dunfermline
HENLEY, Ivor James, builder's labourer	1908 Llanbradach
HERFORD, Dr Martin Edward Meakin	1909 Geneva
HERRING, Frederick William, ladies' hairdresser	1914 Fulham
van HETEREN, Kurt Willibald Tambuza, engineer	1905 Johannesburg
HIGNELL, Ronald, bricklayer	1915 Cardiff
HILL, Frank, motor and marine engineer	1912 Great Yarmouth
HILL, Marie Charles Antoine Thomas ("Tom") horse-breeder	1903 Dublin
HOLE, Arthur Robert ("Jimmy"), retail chemist	1916 Oswestry
HOLLEY, Charles Edward, labourer	1910 Lambeth
HOLLIDAY, William Cuthbert ("Bill"), mechanised vehicle expert	1913 Workington
HOLTOM, Robert Frederick, fireman	1915 Bath
HOPKINSON, Thomas Gordon, company secretary	1911 Nelson
HOWARD, Hon. Hubert John Edward Dominic, independent	1904 Washington
HUMPHRIES, Henry Arthur ("Oomphries"), builder	1896 Liverpool

ILBURY, Frederick, transformer erector	1908 Brentford
INGARFIELD, Leonard	1915 London
JACKSON, Norman, policeman	1915 Denton
JARRETT, Francis Alfred ("Lulu"), miner	1912 London
JOHNS, Ronald Wilby, mechanical draughtsman	1914 South Wales
JOHNSTONE, Reginald Hugh	1895 Stockton
JONES, Sidney	1900 Leamington Spa
JONES, William Christopher, hotel porter	1905 Shrewsbury
JOYCE, Joseph, retired soldier	1887 Bognor
KEEN, Peter Herbert (James), stage manager	1914 London
KENWORTHY, Reginald Watson, test pilot	1896 Wakefield
KILGOUR, John, engineer and turner	1913 Ossett
KILPIN, George	1910 Grimsby
KINGCOTE, Gordon Henry, hotel manager	1884 Monmouth
KUSS, Gerald Valentine, lorry driver	1920 Navan, Eire
LACE, Alfred Clucas ("Tom"), motor racing driver	1897 Ramsgate
LANSDOWN, William Ewart, milkman	1905 Porthcawl
LAVEY, Charles Edward, butler	1905 London
LAW, Robert Galbraith ("Bobby"), dental surgeon	1901 Glasgow
LE MEE-POWER, Colin Adrian Cowper	1910 Bournemouth
LENOX-CONYNGHAM, James Desmond ("Creeping Jesus")	1905 Portrush
LOUREIRO, E.P.	Portugal
LOWE, William Henry	1910 Staines
LUCEY, Denis ("Paddy"), labourer	1915 Curraghglass, Eire
LYONS, Harold Bruce, motor driver and mechanic	1918 East Harptree
McGEE, Patrick Conleth ("Paddy"), journalist	1914 Kilwinning
McKAY, Alexander, technician	1897 Brisbane
McKIBBIN, Leonard George, commercial artist	1906 Bradford

McKIBBIN, Russell, physical training instructor	1912 Bexhill on Sea
MACKIE, Douglas, architect and surveyor	1889 Peckham
McMULLIN, Michael Anthony, student	1913 Nuwara Eliya, Ceylon
McNALLY, Daniel, labourer	1910 Dublin
McNEILL, Edward Goulding, cook	1913 Southampton
MALLOWAN, Cecil Frederick Hubert, schoolmaster	1907 London
MARTIN, Edward ("The Baron"), hairdresser	1914 Oldbury
MAUND, Eric George, motor engineer	1912 Caerphilly
MEDLICOTT, John Irvine, teacher	1914 London
MILLINGTON-HOGG, Godfrey William Albert Lance, riding instructor	1919 London, Ontario
MONTAGUE, John Cook, production engineer	1913 Manchester
MOORE, Charles, assistant cook	1912 Dundalk, Eire
MUNDAY, John Henry	1910 London
MUNRO, Neil	1922 London
NEUMARK, Otto Walter	1921 Brno, Czechoslovakia
NICHOLLS, William George, postman	1908 Surrey
NIGHTINGALE, Christopher Carnac, insurance clerk	1913 London
NINNIS, Robert Douglas Kiallmark, superintendent, Indian police	1897 Streatham
NURK, Karl, game-warden	1904 Estonia
OLIVO, Salvator Antonio, soldier	1910 Chiselhurst
OWBRIDGE, Giles W.G., ski instructor	1921 England
PARKER, George Albert ("Boston"), lorry-driver's mate	1913 York
PATTERSON, Bruce Tyrrell, agriculture student	1921 Aberdeen
PEARCE, James Townsend ("Jimmy"), farmer	1903 Watermouth
PEARSON, Dennis Frederick Alfred	1907 London
PEROWNE, Leonard William, bus driver	1910 South Kensington
PERSHKE, Ivor Frederick, accountant	1915 Beckenham

PHELPS, Jack George ("Lofty"), labourer	1915 West Ham
PHILLIPS, Thomas, mechanic	1904 Sydenham
PHILPOTT, Guy, independent	1903 Ryde
POOKE, Reginald Sydney Bertram, cheesemaker	1907 Plymouth
PORTE, Edward Laurence	1912 London
PRINCE, Harry, plumber	1911 Hendon
PRYSE, David Edward Jones, secretary	1895 London
PUNSHON, Percy Killingworth ("Punch"), radio technician	1910 Canada
PURVES, Ereth Marshall ("Eric"), actor	1919 Amritsar, India
RANKIN, John McK., insurance broker	1910 Glasgow
RATTIGAN, William Douglas Clive ("Bill"), accountant	1908 England
READ, John Edward Thesiger ("Phyllis"), teacher	1910 Vancouver Island
REED, Charles Thomas Michael	1912 Bristol
REYNOLDS, Sylvanus Brian John, independent	1908 Cirencester
ROBERTS, Charles Dennis, stores manager	1908 Hounslow
ROOME, Donald, bricklayer	1905 Derby
ROOSEVELT, Major Kermit, soldier	1889 U.S.A.
ROPER, Charles William, carpenter	1920 Feltwell
RUCK-KEENE, William Edmund, solicitor	1912 Fareham
RYDER, Richard Dudley ("Dick"), accountant	1904 London
SANDBACH, Jack	1909 London
SCOTT, Arnot Hercules Wilmot, soldier	1892 Hong Kong
SCOTT, Nigel William Guthrie, export trader	1912 London
SECCOMBE, Patrick John, schoolmaster	1915 London
SEILERNE, Antoine	1901 Frensham
SEYLER, Paul Clifford, sheep farmer	1914 London
SHAW-KENNEDY, Hugh James, pilot	1902 London
SHERRY, Frederick James, draughtsman	1913 London
SINCLAIR-LOCKHART, Sir Graeme Duncan Power, Bart., independent	1897 Thames, N.Z.

SMITH, John ("Jack"), clerk	1922 Norwich
SMITH, Mark Lindsay ("Smith 824"), market gardener	1919 Lahore
SMITH, Sidney George Rupert ("Smith 24"); ("Trader Smith"), farmer	1917 Woodbridge
SNODIN, Maurice Raymond, schoolmaster	1914 Carlton
SNOWDEN, John Stanley, dispatch clerk	1904 St Albans
STEAD, David Vere, pilot	1906 Melbourne
STEPHENSON, Thomas ("Fingers")	1912 Dunfermline
STUART-MENTETH, Montagu, accountant	1893 Bradford
SUMMERS, Richard John, aero engine fitter	1906 London
TAWELL, Roy Gifford ("Dick"), farmer	1906 Fordham
TAYLOR, Hugh, hotelier	1899 Rawtenstall
THOMPSON, John Edward, hotel porter	1905 London
THOMPSON, Leslie Robert ("Les"), newspaper distributor	1914 Tooting
TIERNEY, William Joseph, labourer	1918 Eire
TILLBROOK, William Harry	1892 Dereham
TOSH, William Henderson, soldier	1900 Dundee
VERNON, Stanley Harold, builder's foreman	1910 Birmingham
VESSEY, Roland, farmer	1903 Sheffield
VON DER LEITH, John Nicholas	1896 New York
WALKER, William Edward, clerk	1911 London
WATKINS, Harold, dental mechanic	1915 Rochdale
WATSON, William Arthur Capron, horse-breeder	1903 London
WAUGH, Albert Henry, hotel proprietor	1883 Wolverhampton
WAY, Robert Edward, horse-breeder	1912 Durban
WEAVER, Denis Robert ("Red"), aircraft engineer	1916 Bristol
WELLMON, Malcolm Harry, pilot	1911 Southsea
WHITE, Albert Edward Barkham, hospital steward	1916 Bristol
WILLIAMS, Bernard James A., hairdresser	1913 London

WINTER, Sir Ormonde, retired soldier	1875 Chiswick
WOODBURN, Alfred Basil Brailsford, transport manager	1911 Bradford
YOUNG, Leslie Edward	1919 Ontario
ZIPFEL, Frederick Leon, private secretary	1914 London

2. Enlisted in Canada (4)

HALL, Samuel John	1914 Canada
HELLENIUS, Rolf August, trapper and prospector	1907 Ylivieska, Finland
WALKER, John Sidney ("Johnnie")	1893 Canada
WALLER, Edward Bloomfield, pilot	1897 Toronto

3. Enlisted in Lapua (13)

BAMFORD, Ernest Ludvig, tourist guide	1902 St Petersburg
BECK, James Cyril, student	1920 Joutselkä, Finland
CRAMPTON, George Ribton	Canada
EAGER, Richard Albert, interpreter	1891 England
GASTER, Benjamin Herman, sergeant	1902 England
HANCOCK, John	Finland
HANCOCK, Robert, commercial artist	1912 Helsinki
HANCOCK, William, journalist and history student	1920 Helsinki
HITCHING, John Joseph Jack O'Brien, journalist & Abwehr agent	1890 Portsmouth
JOHNSON, John William Edgar, auditor	1915 England
MIVILLE, Eric Rodolphe, horse-breeder	Switzerland

and two un-named, born in Russia, 1908 and 1913

4. Anti-Aircraft Technicians (16)

BEST, Charles Alfred	1919 Kent
DOREY, Edward James Frederick sergeant, R.A.O.C.	1914 Portsmouth
FRISBY, William George, sergeant R.A.O.C.	1914 London

GEORGE, Jack	1914 Eccles
HARTGROVE, Cyril Albert, sergeant R.A.O.C.	1907 Leeds
HURST, Jack George, sergeant R.A.O.C.	1911 Wimbledon
LAZARUS, Alan Adolph	1920 London
MASON, William Stanley ("Alan")	1917 Kent
ONGLEY, Percy, sergeant R.A.O.C.	1913 Aden
PARCELL, Sidney William ("Stanley")	1918 South Norwood
SILVERWOOD-COPE, Maclachlan Alan Carl, R.A.	1915 London
SMITH, Alan Malcolm	1916 Boreham Wood
STURGESS, Arthur William	1903 Portsmouth
SUTTON, Ernest Arthur	1918 Crayford
TAYLOR, John Debenham	1920 Walsingham
WEBB, John Henry	1897 West Malling

5. R.A.F. Ground Crews (16)

BENNETT, Reginald Frederick, flight-sergeant	1916 London
BILTCLIFFE, Donald, L.A.C.	1920 York
BRISTOW, corporal	
DE LA PLAIN, Ivan James, L.A.C.	1920 Maidstone
DUCKWORTH, Cyril, L.A.C.	1920 Askham
GALPIN, Walter Cornelius, flight sergeant	1912 Wimborne
INWARD, L.A.C.	
MARSHALL, Robert, L.A.C.	1916 London
MARTIN, Leslie Preston, corporal	1919 Bexhill on Sea
MERRELLS, L.A.C.	1918 Maldon
MITCHELL, L.A.C.	1921 Todmorden
REID, Lionel Thorner, L.A.C.	1920 Walthamstow
RUSSELL, corporal	
SAYCE, corporal	
SHORT, corporal	
WHITE, Raymond Reginald, L.A.C.	1919 Southend on Sea

6. Friends' Ambulance Unit (56)

ARMSTRONG, Anthony	1918
BACKHOUSE, Edward	1919
BROWN, William	1917
BURGESS-SMITH, Elliott	1918
BURNS, Thomas	1913
CADBURY, Brandon	1915
CADOUX, Harold John	1918
CATTERALL, Robert Duncan	1918
CORDER, Stephen Pit	1918
DARBYSHIRE, Brian	1917
DAVIS, Ralph Henry Carless	1918
DICK, Oswald Hector	1915
DICKINSON, Alan Russell	1915
EARLY, Richard Elliott	1908
EVANS, Samuel Vaughan	1917
EVANS, William Rainsford	1918
EWBANK, Walter Frederick	1918
GILLESPIE, John Eustace	1914
GRAVESON, Alfred Hoyland	1918
GREENWOOD, Alan Sutcliffe	1916
HALL, Edwin William Cyril	1919
HARRIS, Michael	1919
HARRIS, Richard Thorpe	1918
HEALTH, John Gordon Wheawell	1912
HEY, Albert	1918
HEYWOOD, John	1918
HILL, Derryck Albert	1917
JOYNES, Ronald Arthur	1917
KING, Kenneth Charles	1917
KYDD, Ian Murray	1917
LIDBETTER, Hubert Martin	1914

LISTER, Douglas George	1917
MACKINTOSH, Stanley Macleod	1918
MENNEL, Francis John	1917
MIALL, William Einar	1917
MOUNSEY, Michael Fryer	1915
PEARSON, Alfred Gordon (Irish citizen)	1919
ROAKE, Paul	1918
ROSS, Hector Gilbert	1915
ROWLANDS, Albert David	1919
ROWNTREE, Michael Hotham	1919
SHARMAN, Ivan Albert	1915
SMITH, Basil William	1919
SMITH, Ralph Reckitt	1915
SYKES, John	1918
TEMPLE, Frederick Stephen	
TOMLINSON, Albert Henry	1918
WATERFIELD, Derick Humphrey	1908
VERNEY, Stephen Edmund	1919
VEYSEY, Roland Hugh	1918
WHITELEY, Roger Cedric	1918
WOOD, John Sterry Graham	1919
WOODCOCK, Dennis Scroxton	1917
WOODS, Frederick William	1917
WOODHEAD, Leonard	1918
WOODHEAD, Maurice	1915

7. First Aid Nursing Yeomanry (19)

BAKER, Miss Grace

BAGGALEY, Miss E.

BENJAFIELD, Miss G.

COGGIN, Mrs Nora

COOPER, Miss P.

CROSBIE, Miss M.

HARRISON, Miss M. ("Peggy") (U.S.A. citizen)
HOLLAND, Mrs Phyllis
KARPELER, Miss K.
KRANS, Miss Lilli (Canadian)
LEE, Miss Joan
McCOMMABLE, Miss J.
NEWBOLD, Miss T.
RAMSDEN, Miss E.
RUNCIMAN, Miss Mary, commandant
SALE, Miss Betty (Australian)
SHIEL, Miss Catherine ("Kathy")
THOMSON, Miss F.
WOOD, Miss K.

8. London Fire Volunteers (8)

BÄCHTOLD, Charles Andrew, commodity broker	1914 London
BAMWELL, James Guy	1911 Edinburgh
CORY, Philip Cecil Donald	1913 Whitchurch
FREAN, Denis Edward, solicitor	1913 Bournemouth
GILKISON, Charles Anthony, film director	1913 York
LATHAM, Wilfred, rubber and cotton wholesaler	1902 Liscard
LOCKE, Allan Frank, fireman	1906 Portsmouth
TATCHELL, Rodney Fleetwood	1909 Purley

9. Volunteers unable to leave the U.K. (186)

ADAMS, Edward Gilbert	1909 London
ANDERSON, Alan Ford	1910 India
ANDRESS, Arnold Leslie	1906 Dunmow
ANDREWS, Thomas Ernest Olvin	1917 Transvaal
APPLEBY, John Leslie	1918 London
ARNOLD, Henry George	1920 Washford

AULT, Kenneth	1916 Monmouth
BAILEY, Raymond Arthur	1917 Ipswich
BALDRY, Kenneth Harvey	1914 London
BAMBER, Paul Kelway	1903 Greenhithe
BANCROFT, Leslie	1911 Fitzwilliam
BARNES, Douglas Stephen	1916 Aberdeen
BARRETT, William John	1916 Ipswich
BELTON, Alfred James	1914 Ewelme
BENNETT, Joseph	1914 Musselburgh
BERRY, Ernest Reginald Sydney	1917 Barnstaple
BERRY, Frederick	1904 London
BLANCKENSEE, Lewis Mervyn	1915 Redland
BLOOMFIELD, Fitzmaurice John Commerell	1897 Waterford
BOOTH, Stanley Keable	1919 Shrewsbury
BORNE, Lucien Louis	1898 France
BOWMAN, Robert Anthony	1918 Devon
BRAND, Geoffrey Hugh Columb	1909 London
BUCKLEY, Cyril Yule (or Tule)	1916 Belfast
BURROWS, Frederick William	1917 Crewe
BURT, Edward James Elliot	1902 Haslemere
CABAN, Freeman Charles Edmund	1912 Brandon
CAIRNS, Walter David	1921 Amballa, India
CAMPBELL-MARTIN, Clifford	1896 Rancegunj, India
CARR, Francis Edwin	1921 Manchester
CHAPMAN, Norman Markham	1914 Beverley
CHILDS, Stanley	1917 Leicester
COCKETT, Albert James	1911 London
COLLINS, Ronald	1910 Isle of Wight
COOPER, Herbert Douglas Haig	1917 Strabane
COX, Ernest Wakefield	1903 Chingford
CROSSLEY, John Richard	1920 Thornton le Dale
CROUCH, Arthur George Bernard	1920 London
CUTHBERT, Robert Guy	1920 Norbury

DAVEY, John	1899 Leicester
DAVIES, Malcolm Haydon	1921 Llanelly
DAWES, Edward	1920 Gillingham
DIPPER, Raymond Willoughby	1921 Northampton
DONKIN, Peter Langlet	1913 Somerset
DOUGLAS, James Sholto	1910 Somerset
DRAPER, Roger Maxwell	1920 Corsham
DRAYSON, Andrew Walter Burnaby	1916 Hanwell
ENGLAND, Richard Geoffrey	1916 Wales
ETTERHAM, Peter Raymond Victor	1920 London
EVANS, James Francis	1917 Fleur de Lys
EVERETT, Robert William Hanmer	1901 Australia
FANCY, John	1913 Lund, Yorkshire
FEARNLEY, Leonard Stanley	1920 Westcliff
FLETCHER, James Bernard	1897 Rock Ferry
FORD, Charles Godfrey	1911 Methil
FORGEARD, Arthur Edward	1911 Jersey
GALE, Emmanuel	1918 Kislovodsk
GALLAGHER, Leonard Henry	1921 Birkenhead
GANDY, Harry	1912 Northampton
GARDNER, Richard Exton	1914 Loughton
GENT, John Thomas Edmund	1921 London
GILL, Louis Frederick	1906 London
GLIBBERY, Albert Robert	1912 London
GLOVER, Reginald Edgar	1918 London
GOULD, Stanley Wilfrid	1919 Newport
GRAY, Brian	1919 Newcastle on Tyne
GRIFFIN, Thomas Neville	1897 London
GRIFFITH, Arthur Stephen	1920 Dorchester
HALLS, Norman Wilfred	1920 London
HARRINGTON, Thomas Wade	1915 London
HARTLAND, Richard	1919 Porthcawl
HILL, Charles Ernest	1912 Metheringham

HILL, Leslie Stuart	1908 England
HILL, Stephen Paull Jewill	1912 Penzance
HITCHCOCK, Raymond	1919 Manchester
HORLE-HOBBS, Basil Henry St Andrew Harle	1919 Redhill
HUTCHINGS, Roger Kennedy Fenwick	1915 Havant
HUTTON, Aymer Stutch	1903 Wales
ILLINGWORTH, George Harrison	1920 Leeds
JAMES, Raymond Wallace	1921 Bridgwater
JOHNSON, Russell	1915 London
JONES, Horace	1910 Manchester
KEATES, Arthur Knightley Rowland	1916 Cheshire
KEENAN, Edward James	1919 Aldershot
KELLER, William Edmund	1913 Toronto
KIMBER, Joseph Henry	1920 London
KNAPP, Reginald William George	1901 Bristol
LAMING, Cyril Henry Robert	1886 Rotterdam
LEAHY, William Joseph	1883 Limerick
LENNY, Charles Arlington	1915 Edinburgh
LIGHTFOOT, Lionel Harvey	1920 London
LINNELL, James Arthur	1910 London
LITTLE, Edwin John	1914 Elstree
LIVERMORE, Robert Mark	1919 Norfolk
LOMBARD, Montan Reginald	1911 London
LONSDALE, Robert Henry	1913 Canada
LOWE, Ronald	1917 Heaton Mersey
LYSAUGHT, Philip Michael Vaughan	1914 Oxford
McCARTHY, William John	1917 Belfast
MACLAGAN, Donald Robert	1920 Belgian Congo
MALAN, Anthony Arthur Noel	1907 India
MALLAM, Dennis Crossland	1911 Heston
MARDON, Gilbert Dennis	1908 Dulverton
MARSH, Alan Edward	1912 Barkworth
MASTERMAN, Cedric Audley	1914 London

MAUDSLAY, Henry Charles	1913 Belfast
MEAGHER, Patric Edward	1910 England
MERCER, Richard Henry	1920 Southport
MERRITT, Leonard John	1913 Worcester
MORGAN, Leonard Lambkin	1915 London
MORRIS, Mervyn Lascelles	1912 South Africa
MORTON, Terence Berkeley	1913 Dublin
MOSES, Arthur	1920 Pontypridd
MURPHY, John Dawson	1919 New Zealand
MURRAY, George Blank	1917 Calgary
NICHOLAS, John Francis	1896 Downderry
NORRIS, Laurence Cecil	1917 Portsmouth
NORSTER, Harold	1912 Gosport
OGILVIE, David Neil Hamilton	1917 Sheffield
O'HEA, James Joseph	1889 London
PAGET, Robert Cecil	1896 London
PALLOT, Alexander Glen	1914 Llandaff
PALMER, Esmond John	1911 Roockie, India
PALMER, William Edward	1921 Dublin
PARKER, Eric Varenius	1909 Porto Rico
PARKER, Ernest Charles	1912 Creswell
PAUL, Frank Dawson	1916 London
PAYNE, Kenneth Johnston	1921 Suffolk
PHEASANT, Douglas	1921 Chelmsford
PHILPOTTS, Fred Geoffrey	1911 Cheltenham
POLDEN, Charles Joseph	1886 London
POMPA, Julius Carmelus	1905 London
RAINBOW, Thomas William	1909 Harwich
RANDELL, Kirkpatrick Graham	1907 New Barnet
REES, Michael	1919 Pembroke Dock
ROBERTSON, Jack Stewart	1913 Dalmuir
ROBERTSON, Johnstone Bolton	1909 Twickenham
ROBERTSON, Kenneth James	1918 Great Yarmouth

ROBSON, Harold	1914 Hexham
ROLLINSON, John Dudley	1911 Wolverhampton
ROSEMOND, Joseph	1916 Dundee
SANDERS, Arthur Thomas Drake	1913 Tiverton
SARLL, John Charles Gratwick	1916 Weymouth
SHIPWRIGHT, Alan Thomas Kingston	1897 London
SIGURDSON, Sigurdjoin Laxdal	1917 Mozart, Canada
SIMPSON, Harold	1914 Oldham
SIMMONS, Arthur Edward	1908 Sussex
SINGLETON, Peter Roland	1921 Bolton
SLADE, Sir Alfred	1898 North Petherton
SMITH, David	1905 Blancoven
SMITH, Ewart William	1909 England
SMITH, Ralph Douglas	1901 Surrey
SMITH, Thomas	1921 Lesmahagow
SPATCHETT, John Henry	1910 Ditchingham
STANSFIELD, Peter Wolryche	1909 Scarborough
STANWAY, William	1916 New Mills
STOCKDALE, James	1921 Colne
STEPHENS, John Frank	1911 Hereford
STRETCH, Benjamin George	1918 Goodwick
SWALLOW, Vincent	1918 Hexham
SWAYNE, Henry Ian Ashton	1914 Southampton
SWIFT, Malcolm Henry	1908 King's Lynn
SWIRE, William	1921 Manchester
TAYLOR, Ernest Norman	1921 Chesterfield
THOMPSON, Stewart Carl	1920 Nottingham
THORNTON, Stanley George	1915 Australia
TREW, Raymond Edgar	1916 Enfield Wash
TURNER, Frederick Cuthbert	1911 New Barnet
TURNER, Robert George	1909 Barnet
TURNER, Sydney Lewis	1912 London
VALE, Eric Stanley	1918 Peterborough

WALKER, Gordon Morrison	1918 Carlisle
WALLACE, Samuel	1913 Belfast
WALLENSTEIN, Maurice Max	1911 London
WARD, Frederick Stephen	1903 Bermuda
WEEKS, Edward Lewis	1920 Isle of Wight
WESTGARTH, George Oswald	1892 Manchester
WILKES, Norman Edmund Robinson	1916 London
WILLIAMS, Albert	1919 Bristol
WINKLES, Henry Stuart	1911 Erdington
WINNALL, Eric Ivan	1891 London
WILSON, Christopher Lea	1921 Isle of Wight
WILSON, George Arthur	1911 Blackburn
WRIGHT, Gordon Ormson Manley	1915 Port Elizabeth
YATES, Alan	1921 Staffordshire

APPENDIX "B"

Agreement of Service

FINNISH AID BUREAU

Conditions of Service and form of Enlistment in the International Volunteer Force for Finland
BRITISH CONTINGENT

Agreement

This Agreement is made on the ....Seventh.............. day of...March..........19.40..: BETWEEN **GEORGE ACHATES GRIPENBERG,** Envoy Extraordinary and Minister Plenipotentiary for Finland to the court of St. James's acting on behalf of the Finnish Government, **HAROLD GIBSON,** the Director of the Committee of the FINNISH AID BUREAU of Thorney House, Smith Square, Westminster, as Agent and on behalf of the said Committee and..........Hubert John Howard.............................. (hereinafter called "the Volunteer").

1. The Volunteer agrees to enlist in the International Volunteer Force for Finland—British Contingent.

2. The Committee undertake to clothe and equip the Volunteer during his period of Service with the Force and to feed and house the Volunteer from the date of enlistment until he arrives in Finland, and from the date of leaving Finland until the date of demobilisation. During his stay in Finland the Finnish Government undertake to be responsible for feeding and housing the Volunteer.

3. The Committee undertake to pay the Volunteer from the date of his enlistment to the date of his demobilisation at the rate of 2/- a day whilst serving as a private soldier. If the Volunteer is appointed to commissioned or non-commissioned rank the Committee will pay him the same amount per day as an officer or soldier of the same rank in the British Army receives. Part of this pay equal to the rate of pay of a Finnish officer or soldier of the same rank serving in Finland, the balance shall be retained by the Committee and paid to the Volunteer upon his discharge, or to his personal representatives if he should be killed during his period of service with the Force. Under special circumstances it may be paid monthly to a nominee of the Volunteer concerned.

4. The Committee undertake to provide free transport to the Volunteer from the place of enlistment to Finland and from Finland back to the place of enlistment upon demobilisation. When in Finland the Finnish Government undertake to provide free transport facilities when the Volunteer is on duty.

5. The Finnish Government and the Committee jointly undertake to provide the Volunteer with all necessary medical and surgical treatment free of charge during his period of service.

6. The Volunteer acknowledges that save for the provisions of paragraph 3 he had no financial claim upon the Finnish Aid Bureau or upon the Committee.

7. Should the Volunteer as the result of his participation in the war be totally or partially incapacitated, the Finnish Government agrees to pay to the Volunteer compensation on a like scale to that applying to conscripts in the Finnish Army, in which shall be taken into account his military rank and the promotion he may eventually have earned during his service in the Volunteer Unit. Should the Volunteer die as a result of bodily injuries received or disease contracted in the course of his military service, the Finnish Government will pay an annuity to those who are dependent upon him for financial assistance in accordance with the provisions of the accident insurance legislation in force for the Finnish Army. The monetary

compensation payable under this clause shall be increased by thirty (30) per cent. in case the recipient is resident outside Finland.

8. Application for the receipt of compensation mentioned in the preceding clause shall be made to the Finnish Ministry of Defence by the Finnish Aid Bureau on behalf of the Volunteer, or in the event of his decease on behalf of his dependents or their legal guardians or trustees, within one year of the date on which the injury was received or death occurred as the result of injury received or disease contracted while on military service with the Volunteer Unit. In respect of subsequent deterioration or improvement of health the provisions of the aforementioned Finnish accident insurance legislation shall apply.

9. The Volunteer hereby undertakes General Service with the Volunteer Force and solemnly binds himself to serve wherever ordered to serve by his superior officers both commissioned and non-commissioned, whether they be of the International Force or of the Finnish Army.

10. This Agreement shall be in force for the duration of the war between Soviet Russia and Finland or until the Volunteer is called up for military service in his own country without prejudice to the right of the Committee to terminate the same upon giving one month's notice to the Volunteer of their intention so to do, or to the right of the Officer Commanding the said Force to terminate the same at a moment's notice if the Volunteer is guilty of misconduct. Except in the event of death the Committee is bound to provide transport for the return of the Volunteer to his place of enlistment.

This Agreement has been drawn up and signed in three copies.

........London....this.......Seventh..........day of......March.....1940...

for and on behalf of the }
FINNISH AID BUREAU by }..........G. A. Lönnberg.-..............................

Signature of Witness...[signature] ......

for and on behalf of the FINNISH AID BUREAU by ...... Arnold Gibson ......

Signature of Witness......

Signature of Recruit.... Hubert J. Howard ......

Signature of Witness......

OATH TO BE TAKEN BY THE RECRUIT ON ENLISTMENT

I, ... Hubert John Howard ......,
swear by Almighty God that I will be faithful to the terms of my engagement and honestly and faithfully defend the Cause of Finland against all enemies and will observe and obey all orders of my military superiors.

...... Hubert J. Howard ......*Signature of Recruit.*

......*Signature of Witness.*

APPENDIX "C"

PETITION presented to Captain H.H. Chandor, 7th May 1940. The proposed point of departure was the port of Petsamo on the Arctic.

Sir,

We have the honour to submit that the NCOs and men of the British Contingent desire strongly to put forward the following proposal with the earnest hope that it will receive favourable consideration.

In view of the international situation and the possibility that communications with England may become still further restricted, the Company desires to make its base near the proposed point of departure at the earliest date, so that immediate advantage may be taken of any opportunity to return to England, where we may be used to the best advantage by our own country.

The Company thinks that if the present state of affairs is allowed to continue indefinitely, it may happen that we shall be unable to make use of any opportunity to return that may occur, due to the great distance that separates us from our proposed point of departure.

In such an event it might well happen that the Company would find itself condemned to a further period of aimless detention in Finland, extending possibly to the whole period of the War.

The Company would be perfectly prepared to continue to complete their training at their new headquarters and undergo the very probable difficulties of accommodation and food supplies.

We ask that this petition be presented through you, our Commanding Officer, at the earliest opportunity to the proper Finnish Authorities.

(Signed) 10 sergeants
15 corporals
91 privates

APPENDIX "D"

SPEECH by Major Magill, 30th May 1940:

"I think Mr Brunow made it very clear about what the Finnish Army's position is, what happens to you tomorrow, what is your status, and what they will do if you decide to stay here as a Unit.

"I am going to say what I hope, and a great many of us who are interested in keeping the British name as good as possible in Finland hope, that you will decide to stick together until you do move . . . well, it comes to Northwards. If you start going off in twos and threes to make you own way home I think I can give you such information about the possibilities as you will see it will not make things any easier.

"Supposing you all decided to go to various places about a hundred miles away and you were therefore scattered. Tomorrow we in Helsinki at the Legation get an answer to the telegram we sent three days ago to take immediate action about you. Well, it cannot be done if you are scattered all over the place, so I would deplore it (a) from the moral point of view, and (b) from the practical point of view if we decide to break up.

"I hope all of you do like . . . particularly at the present moment . . . not to make a bloody bad show in Finland, because you are being watched as a cat watches a mouse. As you might imagine, this country is not free from people who think the Germans are jolly good chaps. There is no end to the amount of lying propaganda which might follow from the fact that you were going off, as you are perfectly entitled to do. Therefore I put it before your officers and NCOs, and I put it before you, that you will decide, whatever hard feelings about positions you may have, to stick together and to move out of this country as an orderly unit and not have to be swept up by the police.

"I will tell you about transport, carrying back to the beginning. You know some of your lads went off. Well, the

Boche got some of them and the Swedes got the rest, and no-one is very happy about it, and the lads in Sweden are waiting exactly as you are. What is the other possibility? In theory Russia is neutral, but in the first place it takes three or four weeks before they consider names, and when they do consider them, if you have given the right one they find you came out here in order to kill as many Russians as possible. So I do not recommend Russia, and I do not think it would be much good if I did.

"A third possibility is the Admiralty, who are the people on whom we had been pinning our hopes all the time, and I can tell you now that there was a day fixed and the whole thing was arranged. You and a great many other people from the other side of the Gulf of Bothnia were all going happily on a ship and live happily . . . or sink happily . . . ever after, but that was all knocked on the head by the Boche behaving in this manner in Holland and Belgium. There is still the possibility of a ship coming to take charge of a large number of you, and those of you who are staying here will be waiting to go at twenty-four hours' notice.

"There is another possibility that if we cannot get a ship to a certain place in the North we can get a ship to another place, and in that case you would be move up and shipped to somewhere in the North of Norway and you would get back that way. A telegram was sent to that effect yesterday when it was known that you were going to be disbanded. I think that shows we are not sitting on our arses saying 'Fuck the volunteers'. The Finns are naturally as anxious to get rid of you because you are a body of fighting men who embarrass them acutely.

"There is one question you have all asked, and I would have asked myself, what are the chances for an individual who sets off himself. I will tell you the position. Assuming you have plenty of money and you could get the police to give you a pass to the Northern war zone. There are a certain number of boats up there, but you will find that all the available space has already been taken up. As an instance I can tell you that we are at the Legation often have very important individuals we want to send home. During the past few weeks we have sent three. At the moment there are five Finnish boats in Petsamo and one of those ships we have managed to get one officer with extremely valuable material.

"There is another harbour in the North, in Norway, and to go there you have to get a visa from the Norwegians which you will find very difficult business unless you can give a very good reason. If you stick together, however, you are a body of men who are very anxious to get shifted, and it will be the combined effort of the Finnish and British governments. Everyone is acutely anxious to get you moving. For God's sake be persuaded that we are doing a lot to get you back and that the difficulties for an individual to get back will be insuperable and you will be a curse to us.

"I have been through you fan mail and these are the main points which I class as intelligent. Discharge papers. The answer is No, who do not get any from the Finnish Army because they do not issue them. Discharge papers will not be issued. Secondly, will you be civilians when you are discharged. Yes, you will. You will wear civilian clothes, and for God's sake remember you are civilians. It is much safer to be civilians. Another point. Will you be interned. No, certainly not, unless you refuse to take off your uniforms and carry rifles. I don't think there is any reason to suppose you would be interned.

"Someone else asks why you should not be sent up North and stay there waiting for your boat. The answer is this, that you are an embarrassment to the Finns. If we sent you up there, a fine body of blackguards, the Germans would get to hear of it and so would the Russians, and they would say there was a force of several thousand British preparing to attack Murmansk. That is the reason the Finns do not want you to go up there.

"I hope for the sake of the British name that you will stick together. I hope you do not wish to make a bloody bad show in Finland. There is no end to the amount of lying propaganda which might follow from the fact that you were going off, as you are perfectly entitled to do, alone.

"There is a possibility that if we cannot get a ship to one

port in the North, we can get it to another, and in that case you would be moved up and shipped to somewhere in the North of Norway and thence home. A telegram was sent to that effect yesterday when it was known that you were going to be disbanded.

"It is immensely difficult to get away individually. As an instance we at the Legation often have very important individuals we want to send home. During the past few weeks we have sent three. At the moment there are five Finnish boats in Petsamo, and on one of these ships we have managed to get one man.

"For god's sake be persuaded that we are doing a lot to get you back and that the difficulties of an individual getting back will be insuperable, and that you will be a curse to us.

"You will be civilians on discharge. Remember you are civilians. It is much safer to be civilians."